Ernest Gyidel

Ukrainian Public Nationalism in the General Government
The Case of *Krakivski Visti*, 1940–1944

With a foreword by David R. Marples

UKRAINIAN VOICES

Collected by Andreas Umland

57 Vakhtang Kipiani
    Ein Land weiblichen Geschlechts
    Ukrainische Frauenschicksale im 20. und 21. Jahrhundert
    Aus dem Ukrainischen übersetzt von Christian Weise
    ISBN 978-3-8382-1891-5

58 Petro Rychlo
    „Zerrissne Saiten einer überlauten Harfe ..."
    Deutschjüdische Dichter der Bukowina
    ISBN 978-3-8382-1893-9

59 Volodymyr Paniotto
    Sociology in Jokes
    An Entertaining Introduction
    ISBN 978-3-8382-1857-1

60 Josef Wallmannsberger (ed.)
    Executing Renaissances
    The Poetological Nation of Ukraine
    ISBN 978-3-8382-1741-3

61 Pavlo Kazarin
    The Wild West of Eastern Europe
    A Ukrainian Guide on Breaking Free from Empire
    Translated from the Ukrainian by Dominique Hoffman
    ISBN 978-3-8382-1842-7

The book series "Ukrainian Voices" publishes English- and German-language monographs, edited volumes, document collections, and anthologies of articles authored and composed by Ukrainian politicians, intellectuals, activists, officials, researchers, and diplomats. The series' aim is to introduce Western and other audiences to Ukrainian explorations, deliberations and interpretations of historic and current, domestic, and international affairs. The purpose of these books is to make non-Ukrainian readers familiar with how some prominent Ukrainians approach, view and assess their country's development and position in the world. The series was founded, and the volumes are collected by Andreas Umland, Dr. phil. (FU Berlin), Ph. D. (Cambridge), Associate Professor of Politics at the Kyiv-Mohyla Academy and an Analyst in the Stockholm Centre for Eastern European Studies at the Swedish Institute of International Affairs.

Ernest Gyidel

UKRAINIAN PUBLIC NATIONALISM IN THE GENERAL GOVERNMENT
The Case of *Krakivski Visti*, 1940–1944

With a foreword by David R. Marples

Bibliografische Information der Deutschen Nationalbibliothek
Die Deutsche Nationalbibliothek verzeichnet diese Publikation in der Deutschen Nationalbibliografie; detaillierte bibliografische Daten sind im Internet über http://dnb.d-nb.de abrufbar.

Bibliographic information published by the Deutsche Nationalbibliothek
The Deutsche Nationalbibliothek lists this publication in the Deutsche Nationalbibliografie; detailed bibliographic data are available on the Internet at http://dnb.d-nb.de.

Cover illustrated by Ernest Gyidel, March 2024

ISBN (Print): 978-3-8382-1865-6
ISBN (E-Book [PDF]): 978-3-8382-7865-0
© *ibidem*-Verlag, Hannover • Stuttgart 2025

Leuschnerstraße 40
30457 Hannover
Germany / Deutschland
info@ibidem.eu

Alle Rechte vorbehalten

Das Werk einschließlich aller seiner Teile ist urheberrechtlich geschützt. Jede Verwertung außerhalb der engen Grenzen des Urheberrechtsgesetzes ist ohne Zustimmung des Verlages unzulässig und strafbar. Dies gilt insbesondere für Vervielfältigungen, Übersetzungen, Mikroverfilmungen und elektronische Speicherformen sowie die Einspeicherung und Verarbeitung in elektronischen Systemen.

All rights reserved. No part of this publication may be reproduced, stored in or introduced into a retrieval system, or transmitted, in any form, or by any means (electronic, mechanical, photocopying, recording or otherwise) without the prior written permission of the publisher. Any person who commits any unauthorized act in relation to this publication may be liable to criminal prosecution and civil claims for damages.

Printed in the EU

"Хорошая газета, говорит тов. Троцкий, лучше, чем плохая дивизия."

"A good newspaper, says Comrade Trotsky, is better than a bad division."*

---

* The quotation is from the report on Leon Trotsky's meeting with the Kuomintang delegation headed by Chiang Kai-shek in Moscow on November 27, 1923: G.M. Adibekov et al., *Politbiuro TsK RKP(b)-VKP(b) i Komintern: 1919-1943 gg. Dokumenty* (Moskva: ROSSPEN, 2004), 223.

Contents

Foreword by *David R. Marples* IX

Disclaimer 1

List of Abbreviations and Terms 2

List of Illustrations 3

Note on Transliteration and Proper Names 4

Acknowledgments 5

Introduction 7

I   The General Government, the Ukrainian Central Committee and *Krakivski Visti* in 1940-1944 23

II   A School of Hate: Images of Poles, Russians/Soviets and Jews in *Krakivski Visti* 75

III "A nation aware of its glorious past and national strength will never disappear": Ukrainian History, Historical Memory and Nation in *Krakivski Visti* 143

Conclusions 199

Bibliography 207

Index of Names 219

Foreword

Wartime Europe often seems unusually close, particularly from my vantage point of Edmonton, Alberta, Canada. It was to this northern city that Mykhailo Khomiak, the chief editor of *Krakivski Visti*, migrated after the Second World War, and his remarkable family soon began to have an impact on the local community and eventually the city and nation too. His daughter Halyna, a lawyer by training, ran unsuccessfully for the New Democratic Party (NDP) in the constituency of Edmonton Strathcona. Another daughter, Chrystia, married the historian and my colleague at the University of Alberta, John-Paul Himka; a younger sister also married a scholar, Myroslav Shkandrij, a professor at the University of Manitoba. Halyna's own daughters attended Harvard University, and the older of the two, another Chrystia, is currently Finance Minister and Deputy Prime Minister of Canada.

More than the above, they were also, for roughly a decade, my close neighbors in a community known by its Ukrainian name *Hromada*, which was initiated to promote "Ukrainianism, socialism, and feminism." Many lively debates ensued, and the metamorphosis from the sort of Ukrainian nationalism embraced by contributors of the wartime newspaper edited by the elderly Mykhailo appeared complete.

I had moved from the UK to Canada to study with the legendary Professor Ivan L. Rudnytsky. Incidentally, he and Khomiak passed away in the same month (April) of 1984, though Mykhailo was the senior by some fourteen years. The 1980s and 1990s, however, were a time of relative innocence, before accusations of collaborationism came to the fore. The 1985 Deschênes Commission, for example, sealed most of the cases and reported tamely that no known Ukrainian war criminals were living in Canada. Thereafter, the question was considered resolved.

Many, including Himka, and my former PhD student Per Anders Rudling (his PhD was actually on Belarus) now disagree and have been at pains to emphasize that Ukrainians in Canada must accept their responsibility for war crimes and a role in the persecution of, inter alia, European Jewry. Matters came to a head last year when the visit of Ukrainian president Volodymyr Zelensky to Canada became the occasion for a member of the Waffen-SS Division *Galizien* to be brought as a guest to the Canadian parliament. There, he received a standing ovation from all the MPs and Zelensky for his role in fighting the Russians in the war and was regarded as a celebratory hero until someone pointed out that the "Russians were on our side" in the conflict. The Speaker of the parliament, who had hosted Yaroslav Hunka, was forced to resign.

Subsequently—as well as earlier—Chrystia Freeland has been the target of activists on the far left who claim, without much hard evidence, that she espouses the same sort of nationalism as the wartime collaborators. In an article for The Wilson Center (May 19, 2022), Zoe Reid and Emily Hardy note that in 2000 she conducted an interview with Vladimir Putin characterizing him as a "cuddly, cooing president" and in 2015 she described herself as a "Russophile."* Her views of Putin obviously changed after the invasion of Ukraine, and Russia banned her from entry in 2014. In the same article, the authors cite her attitude to her grandparents as "political exiles with a responsibility to keep alive the idea of an independent Ukraine." Their legacy has passed to Canada precisely because of the fact that *Krakivski Visti* is available in the Ukrainian Cultural and Educational Centre (*Oseredok*) in Winnipeg, as well as a private copy in Edmonton.

The task of dissecting the issues of a newspaper published under Nazi occupation is a sensitive one. The late Rudnytsky, who was no nationalist and despised the OUN (Organization of Ukrainian Nationalists), once told me that in the 1930s, when western Ukrainians were living under Polish rule, that it was logical that some would support a German invasion since such a development was the only hope of positive change. He noted also that the Germans had been in Ukraine in 1918 and though the early occupation was quite harsh, it bore no relation to what was to follow in the Second World War.

---

* https://www.wilsoncenter.org/microsite/3/node/110533

Some other points are also relevant. The Ukrainians who wrote for *Krakivski Visti* had no state, having been ignored by the victorious powers who assembled in Paris after the First World War. Poland had ignored their rights despite earlier promises of autonomy. Frustrations were evident in the reluctance of many Ukrainians to engage in the legal politics of the Polish Sejm. Thus, they sought an outlet for their intellectual discussions during a war that in 1941 had no obvious end in sight.

In the early years of the war, the Wehrmacht appeared to be unstoppable, and only suffered its first major defeat in Stalingrad in early February 1943. The early indicator was that the occupation might be protracted. One can certainly describe those who found employment under German rule to merit the term 'collaborators.' But the choices were grim. In contrast to those such as the head of the Ukrainian Central Committee, Volodymyr Kubijovyč, who was both a collaborator and anti-Semite, were others who wrote articles on aspects of Ukrainian history and culture that had no other viable outlet.

Thus finding a clear line between intellectuals and ideologues is often very difficult. As Ernest shows, lip service had to be paid to the German war effort, but that aside, it was possible to explore issues linked to the cultural heritage of an emergent nation.

Further east, in Soviet Ukraine, which had joined the USSR in December 1922, early cultural aspirations of the 1920s, ended abruptly with Stalin's rise to power. In 1929-33, mass collectivization was a disaster for Ukraine, and turned into a tragedy with the forced famine that reached its peak in the latter year, and was responsible for the deaths of about four million peasants in the Ukrainian SSR, and perhaps another million in the North Caucasus where a large portion of the population was ethnically Ukrainian.

Following the famine, which Ukrainians called the Holodomor, came the Great Purge of 1937-38, which eradicated Ukraine's cultural and political elite without regard for political ideology. From the vantage point of the Polish part of Ukrainian lands, it was thus logical to look west rather than east for solace. Little could be gained from Soviet rule. Following the Pact between Hitler and Stalin, Ukrainians could witness for themselves the nature of Soviet rule in September 1939, albeit for a brief time. I recall an interview I carried out in Sheffield, England, with a former resident of western Ukraine who had been a child when the Soviet army crossed the border. He told me the main concern of he and other residents was for the state of the horses ridden by Soviet troops. The soldiers themselves looked like beggars and immediately started to root around for products that were scarce further east.

Many Ukrainians living in Poland in the 1920s dabbled with Communism, some even went to Soviet Ukraine to experience firsthand the workers' "utopia." Others joined a branch of the Communist Party of Poland (CPP), known as the Communist Party of Western Ukraine. The party played a role in strikes and protests against the harsher rules and integrationist policies of the Polish state, but by the late 1920s it suffered already from Moscow's suspicion. In the summer of 1938, the Comintern dissolved the CPP and its subordinates.

By that time, many Ukrainians looked to the political right as an alternative and to violent methods to achieve change. The OUN sought an ethnically Ukrainian state for which Ukrainians should be prepared to die. In 1940, when the OUN split into two wings, the Polish state had ceased to exist in its original form, and Ukrainians found themselves under Soviet occupation in the east and German military rule to the west. Kubijovyč, aligned with the older wing of the OUN led by Andrii Melnyk, convinced Hans Frank, head of the General Government, to be allowed to form a Ukrainian Central Committee in Cracow.

In Lviv, the wing of the OUN led by Stepan Bandera, declared an independent Ukrainian state on June 30, 1941, a move that startled the German occupants and toward which they were negative. Over the following weeks, members of the OUN-B present in the occupied area of Ukraine were arrested, including leader Bandera. Thus, while Bandera spent the war under arrest at Sachsenhausen concentration camp, the Melnyk wing continued to collaborate with the Nazis for much of the war. *Krakivski Visti* was one of the more benign consequences. As Ernest notes, it paid lip service to Nazi propaganda, without which it would have been shut down.

But it also provided an outlet for some talented Ukrainian writers whose voices would otherwise never have been heard.

In 2024, the wartime politics have once again come to the fore. Large parts of eastern and southern Ukraine have been occupied by Russian troops. Ukrainian leaders, in Russian propaganda, are equated with wartime Nazis, and therefore Russia has mounted a Special Military Operation to eliminate them. Ukraine in turn has no option but to fight for its own territory, granted to it in 1991 with the dissolution of the Soviet Union. It is in Russia's interest to focus on Bandera, the OUN and UPA, and examples of wartime collaboration such as the Ukrainian Central Committee and the Waffen-SS Division *Galizien*. Stalin is once again a figure to be revered, his atrocities forgotten or ignored, and the Russian narrative also plays down the Holocaust and highlights a "genocide of the Russian people" as the main goal of the Nazis.

The most obvious deduction from recent events is that any prospects of objective truth about this era are long since lost. For both sides, the Second World War has become a symbol either of victory or the beginning of further repressions. The irony that Russia can focus on Ukrainian "Nazis" while replacing the priority of the Jewish Holocaust in its own historical narratives with an alleged Russian one is often overlooked. One can only do, as Ernest has done in this book, and return to the sources available to provide a portrait of different aspects of this tumultuous period.

The wartime period helped to define modern Ukraine, while those who wrote for *Krakivski Visti* either found their way to the West or were taken prisoner or killed. While Bandera himself never moderated his extreme views, others adopted quickly to life in democratic states. Many were employed by the US government during the Cold War for their knowledge of the region and commitment to ending Soviet rule.

In truth, the publication and output of *Krakivski Visti* represented at most a microcosm of the wider conflict, as both an outlet for Ukrainian culture and a means of survival under occupation. How harshly we judge the editors and contributors depends on how we perceive the choices available to those involved. The contributors were not engaged in military activities, committing crimes against minorities or the civil population. No doubt some supported Nazi policies of anti-Semitism and certainly more could be described as anti-Communist. Others were innocent victims of their circumstances: stateless, caught between two vast armies controlled by totalitarian regimes of left and right, and with uncertain futures and hope for raising their families. Nevertheless, the newspaper is a unique reflection of the period, of the lives of those living under occupation and their perceptions of the world around them.

David R. Marples
November 2024

Disclaimer

A significant part of this book discusses in detail, for research purposes only, xenophobic content that appeared in the Ukrainian newspaper *Krakivski Visti* (Cracow News) during World War II. Readers are warned that exposure to such hateful material may be uncomfortable and disturbing. In no way, either directly or indirectly, is this book aimed at supporting ideas of ethnic prejudice or racial hatred.

List of Abbreviations and Terms

Banderites	followers of Stepan Bandera
Melnykites	followers of Andrii Melnyk
OUN	Organization of Ukrainian Nationalists
Ounites	members of the OUN
PAA	Provincial Archives of Alberta
TsDIAL	Central State Historical Archive of Ukraine in Lviv
UAA	University of Alberta Archives
UCC	Ukrainian Central Committee, also referred as the Committee
UNDO	Ukrainian National Democratic Alliance
UPA	Ukrainian Insurgent Army
UPH	Ukrainian Publishing House
WUPR	Western Ukrainian People's Republic

List of Illustrations

1. Audience at the Wawel Royal Castle: Hans Frank (third from right) receives the Ukrainian delegation headed by Volodymyr Kubijovyč (first from left). October 1940, Cracow. Copyright Narodowe Archiwum Cyfrowe/ National Digital Archives, Poland 33

2. Hans Frank (center) celebrates the harvest festival with members of the Ukrainian delegation at the Wawel Royal Castle. The man right behind him is Volodymyr Kubijovyč. October 24, 1943, Cracow. Copyright Narodowe Archiwum Cyfrowe/ National Digital Archives, Poland 34

3. Mykhailo Khomiak, chief editor of *Krakivski Visti*. Early 1940s, Cracow. Copyright Provincial Archives of Alberta, Canada (Michael Chomiak Fonds PR1985.0191) 56

4. Editors of *Krakivski Visti* (from left to right): Ivan Durbak, Lev Lepkyi, Mykhailo Khomiak, Vasyl Kachmar. Early 1940s, Cracow. Copyright Provincial Archives of Alberta, Canada (Michael Chomiak Fonds PR1985.0191) 61

5. Anti-Semitic cartoon in *Krakivski Visti* (no. 6 January 25, 1940) under an official announcement about the exchange of banknotes. The cartoon depicts a working-class man going to a bank and saying to the four men trying to stop him: "No, speculators, you won't profit off my money." 117

Note on Transliteration and Proper Names

The book uses a simplified version of the Library of Congress' romanization of Cyrillic characters. The apostrophe representing soft sign has been omitted everywhere except in quotations and bibliographic records that originally contained it. In my experience, apostrophicide reduces visual clutter and makes the text more readable (compare L'viv to Lviv). As a rule, I have used the spelling of geographic names that reflect their current status; for example, Podlasie instead of Pidliashshia or Lviv instead of Lemberg/Lwów. Exceptions have been made for several toponyms with long-established spelling in English, such as Cracow and Warsaw (rather than Kraków and Warszawa) or Galicia and Volhynia (rather than Halychyna and Volyn).

Acknowledgments

This book is based on my dissertation defended at the University of Alberta in 2019. By its nature, a doctoral thesis is supposed to be a solitary task, but I was fortunate to have two great historians aiding me on the path toward its completion. David R. Marples was an exemplary doctoral supervisor, a true *Doktorvater*. I would have never finished my doctorate without his support, which went far beyond dissertation matters and ranged from friendly advice to employing me as his research assistant for three years. John-Paul Himka, my master's supervisor at the same university, was the reason I ended up in faraway Edmonton in 2012. The dissertation's topic was born in conversations with him. But most importantly, for three years he let me peruse his set of *Krakivski Visti* (inherited from his father-in-law and the newspaper's chief editor, Mykhailo Khomiak), which made my research of the newspaper much easier. After defending the dissertation, I had no plans to publish it. My mind was slowly changed in spring 2023 when I stayed in a quiet and sleepy Swedish town, Dalby. My hosts, both professional historians, convinced me to reconsider, and financial support from the KAW Foundation and Vetenskapsrådet enabled me to finish this book. Last but not least, I am grateful to Andreas Umland for including my book in the *Ukrainian Voices* series. All responsibility for opinions and the accuracy of facts lies with me entirely.

Introduction

In 1977 an important Polish-Jewish historian, Lucjan Dobroszycki (1925-1995), writing about the Polish legal press in the General Government, noted that "there is a surprising paucity of work concerned with the assumptions, methods, and special practices used by the Nazis to influence public opinion. The lack is especially striking on the topic of so important a means of modern communication as the press ... there is no work on the press published in Polish territories by the occupation force itself, on its orders, or with its approval—that is, on the 'legal' press for the subjugated population. It is difficult to attain a complete picture of occupation policies without considering this area."[1] At the time when he made this observation only the Polish underground press had been studied, while the legal press published directly by or under the control of the German authorities in the General Government had received almost no attention.

The primary reason for this historiographical situation at the time was the assumption that the phenomenon of the legal press was insignificant and marginal in the occupied Polish society, which allegedly followed the Resistance in boycotting the public sphere of the General Government. It took Dobroszycki nearly a decade to write a book disproving this assumption and showing "that the [Polish] reptile press was well-nigh universally bought and read, despite being published by the detested occupying power."[2] Subsequent studies of the General Government's legal press support Dobroszycki's conclusion.[3] There is, however, a gap

---

1   Lucjan Dobroszycki, *Reptile Journalism: The Official Polish-Language Press under the Nazis, 1939-1945* (New Haven, CT: Yale University Press, 1994), 1.
2   Dobroszycki, *Reptile Journalism*, ix.
3   See: Klaus-Peter Friedrich, "Publizistische Kollaboration im sog. Generalgouvernement: personengeschichtliche Aspekte der deutschen Okkupationsherrschaft in Polen (1939 - 1945)," *Zeitschrift für Ostmitteleuropa-Forschung* 48 no. 1 (1999): 51-89; Klaus-Peter Friedrich, "Die deutsche polnischsprachige Presse im Generalgouvernement (1939-1945): NS-Propaganda für die polnische Bevölkerung," *Publizistik: Vierteljahreshefte für Kommunikationsforschung* 46 no. 2 (2001): 161-188; Grzegorz Hryciuk, "*Gazeta Lwowska*" *1941-1944* (Wrocław: Wydaw. Uniwersytetu Wrocławskiego, 1996); Lars Jockheck, *Propaganda im*

in the historiography: the Polish and German language legal press of the General Government have been studied relatively well, while the Ukrainian language legal press has not been so fortunate. This study aims to correct this imbalance at least partially, dealing with the most important Ukrainian legal newspaper of the General Government, *Krakivski Visti* (Cracow News), which was published by the Ukrainian Central Committee (UCC), a legal Ukrainian umbrella organization in the General Government. That said, this book is not a comprehensive history of the newspaper (my scope and limitations are discussed further).

Primary Sources

The most important source for a history of *Krakivski Visti* is, of course, its editorial archive, which is located at the Provincial Archives of Alberta (PAA) among the papers of Ukrainian journalist, editor and community activist Mykhailo Khomiak (1905-1984). A lawyer by education, Khomiak was one of the editors of the most important Western Ukrainian newspaper on the eve of World War II — *Dilo* (Action),[4] and shortly after its closure in September 1939, became the deputy editor and then the chief editor of *Krakivski Visti* in 1940-1945. In October 1948 he (as Michael Chomiak) and his family immigrated to Canada.[5] After he died in Edmonton, the family

---

Generalgouvernement: die NS-Besatzungspresse für Deutsche und Polen 1939-1945 (Osnabrück: Fibre, 2006); Józef Lewandowski, "*Goniec Krakowski" (27.X.1939 - 18.I.1945): próba monografii* (Warszawa: [s.n.], 1978); Jolanta Rawska, "*Sprawa polska" w prasie "gadzinowej" (lipiec 1944-styczeń 1945)* (Warszawa: [s.n.], 1980); Maria Świstak, *Nowy Kurier Warszawski: próba monografii* (Warszawa: [s.n.], 1978); Tomasz Andrzej Uchman, *Gazeta Lwowska 1941-1944: próba monografii* (Warszawa: Uniwersytet Warszawski, 1977); Krzysztof Woźniakowski, *Polskojęzyczna prasa gadzinowa w tzw. Starej Rzeszy (1939-1945)* (Kraków: Wydaw. Naukowe AP, 2001); Władysława Wójcik, *Prasa gadzinowa Generalnego Gubernatorstwa: (1939-1945)* (Kraków: Wydaw. Naukowe WSP, 1988).

4   In my dissertation I translated *Dilo* as *Deed* but since then I have seen the newspaper's letterhead in which its name is given as *Action* and *L'Action* in English and French respectively. See: "Posvidka" August 18, 1934. University of Alberta Archives (UAA), Ivan L. Rudnytsky fonds, Accession no. 2020-005, File 35.

5   See Khomiak's autobiography: "Miï zhyttiepys." Provincial Archives of Alberta (PAA), Michael Chomiak fonds, File PR1985.0191/96.

donated his papers to the Provincial Archives in 1985.⁶ The editorial archive of *Krakivski Visti* is a unique collection. According to one estimate, at least 365 Ukrainian periodical titles appeared under German occupation during World War II.⁷ Yet out of all of them the editorial archive of *Krakivski Visti* is the only one known to survive almost entirely. Only the last months (the Vienna period) of the newspaper's history are represented poorly in the papers. The Polish legal press of the General Government survived only slightly better in terms of the archival trail. It seems that the destruction of the last war years was only partially responsible for this lack of survived editorial archives: most likely, they were deliberately destroyed by the newspapers' staff in 1944-45, who might have believed that they would be used against them after the war (they were not wrong).⁸

The editorial archive of *Krakivski Visti* takes up almost five (out of thirty-seven) boxes containing Khomiak's papers. It consists of notebooks in which he recorded his frequent meetings with German officials and the UCC leadership; the editorial chronicle "Chleny Redaktsii 'Krakivskykh Vistei' i spivrobitnyky" (most likely written by Khomiak); German daily information bulletins; business files (salaries, remunerations, etc.); correspondence with journalists and contributors; a collection (selected issues) of other legal press in German, Polish, Ukrainian, and Russian languages; materials about religious affairs in the General Government, primarily on the Ukrainian Orthodox and Greek Orthodox Churches; the Katyn massacre; the Waffen-SS division *Galizien* (primarily official announcements and newspaper articles); *Ostarbeiter* matters; and last but not least the Organization of Ukrainian Nationalists (pamphlets, newsletters, communiqués etc.). Besides the editorial archive, important information about the newspaper is scattered throughout Khomiak's post-war correspondence.

---

6   PAA, Michael Chomiak fonds https://searchprovincialarchives.alberta.ca/mykhailo-chomiak-fonds (accessed May 23, 2024).
7   Kostiantyn Kurylyshyn, *Ukrainske zhyttia v umovakh nimetskoi okupatsii (1939-1944 rr.): za materialamy ukrainomovnoi lehalnoi presy* (Lviv: Lvivska natsionalna naukova biblioteka im. V. Stefanyka, 2010), 5.
8   Dobroszycki, *Reptile Journalism*, 5-6.

The second most important primary source is the newspaper itself. *Krakivski Visti* appeared in two editions, daily (January 1940 – April 1945) and weekly (November 1940 – October 1944). The daily edition ranged between 4 to 10 pages, though it was not uncommon for holiday issues (Easter, Christmas, etc.) to extend to 20 pages. In terms of production quality *Krakivski Visti* was not consistent. Like most newspapers under the German occupation, it was not published on quality paper from the start, but after 1943 it was visibly degraded even further. In terms of content *Krakivski Visti* was also uneven: its worst years were the first and the last. Arguably, the newspaper peaked in 1943 in terms of intellectual quality, variety of topics, and the number of contributors.

It is worth mentioning that after the war Khomiak several times expressed an intent to write memoirs about his journalistic career at *Dilo* and *Krakivski Visti*.[9] Regrettably, he never realized it. In the 1970s one of Khomiak's daughters, Chrystia Chomiak, recorded an audio interview with her father. It deals mostly with family history and stops at the events of the Polish-Soviet War of 1920.[10] In 2010, another daughter, Maria Hopchin, and her husband, Bruce Hopchin, videotaped an interview with Khomiak's first cousin, Benedict Blawacky (1920-2014). Both Chrystia and Maria were kind enough to make the interviews available to me: without a doubt they are important sources for Khomiak's biography and family history, but unfortunately, they contain very little about *Krakivski Visti* per se.

Historiography

As a primary source *Krakivski Visti* has been used by researchers of Ukrainian wartime history since the 1950s. John A. Armstrong, a renowned American political scientist whose early work focused

---

9 See for example: Letter from Mykhailo Khomiak to Kost Pankivskyi March 29, 1959. PAA, Michael Chomiak fonds, File PR1985.0191/208; Letter from Mykhailo Khomiak to Volodymyr Kubijovyč September 13, 1960. PAA, Michael Chomiak fonds, File PR1985.0191/184.
10 The interview was recorded in December of either 1975 or 1977. Personal communication from John-Paul Himka.

on Ukrainian nationalism, was the first to remark on its quality and importance: "[it] stood head and shoulders above any other Ukrainian publication in the German-dominated areas. *Krakivs'ki Visti* (Cracow News, as it was named after the Germans forbade the use of 'Ukrainian' in the title) was one of the few papers which did not become a party organ but consistently served as a forum for a broad variety of Ukrainian viewpoints. Moreover, it was the only paper of this nature which possessed considerable material resources and attracted numerous contributions from writers of real talent. It was subjected to a censorship stricter than that inflicted on Ukrainian papers in Greater Germany (although much less severe than that of the papers later established under German rule farther east); nevertheless, it was able to reflect a considerable range of Ukrainian life and thought. As a result it is an invaluable witness of the events of the war years."[11] Four decades later another important researcher, Karel C. Berkhoff, pointed out the importance of the Ukrainian legal press as a primary source for the history of Ukrainian lands under German occupation and noted that this is "especially the case" with *Krakivski Visti*.[12]

While as a primary source *Krakivski Visti* has enjoyed attention and recognition, as an object of study for a long time it did not. The very first account of the newspaper's history appeared thirty years after its closure—in Volodymyr Kubijovyč's history of the Ukrainian Central Committee (UCC), which was based on its archive.[13] The author planned to write a full history of the UCC from 1939 to 1945 but finished only the first volume covering the period of 1939-1941.[14] Kubijovyč reviewed the newspaper's circulation in 1940-41, changes in its editorial board, commented on the most prominent figures among its journalists and contributors, and on the

---

11 John A. Armstrong, *Ukrainian Nationalism, 1939-1945* (New York, NY: Columbia University Press, 1955), 52.
12 Karel C. Berkhoff, "Ukraine under Nazi Rule (1941-1944): Sources and Finding Aids: Part I," *Jahrbücher für Geschichte Osteuropas* 45, no. 1 (1997): 93.
13 Volodymyr Kubijovyč, *Ukraintsi v Heneralnii Hubernii, 1939-1941: istoriia Ukranskoho Tsentralnoho Komitetu* (Chicago, IL: Vyd-vo Mykoly Denysiuka, 1975), 272-278.
14 Letter from Volodymyr Kubijovyč to Mykhailo Khomiak March 1, 1976. PAA, Michael Chomiak fonds, File PR1985.0191/185.

relationship of the editorial board with German censorship. In this short account (seven pages) he also made two important claims about the newspaper. First, he confirmed that *Krakivski Visti* was an organ of the UCC "to a certain degree" (when the newspaper appeared, it never officially acknowledged this connection).[15] Second, he set *Krakivski Visti* apart from the rest of the legal press that appeared in the General Government: it was not "a German newspaper [published] in Ukrainian, but a Ukrainian newspaper edited under German reality."[16] The question to what degree *Krakivski Visti* served the political goals of the German occupation regime and reflected Nazi ideology in its content, in particular that of anti-Semitism, he avoided completely. Besides the UCC's archive in his possession, Kubijovyč might have also relied on a short history of the newspaper that Khomiak prepared for him in 1960.[17]

Two decades later Canadian historian John-Paul Himka produced three research pieces (1996, 1998 and 2013) on *Krakivski Visti*. The first and third articles were studies of specific episodes from the newspaper's history—an anti-Semitic campaign organized on German orders in 1943;[18] reporting of NKVD mass murders in 1941 (prison massacres in Western Ukraine) and 1943 (exhumation of victims in Vinnytsia).[19] The second article was a short overview of the newspaper's history.[20] In a sense, it complemented the abovementioned Kubijovyč's account which was limited to 1940-1941.

---

15 Kubijovyč, *Ukraintsi v Heneralnii Hubernii*, 276.
16 Ibidem.
17 In his letter from August 13, 1960 Kubijovyč asked Khomiak to write an entry on *Krakivski Visti*—"12 sentences"—for the *Entsyklopediia Ukrainoznavstva*. In response Khomiak prepared a twelve-pages long typescript which he sent to Kubijovyč with a letter from September 13, 1960. Both letters and the typescript's copy are located in: PAA, Michael Chomiak fonds, File PR1985.0191/184.
18 John-Paul Himka, "*Krakivski visti* and the Jews, 1943: A Contribution to the History of Ukrainian-Jewish Relations during the Second World War," *Journal of Ukrainian Studies* 21, no. 1-2 (Summer-Winter 1996): 81-95.
19 John-Paul Himka, "Ethnicity and the Reporting of Mass Murder: *Krakivs'ki visti*, the NKVD Murders of 1941, and the Vinnytsia Exhumation," in *Shatterzone of Empires: Coexistence and Violence in the German, Habsburg, Russian, and Ottoman Borderlands*, ed. Omer Bartov and Eric D. Weitz (Bloomington: Indiana University Press, 2013), 378-98.
20 John-Paul Himka, "*Krakivs'ki visti*: An Overview," *Harvard Ukrainian Studies* Vol. 22 no. 1/4 (1998): 251-261.

Himka's pieces were the first research based on the newspaper's editorial archive and were rich in detail and original interpretation. He was the first scholar to show how *Krakivski Visti* served the ideological needs of the occupiers.

The third author who produced original research on *Krakivski Visti* was Ukrainian historian Larysa Holovata, who wrote an excellent history of Ukrainian legal publishing in the Protectorate of Bohemia and Moravia and the General Government.[21] Her work drew a lot on Canadian, Polish, Russian and Ukrainian archives, though she had no access to Khomiak's papers. One of the central subjects of Holovata's book was the Ukrainian Publishing House (*Ukrainske Vydavnytstvo*), which published *Krakivski Visti*. Holovata discussed in detail the early history of the newspaper (1940-1941), its relationship with the Ukrainian Central Committee, and its main contributors.[22] Unfortunately, she paid little attention to the newspaper's content.

Two more studies deserve to be mentioned though they do not deal with *Krakivski Visti* specifically. Nonetheless, they provide important context to the newspaper's history. The first is *Reptile Journalism* by the Polish historian Lucjan Dobroszycki, which I quoted at the beginning of this introduction. Dobroszycki was a Holocaust survivor best known for his chronicle of the Łódź ghetto.[23] Originally written in Polish, *Reptile Journalism* appeared in German (1977) and English translation (1994).[24] Though limited in focus — it dealt exclusively with the Polish language press published for the Poles — it is an indispensable work for anyone interested in the legal press of the General Government. Some of the observations that Dobroszycki made on the basis of the Polish material are worth examining against the Ukrainian legal press, including *Krakivski Visti*.

---

21 Larysa Holovata, *Ukrainskyi legalnyi vydavnychyi rukh Tsentralno-Skhidnoi Yevropy, 1939-1945* (Kyiv-Lviv, 2013).
22 Holovata, *Ukrainskyi legalnyi vydavnychyi rukh*, 293-319.
23 Lucjan Dobroszycki, ed., *The Chronicle of the Łódź ghetto, 1941-1944* (New Haven, CT: Yale University Press, 1984).
24 Lucjan Dobroszycki, *Die legale polnische Presse im Generalgouvernement, 1939-1945* (München: Selbstverlag des Instituts für Zeitgeschichte, 1977); Lucjan Dobroszycki, *Reptile Journalism: The Official Polish-Language Press under the Nazis, 1939-1945* (New Haven, CT: Yale University Press, 1994).

For example, he noted that though the "German propaganda did not achieve its goal [that] does not mean, however, that it had no effect."[25] The Polish resistance thought the same. As soon as 1941, a Polish resistance publication was already alarmed at the influence of the enemy's propaganda on the Polish population: "You can know every one of the Nazis' lies precisely; you can believe not a single word of the reports — a vestige of the force of conviction remains even in the lies and hatred. The Germans are sure that, aside from imbeciles, no one in Poland takes the idiocy of their propaganda seriously. Yet they invest enormous sums in this propaganda; for they know that even the critical listener or reader cannot completely escape the influence of the constantly repeated lies."[26] One of those influences, according to Dobroszycki, was anti-Semitism which was also reinforced by the resistance publications: "The consequences of Nazi propaganda against the Jews are a special problem. Here the effect of the propaganda was especially sweeping because it was supported by the underground press of all Polish parties from the center to the right."[27]

The second work is by the Ukrainian historian Kostiantyn Kurylyshyn.[28] In his book he attempted to summarize what one could learn from reading the Ukrainian legal press of the General Government and *Reichskommissariat* Ukraine about Ukrainian national life in those territories. His work is not similar to Dobroszycki's: Kurylyshyn was not concerned with the history of the press, how the occupation authorities shaped it and what effect it had on the local population. His book is largely descriptive and reads as an assortment of paraphrased newspaper articles structured by a subject, including a chapter on the "anti-Jewish issue."[29] According to him, there were two kinds of "anti-Jewish materials" published in the press: propaganda articles and official acts. The

---

25 Dobroszycki, *Reptile Journalism*, 117.
26 Ibidem.
27 Dobroszycki, *Reptile Journalism*, 120.
28 Kostiantyn Kurylyshyn, *Ukrainske zhyttia v umovakh nimetskoï okupatsii (1939-1944 rr.): za materialamy ukrainomovnoi lehalnoi presy* (Lviv: Lvivska natsionalna naukova biblioteka im. V. Stefanyka, 2010).
29 Kurylyshyn, *Ukrainske zhyttia*, 95-123.

whole chapter deals with the latter because Kurylyshyn chose not to discuss the former: "We are not going to analyze this layer of ideologically anti-Jewish publications."[30] In addition, he denied that the "layer" contained original Ukrainian submissions, in his words it was just "special materials" produced by "Nazi propaganda" which were "obligatory" for publication in the legal press.[31]

The question of collaboration

Neither Dobroszycki nor Kurylyshyn dealt with *Krakivski Visti* (the former did not mention it at all, the latter mentioned it only in passing), but they both addressed the important question whether the legal press under German occupation should be regarded as collaborationist on respectively Polish and Ukrainian material. Dobroszycki had no issues with regarding it as such and throughout the whole book he applied the scornful term used by the Polish Resistance, "reptile press" (*prasa gadzinowa*), to describe the Polish legal press.[32] This was also the position of the Polish government-in-exile and of the Polish state after 1945, which put staff of the legal press on trial as German collaborators: transcripts of those trials made for an important primary source for Dobroszycki.[33] However, he was also quick to make two reservations. The first was that "in the true sense of the word" only a tiny section of the Polish Far Right collaborated with the Germans; for the remainder work in the legal press was "quite simply a well-paid job offering relative security and a sense of stability in difficult times" and their "collaboration was based neither on firm conviction nor on ideological motives."[34] His second reservation was that the German occupiers, not the occupied Poles, defined the nature and scope of the collaboration. A Polish analog of Quisling never appeared during the war not because of the staunch Resistance character of the Polish nation,

---

30 Kurylyshyn, *Ukrainske zhyttia*, 97.
31 Ibidem.
32 The term *prasa gadzinowa* predates World War II. On its origins see: Dobroszycki, *Reptile Journalism*, 2-3.
33 Dobroszycki, *Reptile Journalism*, 6-7, 18.
34 Dobroszycki, *Reptile Journalism*, 75.

as Polish patriots would like to believe, but because "the Germans never seriously attempted to produce such a figure."[35]

Kurylyshyn paid even greater attention to the question of whether the legal press under German occupation was a form of collaboration, dedicating a special chapter to the issue.[36] Based on the definition proposed by the prominent Ukrainian historian Yaroslav Dashkevych (1926-2010), which equates collaboration to state treason,[37] Kurylyshyn categorically denied that Ukrainian legal activities under German occupation, including the legal press, could be described as collaboration.[38] Since a Ukrainian state did not exist at the time, there are no formal, legal grounds for any implication in treason. Thus, according to Kurylyshyn, by definition the Ukrainian legal press and organizations under the German occupation cannot be classified as collaborationist. This conclusion, he added, also applies to those Ukrainians who volunteered to serve in the Wehrmacht (in the battalions *Nachtigall* and *Roland*) and the Waffen-SS (division *Galizien*).[39] However, the Polish case, according to him, was different. Poles had their own state which they had lost due to the German invasion of 1939. Hence those Poles who cooperated with German occupiers in the General Government were collaborators, whereas Ukrainians in the same situation were not.[40]

How was the question of collaboration tackled by the three authors who wrote about *Krakivski Visti*? Most likely, Kubijovyč would have agreed with Dashkevych and Kurylyshyn: his history

---

35 Dobroszycki, *Reptile Journalism*, 152.
36 Kurylyshyn, *Ukrainske zhyttia*, 11-26.
37 "[T]he definition of collaboration, as is known, refers to a voluntary cooperation of citizens of their own, but already conquered state with the occupying power against this very own state—and that is why collaboration is equal to state treason ... The real collaborators are those who acted against their own nation in the interests of a foreign state and a foreign nation." See: Yaroslav Dashkevych, "Vstupne slovo, abo pro problemy kolaborantstva," in *Persha Ukrainska dyviziia Ukrainskoi natsionalnoii armii: istoriia stvorennia ta natsionalno-polityche znachennia. Materialy naukovo-praktychnoi konferentsii. Dopovidi ta povidomlennia*, ed. Yaroslav Dashkevych (Lviv: Novyi chas, 2002), 9.
38 Kurylyshyn, *Ukrainske zhyttia*, 24.
39 Kurylyshyn, *Ukrainske zhyttia*, 22.
40 Kurylyshyn, *Ukrainske zhyttia*, 17.

of the UCC implied that Ukrainian legal activities under German occupation did not constitute a form of collaboration (a topic to which he, as the head of the UCC, was naturally sensitive).[41] Himka offered no opinion on the question, but the factual material presented in his research — participation of *Krakivski Visti* in the ideological campaigns of the German authorities with original contributions — supports the argument that it was.[42] Holovata rejected a portrayal of the Ukrainian legal press as a "reptile" in the sense that it was betraying Ukrainian national interests.[43] But, unlike Kurylyshyn, she recognized that the Ukrainian legal press contained original anti-Semitic materials and "spread the ruling [Nazi] ideology" which was a "payment for the legal status."[44]

Collaboration under German occupation during World War II remains a controversial issue due to its sensitive nature and challenges to national myths, historical (and often family) memory and politicization. The most recent debate in *The Slavic Review* in 2005-2006 showed how polarized historians can be on this subject.[45] The very definition of what constituted collaboration and what did not in German-occupied Europe remains highly contested despite some definitions approaching almost a page in length (their length, I must add, confuses rather than clarifies the issue).[46] In the context

---

41 Kubijovyč's memoirs also make it clear that he did not consider himself "a German collaborator." See: Volodymyr Kubijovyč, *Meni 70* (Munich: Logos, 1970), 73-75; Volodymyr Kubijovyč, *Meni 85* (Munich: Molode zhyttia, 1985), 84, 199, 212. In August 1946 the American military police arrested Kubijovyč in Bavaria. Six weeks later it released him after questioning about "my cooperation [spivpratsia] with Germans" during the war. Kubijovyč considered the fact of his release as being "vindicated" from the accusation of wartime collaboration and even joked in his memoirs that the arrest "perhaps, gives me a right to belong to an organization of Ukrainian political prisoners." See: Kubijovyč, *Meni 70*, 76; Kubijovyč, *Meni 85*, 146, 197, 200.
42 At my dissertation defense Himka said that he dislikes using the term collaboration because of its politicization.
43 Holovata, *Ukrainskyi legalnyi vydavnychyi rukh*, 51-52.
44 Holovata, *Ukrainskyi legalnyi vydavnychyi rukh*, 48, 57.
45 See articles in: *Slavic Review*, Vol. 64, No. 4 (Winter, 2005): 711-798. The discussion was followed by some highly polemical letters: *Slavic Review*, Vol. 65, No. 4 (Winter, 2006): 885-893.
46 A good overview of the debates on collaboration in German-occupied Europe can be found in: Leonid Rein, *The Kings and the Pawns: Collaboration in Byelorussia during World War II* (New York: Berghahn Books, 2011), 11-55.

of the Second World War, I define collaboration as a dynamic spectrum of activities that advanced military, political, and ideological goals of the occupying power, carried out by the occupied at the occupiers' behest. Within the phenomenon I distinguish between ideological and situational (or circumstantial) collaboration. The former was motivated primarily by alignment with the occupiers' ideology (Communism, Fascism, Nazism, etc.) and its goals in the occupied territories, while the latter falls within the category of adapting to (or taking advantage of) circumstances of occupation. This simple theoretical framework to describe the phenomenon of collaboration of course does not imply that the personal experiences of collaborators were an either/or choice between ideological and circumstantial motives. The same person could have collaborated for a variety of reasons. Many German collaborators who can be classified as situational were also motivated by anticommunism and anti-Semitism to a degree.

This book classifies *Krakivski Visti* as a collaborationist newspaper due to the simple fact that its existence was allowed, controlled, and directed by the German occupation regime. The newspaper served the regime's ideological and political goals in its **content** and in the **form** of its presentation. I recognize that the newspaper's staff and contributors most likely did not dream of working for Nazi Germany. But that sentiment could also be applied to the two classical examples of German collaborators during World War II — the French Marshall Philippe Pétain and the Soviet General Andrei Vlasov — none of whom envisioned in 1939 their future collaboration with the Third Reich. The intentions of collaborators should be noted and studied, but in German-occupied Europe the limits and types of collaboration were set by the occupiers, not the occupied. By regarding the legal press and other legal activities that served the military, political and ideological goals of German occupiers as a collaboration I do not seek to pass a moral judgment or engage in virtue signaling. This book is not an exercise in moralizing. I am aware that the term carries negative connotations, but I use it as purely descriptive to stress the fact that collaboration, not resistance, was a norm in Hitler's New Europe.

In addition, I would argue that we need to divorce the issue of collaboration during World War II from associating it strictly with state or national treason because it limits our understanding of the phenomenon and how widespread it was. The association mainly echoes the political results of the war's outcome when the victors decided who was a "traitor" and who was not. Equating collaboration with treason of national or state interests (or equating resistance with loyalty to them) has been one of the most significant obstacles for frank and dispassionate studies of the phenomenon in World War II historiography. It promotes a collectivist perspective, neglecting that many people were guided by individual, not group, interests in their choices during the war. A Ukrainian who in 1943 joined the Ukrainian Insurgent Army (UPA) to fight *against* Germans or enlisted in the Waffen-SS division *Galizien* to fight *for* Germans may not necessarily have done so because of his nationalistic feelings, but because he considered it a better fate than being sent to forced labor in the Third Reich.

This equation (collaboration=treason) is also one of the reasons why in the Ukrainian case such intelligent scholars as Dashkevych and Kurylyshyn would rather engage in mental gymnastics that would allow them to claim that Ukrainian collaboration was non-existent without ever bothering to address the fact that German civilian and military administrations in the occupied Polish and Soviet territories never experienced a shortage of Ukrainian helpers.[47] The legalistic argument that Ukrainians were not collaborators because they had no state of their own reminds me of the argument that a wife cannot be raped by her husband. The underlying motivation behind both arguments is to distort the character of engagement and to avoid responsibility for actions. Whether one was a collaborator or not is determined primarily by his/her

---

47 One of the few scholars who noted this was Jan Tomasz Gross. In his first book he pondered the question "why did the Ukrainians collaborate so willingly" under the German occupation. He believed that the answer was "complex," but part of it was "that the Germans unleashed Ukrainian nationalism and let it unburden itself on other nationalities" in the occupied territories. See: Jan Tomasz Gross, *Polish Society under German Occupation: The Generalgouvernement, 1939-1944* (Princeton, NJ: Princeton University Press, 1979), 192.

relationship with the occupier under the occupation. Another frequent argument is that Ukrainian nationalists were not collaborators because they pursued their own national interests in working with German occupiers. This is a simple non sequitur: one does not exclude the other.

The main argument, limitations and issues of terminology

This book's central argument is that *Krakivski Visti*, unlike most Ukrainian legal newspapers under German occupation, enjoyed a degree of intellectual autonomy and, besides reproducing the ideology of the occupiers, developed its own ideological layer. The first chapter discusses the circumstances that made this development possible and provides an overview of the newspaper's history, its editors, contributors, distribution and reception. Chapters Two and Three discuss the newspaper's own ideological layer, which I describe as a loyalist Ukrainian nationalism, that is the advancement of the Ukrainian national cause as far as possible within the legal framework set by German occupiers through maintaining a loyalist relationship with them. The second chapter covers content that identified historical enemies of Ukraine and their specific threats: Poles, Jews, and Russians/Soviets. On the surface, these materials may appear as a reproduction of Nazi propaganda, but the authors of *Krakivski Visti* had their own Ukrainian reasons, which had little or nothing to do with Nazi ideology, for writing those texts. Though framing them in Nazi ideological language might have had a radicalizing influence and made them look more volatile, the parts of the chemical reaction were in place before the Germans arrived in 1939. The third chapter deals with content that promoted Ukrainian identity (articles on Ukrainian history, culture and memory) and discussed its internal challenges such as *latynnyky* and mixed marriages. In terms of cultural significance, *Krakivski Visti* was arguably one of the most important Ukrainian newspapers during World War II.

My analysis of the newspaper's original layer is limited in chronology and scope (mostly by intent). I do not discuss the period when *Krakivski Visti* was moved from the General Government to the Third Reich (October 1944 – April 1945) for reasons detailed in the first chapter: loss of its unique status, many contributors and most of its original intellectual value. Despite my efforts, the newspaper's weekly edition was mostly inaccessible to me. Though Mykhailo Khomiak frequently appears throughout this book, I did not seek to write his wartime biography.

To understand this book better, a reader must be aware of two terminological issues. The first is Nazi vs German. We live in the age of term dissolution. The time when *Nazi* used to mean a concrete historical phenomenon is gone. Today, the term seems to have lost any heuristic value, at least in the public discourse, where it gets easily thrown at almost anyone and anything, often without any discernible justification. The situation in the academic discourse is different, but it suffers from another troubling tendency — supplanting German with Nazi in the context of World War II, for example, describing German invasions of Poland or France as Nazi invasions.[48] One can read about Nazi soldiers, Nazi generals, Nazi occupation, etc. If this trend continues, there will eventually be a time when people will be surprised to learn that Nazis were Germans. This book uses the term Nazi in its narrow historical sense as pertaining to the Third Reich's leadership, Nazi party, propaganda and ideology. Such terms as German invasion or German occupation reflect more accurately the historical experience of the occupied populations (Jews, Poles and Ukrainians) in the General Government who thought of their occupiers as Germans rather than Nazis.

The second problematic term is *Ukrainian nationalism*. In discussing the period of 1930s-50s, the term usually implies the Organization of Ukrainian Nationalists (OUN) and its three offshoots (Banderites, Melnykites and *dviikari*). In research works dealing strictly with the OUNs this is not an issue; however, it becomes a

---

48   Julian Jackson, *The Fall of France: The Nazi Invasion of 1940* (Oxford; New York: Oxford University Press, 2003); Rush Loving, *Fat Boy and the Champagne Salesman: Göring, Ribbentrop, and the Nazi Invasion of Poland* (Bloomington, Indiana: Indiana University Press, 2022).

problem when one needs to distinguish other nationalist organizations/parties or Ukrainian nationalists without an affiliation such as Mykhailo Khomiak or Volodymyr Kubijovyč. So far three solutions have been offered for better terminological clarity. The first is reserving *integral nationalism/integral nationalists* for the OUNs and their members. The second solution proposes to use capital *Nationalism* for the OUNs and lower-case *nationalism* when discussing other nationalist organizations/parties or Ukrainian nationalism in general. The solution is borrowed from fascism studies which use capital *Fascism* to denote the specific fascism of Mussolini's Italy and lower-case *fascism* for generic fascism, that is similar movements. This book employs the third solution of using *Ounites* to distinguish members of the OUN from other Ukrainian nationalists. It is based on the Ukrainian term *ounivtsi* which has been used in Ukrainian-language memoir literature and historiography for quite some time.

I The General Government, the Ukrainian Central Committee and *Krakivski Visti* in 1940-1944

The General Government and its legal press

The Second World War started on September 1, 1939 with the German invasion of Poland, which was followed by the Soviet invasion of the country from the east on September 17. By the end of the month the Polish campaign was over. The two victors partitioned Poland primarily among themselves, with Slovakia and Lithuania being two other, minor beneficiaries. Moscow and Berlin divided the conquered territory with ethnic lines in mind: an absolute majority of Poles ended up under the German occupation while an absolute majority of minorities (primarily Ukrainians and Belarusians) under the Soviets. A resettlement commission was created promptly for ethnic Germans who wished to live in the German-occupied rather than the Soviet-occupied parts of the former Polish state. By the end of October 1939 Moscow incorporated its new conquests, Western Ukraine and Western Belarus, into the Soviet Union, where they legally became ordinary Soviet provinces.[49] The German policy was more nuanced: a smaller part similarly to the Soviet case became an integral part of the Third Reich, but from the rest, roughly one-third of the former Polish state, they created the *Generalgouvernement für die besetzten polnischen Gebiete* (General Government for the Occupied Polish Territories) in October 1939,[50] renamed to just *Generalgouvernement* in July 1940.[51] It is a common mistake in the historiography to believe that the General

---

49 Vladyslav Hrynevch, *Nepryborkane riznoholossia: Druha svitova viina i suspilno-politychni nastroi v Ukraini, 1939 – cherven 1941 rr.* (Kyiv-Dnipropetrovsk: Vydavnytstvo "Lira," 2012), 208-233.

50 Gross, *Polish Society under German Occupation*, 45; Diemut Majer, *"Non-Germans" under the Third Reich: The Nazi Judicial and Administrative System in Germany and Occupied Eastern Europe, with Special Regard to Occupied Poland, 1939-1945* (Lubbock, TX: Texas Tech University Press in Association with the United States Holocaust Memorial Museum, 2013), 236.

51 Majer, *"Non-Germans" under the Third Reich*, 760.

Government was officially a part of the Third Reich.[52] Though most of the Reich's laws were eventually extended to its territory, the General Government was never formally incorporated and was regarded as "affiliated" territory in relation to Nazi Germany, preserving its "semiautonomous" character until the very end.[53] As Diemut Majer noted in her extensive legal study, the "General Government had foreign exchange, currency, customs, and economic borders, and in that respect was a foreign country ... it had its own police borders with the Reich and its own postal and rail administration."[54] With few exceptions, traveling inside and outside of the General Government required a special permit.[55]

This new entity was more akin to an early modern colonial dominion with its ruler having the authority of a viceroy, essentially the "first colony" of the Third Reich.[56] The Nazi leadership's immediate goals in the General Government were neutralizing the Polish threat to the occupation regime and preparing a staging ground for the future invasion of the Soviet Union. But in the longer term its main goal was ruthless economic exploitation.[57] The Third Reich required food and workers. As long as that task was fulfilled, Berlin did not care much about the internal affairs of the territory. The task was assigned personally by Hitler to Hans Frank (1900-1946), a participant in the Beer Hall Putsch of November 1923 and the Nazi party's main lawyer since the late 1920s.[58] Contemporaries

---

[52] See for example: Paul Robert Magocsi, *With Their Backs to the Mountains: A History of Carpathian Rus' and Carpatho-Rusyns* (Budapest/New York: Central European University Press, 2015), 281.
[53] Majer, *"Non-Germans" under the Third Reich*, 264-270.
[54] Ibidem, 761.
[55] In his memoirs Lev Bilas even referred to his permit to visit and stay in the General Government as a "visa," which required a passport to be issued: Lev Bilas, *Ohliadaiuchys nazad. Perezhyte 1922-2000 i peredumane* (Lviv: Instytut ukrainoznavstva im. I. Krypiakevycha NAN Ukrainy, 2005), 134.
[56] Majer, *"Non-Germans" under the Third Reich*, 261-262.
[57] Gross, *Polish Society under German Occupation*, 46-50; Majer, *"Non-Germans" under the Third Reich*, 261-264.
[58] On Frank see: Martyn Housden, *Hans Frank: Lebensraum and the Holocaust* (New York: Palgrave Macmillan, 2003); Dieter Schenk, *Hans Frank: Hitlers Kronjurist und Generalgouverneur* (Frankfurt am Main: S. Fischer, 2006). The most famous (and perhaps the most biased) biographies of Hans Frank were written by his youngest son, Niklas Frank, who turned it into his life's cause to expose his

and later scholars often regarded Hans Frank as a weak figure whose only defining feature was his unconditional loyalty to Hitler. Joachim Fest had famously described him as "weak, unstable and full of strange contradictions... an insecure and vacillating character."[59] Weakness, however, is a relative term. Perhaps he appeared so in the presence of such a dominant figure as the Führer, but far away from him he was hardly a weakling.[60] Given a free hand in the General Government as long as he met Berlin's demands for food and labor, Frank developed and implemented his own policies.[61] One of his first major decisions was to have Cracow, the former capital of the medieval Polish kingdom and an important Habsburg city in 1846-1918, as the capital of the General Government.[62] Within the city he chose Wawel, the castle of the Polish kings built in the 14th century, as his residence.

Frank developed his own policies for the press in the General Government. The public sphere was severely narrowed under the pretext of a paper shortage. Another feature of the General Government's legal press was the parcellation of information along ethnic lines. Germans, Poles and Ukrainians (and briefly even Jews) had their own legal newspapers in their respective languages (the press for Jews was, however, published in Polish). While some content was universal for all of them, they also had differences. They all

---

father as a Nazi criminal: Niklas Frank, *Der Vater: eine Abrechnung* (München: C. Bertelsmann, 1987); Niklas Frank, *Bruder Norman!: "Mein Vater war ein Naziverbrecher, aber ich liebe ihn"* (Bonn: Dietz, 2013).

59 Joachim C. Fest, *The Face of the Third Reich*, trans. Michael Bullock (London: Weidenfeld and Nicolson, 1970), 209.
60 In Fest's interpretation the brutality that Frank showed in the General Government was not genuine: "Frank gazed with secret admiration at the men of violence around him, who obviously carried out every task entrusted to them without a moment's hesitation. Greedy for their approval, he imposed their role on himself, at times showing himself harder, more cynical and more merciless than they." See: Fest, *The Face of the Third Reich*, 210.
61 In April 1943 Frank was even denounced in a report to the head of SS, Heinrich Himmler, for wanting to make the General Government completely independent from the Third Reich. See: Majer, *"Non-Germans" under the Third Reich*, 761.
62 For a general history of the General Government see the somewhat outdated but still important work: Jan Tomasz Gross, *Polish Society under German Occupation: The Generalgouvernement, 1939-1944* (Princeton, NJ: Princeton University Press, 1979).

praised Axis victories and wrote about the blessings of German rule. German and Ukrainian newspapers were allowed to publish anti-Polish pieces, but the Polish legal press was not allowed to return the favor or engage in polemics with them. Frank's control over the legal press in the General Government led to bureaucratic disputes, which were never resolved, with Reich Minister of Propaganda and Public Enlightenment Joseph Goebbels, who believed that media policies belonged to his domain not only within Nazi Germany but in conquered territories too.[63] This was the environment (of competing agencies) that made *Krakivski Visti* possible. If Frank had allowed Goebbels to take full control of the press in the General Government, the newspaper most likely would not have developed its unique character.

The Ukrainian Central Committee, Volodymyr Kubijovyč and Ounites

In October-December 1939 Cracow became a convergence point for thousands of Ukrainians—mainly refugees from the Soviet-occupied Western Ukraine who often risked their lives to cross the border illegally; others were freed from Polish prisons (such as Stepan Bandera) or German captivity (taken as POWs during their service in the Polish Army).[64] By the end of 1939 the city had a sizable colony of Ukrainian intelligentsia, politicians and public figures. Besides them, there were other Ukrainians in the General Government. These were the Eastern Slavic inhabitants of Chełm (*Kholmshchyna*), Lemko (*Lemkivshchyna*), Nadsanie (*Posiannia*) and Podlasie (*Pidliashshia*) regions—territories that the Ukrainian national project since the 19th century had regarded as part of imagined Ukraine. These regions were viewed by the Ukrainian national activists as heavily Polonized and denationalized. That "Ukrainians" here were often not aware of their "true" identity and typically identified themselves as "locals" (*tuteishi*) or with some kind of

---

63 Dobroszycki, *Reptile Journalism*, 55.
64 Kubijovyč estimated their total population in the General Government at 20,000 – 30,000: Kubijovyč, *Ukraintsi v Heneralnii Hubernii*, 33.

regional identity (*boiky, lemky*) was often lamented by the Ukrainian national leaders in the late 19th and early 20th centuries.[65] The ethnic composition of the General Government had changed after the German invasion of the Soviet Union in June 1941, significantly increasing its Ukrainian population, by incorporating Galicia (*Halychyna*), as a separate, fifth, district.

The Poles were seen by Frank as the most serious threat to the occupation due to their numbers (estimated at around 12 million by Germans) and historical tradition of rebelling against occupiers.[66] The three largest ethnic minorities of the General Government were treated each in its own way. The local Germans, *Volksdeutsche*, had to be brought up to the Nazi standards of Germanhood and rapidly go through the same process of Nazification that German society had been subjected to since 1933. The Jews were treated the worst: for the time being, they had to be segregated until a comprehensive solution could be found for them. The Ukrainians, while regarded as racially inferior to Germans, were put in a privileged position compared to Poles and Jews. Frank decided to exploit existing ethnic antagonisms of the defeated Poland to Germany's advantage. The interwar Polish state had failed to promote loyalty among its national minorities. At the time when Poland fell to German arms the Ukrainians were one of the most dissatisfied minorities.[67]

Frank considered Ukrainians "the born deadly enemies of the Poles" because, as he believed, more than a million of them had perished under interwar Polish rule.[68] He summarized his political line with regard to Ukrainians in his diary on August 5, 1942: "I must state that in the interests of German policy [in the General

---

65 Kubijovyč, *Ukraintsi v Heneralnii Hubernii*, 20-31. By Kubijovyč's estimate, there were 525,000 Ukrainians and 170,000 "Polonized Ukrainians" in the General Government at the time of its creation.
66 Gross, *Polish Society under German Occupation*, 3-4, 73.
67 Ibidem, 18-20.
68 Housden, *Hans Frank*, 125. The figure of over one million of Ukrainians was also repeated in the German propaganda in the General Government, see: "1,220.000 ukraintsiv zhertvamy polskoho teroru," *Krakivski Visti* no. 19 March 13, 1940, 6. This article originally appeared in *Krakauer Zeitung* (March 7, 1940) and claimed that "even according to Polish statistics, 1,200.000 Ukrainians, or 21,6% of their total, had perished as a result of 21 years of the Polish rule."

Government], strained relations are being maintained between the Poles and the Ukrainians. The 4.5 or 5 million Ukrainians whom we have in this country are extraordinary important as a counterweight to the Poles. I have therefore always tried to keep them in some form of politically satisfied frame of mind, in order to prevent them joining in with the Poles."[69] Frank was not the only one who regarded Ukrainians as a reliable buffer against Poles. The SS, which operated independently in the General Government, did so as well. For example, during the forcible removal of the Polish population from a part of the Lublin district to clear the territory for German resettlement in 1942-1943 (*Aktion Zamosc*), the SS also settled Ukrainians around the German colonies, who in their mind would provide the German settlers with reliable anti-Polish security.[70]

Despite regarding Ukrainians as racially inferior, German policy toward them in the General Government, with some degree of perversion, can be termed as affirmative action—Ukrainian identity was promoted and privileged compared to how Jews and Poles were treated. Initial Ukrainian expectations of the Germans were optimistic. The horrors of the Nazi regime were yet to come. Most Western Ukrainians, from all sectors of society, based their expectations on their experiences with German (this includes what we would today call Austrian) order and culture before World War I. A genuine Germanophilia, both political and cultural, was widespread among Western Ukrainians on the eve of World War II. As Ivan L. Rudnytsky put it in 1983: "Germany was traditionally the one country of Western Europe which had represented the West for the [Western] Ukrainians. For one [Western] Ukrainian who knew French or English, there were a hundred who knew German. Germany stood for European civilization. This might seem paradoxical,

---

69 Stanisław Piotrowski, *Hans Frank's Diary* (Warszawa: Państwowe Wydawnictwo Naukowe, 1961), 267.
70 Housden, *Hans Frank*, 188, 192.

thinking of what happened [during the war]. But this was the historical experience of the [Western] Ukrainian people."[71]

By the end of the 1930s, high hopes for German liberation from both Polish and Soviet rule were held not only by Ounites but also by most Western Ukrainian national activists, even democratic ones. Prominent Ukrainian interwar female activist and democrat Milena Rudnytska, according to her son, was among them too: "My mother and I did not belong to enthusiasts of the Third Reich, we were more skeptical than the majority of our countrymen, but even we thought that following its own interests Germany would have to allow, if not for the creation of an independent Ukraine, then for a more or less autonomous 'protectorate,' which compared with the Bolshevik regime would still be a progress."[72] Ukrainian journalist Mariia Strutynska, reflecting in 1943 on the reality of German occupation, wrote with sadness in her diary that in 1939 "we did not expect this [German] devil, but the arrival of a cultured state."[73] Even laymen expected the German conquest to be some sort of a solution and desirable event. Ukrainian historian Lev Bilas remembered how in summer 1939 (he was 17 at the time), while touring the Galician countryside, a Ukrainian peasant had suddenly asked him when "Uncle Hitler is going to come?" Bilas prophetically replied that he would come soon.[74]

However, after the German arrival Ukrainians were not in an advantageous political situation. They were without any political representation except one, underground organization—the OUN. On September 22, 1939 when the Red Army occupied Lviv, all Ukrainian legal parties, which had their headquarters in the city, disbanded under the pretext that they did not want to operate

---

71 "Round-Table Discussion," in *Ukrainian-Jewish Relations in Historical Perspective*, ed. Howard Aster and Peter J. Potichnyj 2nd ed. (Edmonton: Canadian Institute of Ukrainian Studies, University of Alberta, 1990), 489.
72 Letter from Ivan L. Rudnytsky to Mykhailo Dobrianskyi February 1, 1950. UAA, Ivan L. Rudnytsky fonds, Accession no. 1984-155, File 751.
73 Mariia Strutynska, *Daleke zblyzka* (Winnipeg: Vydavnycha Spilka "Tryzub," 1975), 185.
74 Bilas, *Ohliadaiuchys nazad*, 63.

under the Soviet regime (which would ban them anyway).[75] An unintended consequence of this development was that even those who did not sympathize with the OUN had to turn toward it, since now it was the only organized Ukrainian political force left. Some of the OUN leaders were already thinking about creating a legal façade through which to deal with the German occupation regime. Also, in some localities where Polish authority had already vanished, but German authority had not yet been established, Ukrainian activists in October 1939 organized their local, ad hoc committees to fill the power vacuum.

Eventually, the Ukrainian exiles in Cracow under the initiative and influence of Melnyk's faction of the OUN (formally still a single organization) offered the Germans an opportunity to unify these committees under a central one — later named the Ukrainian Central Committee (*Ukrainischer Hauptausschuss*) — which was supposed to serve as an umbrella organization representing the entire Ukrainian population vis-à-vis the occupiers.[76] Frank gave his blessing for its creation in November 1939 during a meeting with a Ukrainian delegation led by Roman Sushko (1894-1944), a prominent Ounite and Melnyk sympathizer. It was Sushko whom the delegation proposed for the head of the Committee, but Frank told them to pick a different candidate because of political reasons.[77]

The selection was decided in favor of Volodymyr Kubijovyč (1900-1985) — a scholar, Ukrainian nationalist (but without any party affiliation) and soon-to-be German collaborator. Sushko was appointed his deputy. Kubijovyč was an odd choice for such a

---

75 Ivan Nimchuk, *595 dniv sovietskym viaznem* (Toronto: Vydavnytsvo i Drukarnia OO. Vasyliian, 1950), 25-26.
76 Kubijovyč, *Ukraintsi v Heneralnii Hubernii*, 58-59. The initial proposed name was Ukrainian National Association (*Ukrainske Natsionalne Obiednannia*).
77 According to Kubijovyč the meeting with Frank occurred after November 16: Kubijovyč, *Ukraintsi v Heneralnii Hubernii*, 65-66. Kucheruk dates it by November 12 based on archival documents: Oleksandr Kucheruk, "'... Vse, shcho zviazane z vyzvolenniam Ukrainy' (Do genezy vidnosyn Orhanizatsii Ukrainskykh Natsionalistiv ta Ukrainskoho Tsentralnoho Komitetu na pochatku Druhoi svitovoi viiny)," *Ukrainskyi vyzvolnyi rukh* no. 18 (2013): 27-28. A third date of the meeting, November 19, is given by Yevhen Yulii Pelenskyi: Ye. Yu. Pelenskyi, "Pered dvoma rokamy," *Krakivski Visti*, no 1 (448) January 2, 1942, 3.

political position as head of the Ukrainian Central Committee.[78] He was the offspring of a mixed Polish-Ukrainian marriage and grew up in the Lemko region but mostly in a Polish cultural environment.[79] By his own admission, in his 30s he knew Polish better than Ukrainian and was thinking in the former until he forced himself to switch to the latter.[80] According to people who met him in person he spoke Ukrainian with a Lemko accent.[81] In 1918-1919 Kubijovyč served in the Ukrainian Galician Army (field artillery branch) and fought against the Poles until he got sick with typhus.[82] In fall 1919 he resumed his studies in Cracow and received a doctorate in geography from the Jagiellonian University (1923, habilitation in 1928), specializing in the anthropogeography of the Carpathian Mountains.[83] In the 1930s, he turned his academic activity to the "national cause" (inspired by Polish patriotism, ironically) and worked on statistics and mapping of Ukrainian ethnicity, primarily

---

78 Kubijovyč's own speculation was that three factors played in favor of his candidature. He was a known scholar with connections to the German universities. During the interwar period he was not a member of any Ukrainian party and thus stood above any political rivalries. Kubijovyč was a "native" of the General Government in the sense that he was born and lived almost entire his life in that part of Poland which came under the German occupation in 1939. See: Volodymyr Kubijovyč, *Meni 70* (Munich: Logos, 1970), 38-39; Volodymyr Kubijovyč, *Meni 85* (Munich: Molode zhyttia, 1985), 89-90; Kubijovyč, *Ukraintsi v Heneralnii Hubernii*, 68.
79 Kubijovyč, *Meni 85*, 7, 11-12. Like his father, Kubijovyč also married a Polish woman. From the marriage he had two daughters. Both his first wife and the daughters remained in Poland after 1945. See: Kubijovyč, *Meni 85*, 28-29, 37, 53. Kubijovyč's cousin, Polish scholar Kazimierz Dobrowolski (1894-1987), claimed that they also had Jewish blood because the Dobrowolski line (Kubijovyč's mother belonged to it) descended from converted Jews. Kubijovyč recalled Dobrowolski telling him that "having a few drops of Jewish blood is good, and maybe to this we owe our academic contributions, but only a few drops—no more." See: Kubijovyč, *Meni 85*, 22.
80 Kubijovyč, *Meni 85*, 36-37.
81 Inna Zabolotna, "Roky nimetskoi okupatsii na Zakhidnii Ukraini za spohadamy Ivana Krypiakevycha," *Ukrainskyi arkheohrafichnyi shchorichnyk* vol. 10 no. 7 (Kyiv—New York: Vydavnytstvo M. P. Kots, 2002): 405; Roman Kolisnyk, "Moie znaimostvo z profesorom Volodymyrom Kubiovychem," in *Profesor Volodymyr Kubiovych*, ed. Oleh Shablii (Lviv: Vydavnychyi tsentr LNU imeni Ivana Franka, 2006), 357.
82 Kubijovyč, *Meni 70*, 13; Kubijovyč, *Meni 85*, 20, 25-26, 32, 38.
83 Kubijovyč, *Meni 85*, 38-40.

focusing on its Western borders.[84] This displeased the Polish authorities and nationalistic public who saw in his scholarship a security threat to Poland's eastern borders. Kubijovyč had received plenty of warning signs in the Polish press that his work was not perceived as politically harmless or innocent.[85] He persevered, even after some Polish students started to boycott his lectures in the late 1930s.[86] In the end, the Polish authorities forced his expulsion from the Jagiellonian University on June 16, 1939 (he had taught there since 1928).[87] He did not remain unemployed for long. The war would soon provide him with the greatest opportunities of his life, and from a jobless professor he would rise to a leader in charge of millions of people.

As a scholar Kubijovyč had a good reputation (at least in Ukrainian circles), but he lacked administrative experience. Educated in a Polish school and university within Polish ethnic territories, he stood apart from Galician Ukrainians, many of whom considered themselves model Ukrainians. For them he was an outsider, who in the interwar period "rarely visited Lviv, did not know [Galician] Ukrainian relations and [Galician] Ukrainian human potential."[88] He also had a character that was easier to respect than to like. Ukrainian historian Ivan Krypiakevych (1886-1967), who knew Kubijovyč personally, described him in 1944 as "ambitious," "power-

---

84 "[In the 1930s] I took an active part in the struggle between two nationalities, Polish and Ukrainian, but as a scholar, not as a politician. That I became a Ukrainian obliged me to do something [for the Ukrainian cause]. In my patriotism I followed the [example of] Polish patriotism, Poles were passionate and self-sacrificing patriots." See: Kubijovyč, *Meni 85*, 37. Another source of the motivation was marrying a Polish woman in 1929: "Strange as it may seem, but my marriage to a Polish woman did not bring me closer to Poles, on the contrary it pushed me to work more intensely on the Ukrainian front; to some extent it felt like paying the debt to the Ukrainian cause for my marriage to a Polish woman." See: Kubijovyč, *Meni 85*, 54.
85 Paweł Markiewicz, "Volodymyr Kubijovych's Ethnographic Ukraine: Theory into Practice on the Western *Okraiiny*," *Jahrbücher für Geschichte Osteuropas* 64, no. 2 (April 2016): 237.
86 Kubijovyč, *Meni 85*, 56.
87 Markiewicz, "Volodymyr Kubijovych's Ethnographic Ukraine," 238. For Kubijovyč's description of the expulsion see: Kubijovyč, *Meni 85*, 61-63.
88 Ivan Kedryn, *Zhyttia – podii – liudy. Spomyny i komentari* (New York: Chervona Kalyna, 1976), 361.

hungry," "energetic" and "cold."[89] According to him, Kubijovyč enjoyed a "good reputation among the Germans. He knew how to talk to them because he himself had the German cold character and as a type was close to a German, and that is why he often achieved what he wanted."[90] It seems that the occupation regime was indeed satisfied with Kubijovyč: he remained the head of the UCC until its very end in 1945. In his memoirs he made no mention of Germans ever trying to replace him.

Audience at the Wawel Royal Castle: Hans Frank (third from right) receives the Ukrainian delegation headed by Volodymyr Kubijovyč (first from left). October 1940, Cracow. Copyright Narodowe Archiwum Cyfrowe/National Digital Archives, Poland

In running the UCC Kubijovyč strove for total control of the organization with little tolerance to criticism or internal opposition. In German his position was called *Leiter*, a mere director, but in Ukrainian he referred to himself as *Providnyk*, a Leader, of the UCC, a much more ambitious title.[91] When Levko Lukasevych met

---

89 Zabolotna, "Roky nimetskoi okupatsii," 406.
90 Ibidem.
91 Adolf Hitler and Benito Mussolini were referred to as *Providnyk* in Ukrainian. The OUNs also used the title for its own leaders.

Kubijovyč in 1941, he saw a man who was "sick on *vozhdyzm*," that is cult of personal leadership.[92] "He liked authoritarian order" recalled Krypiakevych in 1944.[93] Yurii Shevelov wrote in his memoirs that Kubijovyč, with whom he became well acquainted in 1943-1944, displayed a "distinct inclination toward Fuhrerism" and "megalomania of being the leader of the [Ukrainian] nation."[94]

Hans Frank (center) celebrates the harvest festival with members of the Ukrainian delegation at the Wawel Royal Castle. The man right behind him is Volodymyr Kubijovyč. October 24, 1943, Cracow. Copyright Narodowe Archiwum Cyfrowe/National Digital Archives, Poland

In his history of the UCC, Kubijovyč did not shy away from addressing this issue, though he depersonalized his answer. He

---

92 Levko Lukasevych, *Rozdumy na skhylku zhyttia* (New York: St. Sophia Ukrainian Orthodox Publishers, 1982), 223.
93 Zabolotna, "Roky nimetskoi okupatsii," 406.
94 Yurii Shevelov, *Ya – mene – meni... (i dovkruhy)* vol. 1 (Kharkiv: Vydavets Oleksandr Savchuk, 2017), 443-444, 577. In this memoir, which was written in the 1980s, Shevelov described Kubijovyč as one of few Ukrainians who had "the character and bearing of a statesman" (Ibidem, 459), adding: "He was ruthless and stubborn, with unwavering will, qualities that make a true politician out of tens of thousands of people around. He could have been a leader of the nation [vozhd natsii]. After the celebration of his 80th birthday in New York, he admitted to me that that was his ambition." See: Ibidem, 577.

recognized the negative sides of the leadership (*providnytska*) system: "its biggest flaw is that it does not have a space for criticism, it does not allow healthy competition between different groups and the leadership's connection with society is rather weak."[95] But he defended the system as a "good" short-term solution in "exceptional circumstances," such as war, which require "fast and decisive decisions." In the case of the UCC, "the leadership system was completely appropriate and in line with the spirit of the times."[96] In addition, he claimed that the leadership system was imposed on the UCC by the occupying regime, which was very sensitive to any "democratic deviations."[97]

That said, in the UCC's first year and a half Kubijovyč was hardly an all-deciding and all-controlling *Providnyk*. By his own admission, the OUN (specifically a small group of well-connected Melnykites headed by Roman Sushko) played a crucial role in setting up the UCC and staffing it with Ounites at key positions both in the central and district apparatus.[98] "There was nothing strange in that the strongest group seized the most important positions," wrote Kubijovyč.[99] The Ounization of the UCC, according to him, had positive and negative sides. The positive was that the Ounites were energetic, passionate and dedicated to the Ukrainian national cause. The negatives were lack of experience, skills and patience; inability to do continuous "grey" work that does not produce quick results; combatting other Ukrainian nationalists as political enemies; using positions in the UCC as a cover for OUN-related activities (propaganda, collecting money, etc.).[100] In terms of loyalty the Ounites put their organization above the UCC and were not afraid to commit "disloyal actions" such as copying the Committee's internal documentation or even stealing its equipment.[101]

---

95 Kubijovyč, *Ukraintsi v Heneralnii Hubernii*, 333.
96 Ibidem, 332.
97 Ibidem, 331.
98 Ibidem, 334-335. Ivan Kedryn in his memoirs described Roman Sushko as "the grey eminence" of the UCC. Kubijovyč, he wrote, often could not resolve an issue without Sushko's decision: Kedryn, *Zhyttia – podii – liudy*, 362.
99 Kubijovyč, *Ukraintsi v Heneralnii Hubernii*, 336.
100 Ibidem, 335-337.
101 Ibidem, 338-339.

Two factors weakened the OUN's hold over the UCC and allowed Kubijovyč to strengthen his personal authority. The first was the breakup of Ounites into two competing factions, Banderites and Melnykites, within the OUN and then their formal separation into two OUNs over the course of 1939-1941. In this struggle, the UCC became an important battlefield between the two factions. Melnykites were in the minority in the UCC apparatus, but they controlled top positions and had better connections in the occupying administration and, most importantly, in Berlin. Banderites dominated in low-ranking positions and in local committees. According to Kubijovyč, they enjoyed some victories in their attempt to take over the UCC, but in the end Melnykites came out on top. The latter managed to preserve their presence atop the UCC's hierarchy and even became a majority among "loyal" Ounites who remained to work for the UCC. Other Ounites either left or were replaced by "local" cadres resulting in a decrease of the Ounites' share in the UCC's personnel.[102]

The second factor was the German invasion of the Soviet Union in June 1941. The spectacular successes of the German advance inspired "hundreds" of young Ounites in the General Government to abandon their "public work," which included working for the UCC, and join the *pokhidni hrupy* (expeditionary groups) that both OUNs sent out in the wake of German troops.[103] But senior Melnykites such as Sushko remained in their positions at the UCC after 1941. It should be noted that the general political line of Melnykites in the General Government and that of Kubijovyč's—maintaining and developing Ukrainian national life within legal boundaries set by the occupation regime—continued to overlap until the very end, which perhaps was not a coincidence.[104] Later in his memoirs

---

102 Ibidem, 343-346; Kubijovyč, *Meni 85*, 95.
103 Kubijovyč, *Meni 70*, 45; Kubijovyč, *Meni 85*, 97.
104 Kedryn claimed that after 1941 the UCC became fully emancipated from Ounites: "Following the breakup of the OUN, Melnykites completely took over the UCC apparatus, but things changed after the Germans marched East [in 1941]. Both Melnykites and Banderites dispersed and went to Ukraine in their 'expeditionary groups,' then came German repressions against both wings of the OUN, and when the UCC expanded [its authority] to entire 'General Government,' which [now] included Eastern Galicia, the UCC emancipated itself

Kubijovyč wrote that the UCC's reputation as a "Melnykite" organization was "not entirely deserved."[105] In his history of the UCC he described the Committee as a "non-partisan and, to some extent, above-party organization."[106] As its leader "I did not consider myself subordinated to the OUN."[107]

This postwar recollection is challenged by the documents from 1940-1941. They show Kubijovyč actively pursuing Melnykite involvement with the UCC: at a three-day conference between the UCC leadership and Melnykites in Berlin in December 1940 it was Kubijovyč who was convincing Andrii Melnyk, not the other way around, to allow "as many nationalists [that is, Melnykites] as possible" to be employed by the UCC and that "95% of the [Melnykite] OUN's work can be done" through the UCC's legal framework.[108] The conference resulted in a ten-point agreement that defined the relationship between the UCC and Melnyk's OUN as "cooperation" (*spivdilannia*). The points included the UCC submitting to the OUN's ideological primacy; the UCC agreeing to be used as a framework through which the OUN could operate in the General Government; besides Melnykites the UCC had the right to employ other Ukrainian nationalists if really necessary, except "mutineers" (meaning Banderites); "saboteurs" (Banderites again) still working in the UCC apparatus had to be removed "as soon as possible." In return, the OUN promised to support the UCC activities "by any means possible" and promote "the authority of its leadership in the Ukrainian community." Both parties agreed to keep their "cooperation" in secret.[109]

Later, in May 1941, Kubijovyč sent a letter to Melnyk about the necessity to consolidate "Ukrainian forces under one strong National Leadership" in anticipation of a Ukrainian state ("hopefully soon"). Melnyk, he wrote, should: rise above the "narrow

---

from the OUN's monopolizing influence and became an independent Ukrainian public entity." See: Kedryn, *Zhyttia – podii – liudy*, 363.

105 Kubijovyč, *Meni 70*, 44; Kubijovyč, *Meni 85*, 95.
106 Kubijovyč, *Ukraintsi v Heneralnii Hubernii*, 334.
107 Ibidem, 338.
108 Kucheruk, "'... Vse, shcho zviazane z vyzvolenniam Ukrainy,'" 33.
109 Ibidem, 36-38.

framework" of the OUN and political divisions to become "the leader of the Nation" (*vozhd Natsii*); start relying on people based on their "character, ability and professionalism" rather than their political affiliation; submit the OUN to a "complete and radical sanation" (*sanatsiia*); establish "cooperation" with the UCC based on an "equally mutual approach to accomplishing tasks and on trust."[110] This willingness to recognize Melnyk as the head of a future Ukrainian state makes Kubijovyč's reaction to the Banderite proclamation of the Ukrainian State on June 30, 1941 in Lviv even more strange. Upon learning the news on the radio, he assembled (despite "having doubts") the UCC staff to welcome "the creation of a new Ukrainian government" (which was formed by the Banderites) and "called for loyalty toward it."[111] Two days later, however, Kubijovyč traveled to Lviv to see the real situation and, if his memoirs were to be believed, found out that no Ukrainian organization, including the Banderite government, qualified to be a "real Ukrainian center" in Galicia.[112] Soon he would learn that Galicia would be incorporated into the General Government as the fifth district despite Ukrainian protests (ignored by the occupiers). Initially Kubijovyč resisted German orders to extend the UCC operations into the new district but eventually, after Germans closed down the local committee (*Ukrainskyi Kraiovyi Komitet*), was forced to do so in February 1942.[113]

Besides Kubijovyč's commitment to the Ukrainian national cause in family life and academic work, we know nothing about his political or social views in the interwar period. His memoirs provide no information in this regard.[114] During the war he was quick to adopt Nazi public rituals such as celebrating birthdays of Hitler and Frank in the General Government or using the Hitler salute.[115]

---

110 Ibidem, 30-31.
111 Kubijovyč, *Meni 85*, 97.
112 Ibidem, 98.
113 Ibidem, 99-100, 103.
114 In his history of the UCC he wrote one sentence on this matter: "Before the war I took no part in political life." See: Kubijovyč, *Ukraintsi v Heneralnii Hubernii*, 67.
115 There was an attempt to introduce a similar public celebration for Kubijovyč too. In 1943 the UCC declared the feast of St. Volodymyr as the name day to honor Kubijovyč for the sake of "nurturing [his] authority." See: Kost

His correspondence with German authorities reveals that he became skilled at adopting Nazi political language and using it in his proposals and requests.[116] He was, at least outwardly, quite loyal toward the occupation authorities. But behind those public displays of loyalty to the German officials and Nazi symbols most likely lay not conviction but calculation. There is no documentary evidence to suggest that he *genuinely* sympathized with the Nazi ideology. That does not mean that he was without a bias. Kubijovyč, like many people of his time, favored racial thinking and retained it even in the postwar years. In 1947 Ukrainian émigré scholars in Germany reestablished Shevchenko Scientific Society (*NTSh*) which was closed by the Soviets in Lviv in 1940. Ivan Rakovskyi (1874-1949) was elected its head, Kubijovyč—general secretary.[117] Two years later the Society published "Vstup do rasovoi budovy Ukrainy" (Introduction to Racial Structure of Ukraine) by Rostyslav Yendyk (1906-1974).[118] Yendyk was a Ukrainian nationalist and racial theorist, who before the war wrote a praising biography of

---

Pankivskyi, Vasyl Hlibovytskyi, "V spravi vshanuvannia Imianyn Providnyka," *Krakivski Visti* no. 160 (898) July 25, 1943, 3.

116 See: Wasyl Veryha, comp., *The Correspondence of the Ukrainian Central Committee in Cracow and Lviv with the German Authorities 1939–1944*, 2 vols., Research Report No. 61 (Edmonton: Canadian Institute of Ukrainian Studies Press, 2000). Historian Tarik Cyril Amar offered an interesting observation on this matter: "The face Kubiiovych presented to the Germans was that of a kindred spirit, an up-to-date right-wing *völkisch* totalitarian, aware of the opportunities offered by a new order. The question of which Kubiiovych was truer (or perhaps preferable to himself in hindsight), the fluent speaker of Nazi or one who was just lying in it, is moot. What is pertinent is that it was possible to effectively speak Nazi to Nazis and then become an 'innocent nationalist' during the Cold War. Kubiiovych's truth, if any, was that he mastered both." See: Tarik Cyril Amar, *The Paradox of Ukrainian Lviv: A Borderland City between Stalinists, Nazis, and Nationalists* (Ithaca; London: Cornell University Press, 2015), 129.

117 Kubijovyč, *Meni 85*, 203-204.

118 Rostyslav Yendyk, *Vstup do rasovoi budovy Ukrainy* (Munich: Nakladom Naukovoho Tovarystva im. Shevchenka, 1949). On Yendyk see: Oleksandr Zaitsev, *Ukrainskyi integralnyi natsionalizm (1920-1930-ti) roky: narysy intelektualnoi istorii* (Kyiv: Krytyka, 2013), 342-343, 359-361; Myroslav Shkandrij, *Ukrainian Nationalism: Politics, Ideology, and Literature, 1929-1956* (New Haven, CT: Yale University Press, 2015), 97-98. Yendyk's racial views on Ukrainians were summarized in: "Rasovi probliemy," *Krakivski Visti*, no. 120 (275) June 6, 1941, 5. According to the summary, Yendyk considered Jews a group whose "great harmfulness is evident."

Hitler[119] and admired the work of German "racial scientist" Hans F. K. Günther (1891-1968) whose ideas he popularized in Ukrainian.[120]

"Vstup do rasovoi budovy Ukrainy" reads as if it was written in the 1930s Nazi Germany which adopted "racial science" as an academic discipline and as a political practice: the book, which presented itself as a scientific work, praised European racial theorists (especially Gobineau and Günther), advocated racial worldview, racial purity and racial determinism. In a letter from 1952 Kubijovyč wrote that he liked the book, but as the Society's general secretary he was forced, for external reasons, to stop its distribution: "Without a doubt, it is a good book, but he [Yendyk] also put in it some comments about Jews, that now offend oversensitive Jews."[121] In other words, the book was not wrong, it was merely untimely. Kubijovyč ordered to move all its copies to a basement, but news about a forbidden book made it popular so "certain people have been stealing it and selling it in America," where it caused a scandal in the "socialist and Orthodox newspapers." To prevent further theft and circulation, the remaining copies of the book were "destroyed." The whole affair—"Yendykiada" in Kubijovyč's words—showed him the absurdity of the US press, which may write any "stupidities" about everyone, including the President, "but is not free to touch Jews-Masonry [zhydiv-masonerii]."[122] Yendyk must had not been happy with how Kubijovyč handled backlash to his magnum opus, but it seems that their relationship had survived this negative episode. When the latter launched his project of *Entsyklopediia Ukrainoznavstva*, the former contributed articles on Ukrainian anthropology and races.[123]

Nominally the UCC was one of the three social aid organizations Germans allowed to Ukrainians, Poles (*Rada Główna*

---

119 Rostyslav Yendyk, *Hitlier* (Lviv, 1934).
120 Rostyslav Yendyk, "Hans F. K. Ginter," *Krakivski Visti* no. 39 (195) February 24, 1941, 6.
121 Letter from Volodymyr Kubijovyč to Mykhailo Khomiak November 17, 1952. PAA, Michael Chomiak fonds, File PR1985.0191/184.
122 Ibidem.
123 See Yendyk's signed articles "Antropolohiia na Ukraini" (1955, vol. 1: 52) and "Rasy ї rasovi formatsii Ukrainy" (vol. 2: 2468-2470).

Opiekuńcza), and Jews (*Jüdische Soziale Selbsthilfe*). However, by Kubijovyč's own admission the UCC had more authority over its own ethnic group than the Polish and Jewish committees over theirs.[124] Due either to Frank's attitude to Ukrainians or his desire to unload certain functions from the German administration (or both) Kubijovyč and the UCC were able to enforce their views and policies on many aspects of Ukrainian life under German occupation. Culture, education, healthcare and many other aspects of everyday life of Ukrainians in the General Government were almost entirely under the control of the UCC. In certain areas, the UCC operated even beyond its German mandate and engaged in activities that, according to Kubijovyč, were "borderline illegal," such as helping Ukrainian political prisoners, refugees from the *Reichskommissariat* Ukraine, and Ukrainian academics in the *Reichskommissariat* and in the Protectorate of Bohemia and Moravia. To avoid German ire an effective solution was found. The UCC staff produced two sets of reports, a complete one in Ukrainian for the Committee's leadership and one in German for the occupation authorities, which simply omitted information that could get the UCC into trouble.[125] No bureaucratic trail, no problem. The UCC's power also expanded spatially to Galicia, the fifth district of the General Government, in February 1942.[126] Arguably the peak of the Committee's influence was reached in 1943 when it became directly involved in military recruitment for the Waffen-SS division *Galizien*.[127]

Kubijovyč had an ambitious program of developing and elevating Ukrainians as an ethnic group into a modern nation. On several occasions he tried to persuade Hans Frank to expand his pro-Ukrainian policies and the UCC's authority, turning it into a quasi-government for Ukrainians. On June 21, 1941 (just one day before Germany's invasion of the Soviet Union) Kubijovyč proposed to

---

124 Kubijovyč, *Meni 85*, 91.
125 Kubijovyč, *Ukraintsi v Heneralnii Hubernii*, 114; Kubijovyč, *Meni 85*, 92.
126 Kubijovyč, *Meni 85*, 103. In 1941 the UCC also tried to expand outside the General Government, to Volhynia, but was not successful: Kubijovyč, *Meni 85*, 102.
127 Per Anders Rudling, "'They Defended Ukraine': The 14. Waffen-Grenadier-Division der SS (Galizische Nr. 1) Revisited," *The Journal of Slavic Military Studies*, 25:3 (2012): 339.

Frank to establish a purely ethnic Ukrainian enclave in the General Government, which would be free of "the Polish and Jewish element by resettlement."[128] Naturally, the UCC would be in charge of the proposed enclave. A month later, on August 29, he submitted another proposal, this time regarding the Jewish properties:

> Considering that all Jewish property originally belonged for the most part to the Ukrainian people and only through ruthless law-breaking on the part of the Jews and through their exploitation of members of the Ukrainian people did it pass into Jewish possession, we deem it a requirement of justice, in order to make restitution to the Ukrainian people for moral and material damages, that a very considerable portion of confiscated Jewish property be returned to the Ukrainian people. In particular, all Jewish land holdings should be given to Ukrainian peasants.[129]

None of these proposals were implemented. It seems that at the time Kubijovyč had not realized yet that though Germans treated Ukrainians favorably compared to Poles and Jews there were also limits to this positive discrimination. There was a certain duality in the pro-Ukrainian policies of the occupation authorities—the advancement of Ukrainians was encouraged, but the occupiers had no interest in strengthening the Ukrainian minority above its counter-balancing role against Jews and Poles. Protecting the superior position of the German minority in the General Government excluded any possibilities of a Ukrainian enclave or a massive increase of Ukrainian landholdings. The occupation regime needed Ukrainian peasants in the function of agricultural workers in the Third Reich, not as a wealthy peasant class in the General Government. That place was already reserved for Germans. Some of Kubijovyč's German connections privately warned him that he personally and all Ukrainians in the General Government existed at the occupier's mercy. When the UCC was founded, its charter was written by SS-*Obersturmbannführer* Fritz Arlt, one of the Ukrainian

---

[128] Veryha, comp., *The Correspondence*, vol.1: 242. Cited after: Himka, "Ethnicity and the Reporting," 396.
[129] Veryha, comp., *The Correspondence*, vol.1: 342. Cited after: Himka, "Ethnicity and the Reporting," 397.

sympathizers in the occupation administration.[130] After studying national relations in the General Government Arlt concluded that *immediate* German interests would benefit from supporting Ukrainians, to which extent he himself wrote a brochure on the Ukrainian question for German officials in the General Government.[131] Yet he also cautioned Kubijovyč about German interests and friends: "I like Ukrainians and will help them gladly, but if I received an order to annihilate you [Ukrainians], I would have carried it out. Keep this in mind."[132]

Indeed, Frank's pro-Ukrainian policies were purely tactical and designed to last only as long as the occupation authorities found them useful against Poles and Jews in the General Government, whose removal he estimated (in March 1941) would take from fifteen to twenty years.[133] Once they were no longer useful, the Ukrainians would share the same fate as the Poles: in March 1942 Frank noted in his diary that both ethnic groups would have to be removed from the General Government in the postwar decades[134] and in January 1944, at a meeting with Cracow district officials Frank declared that when the war is over "as far as I am concerned, we can make mincemeat of the Poles and the Ukrainians and all the other people hanging around here."[135] In his memoirs, Kubijovyč wrote that he had some inkling about what fate Ukrainians could expect under the German occupation from confidential

---

130 Kubijovyč, *Meni 85*, 167. The UCC's charter (German original and Ukrainian translation) were republished in: Kubijovyč, *Ukraintsi v Heneralnii Hubernii*, 454-479. On Arlt see: Frank Mecklenburg, "Von der Hitlerjugend zum Holocaust. Die Karriere des Fritz Arlt," in *Deutsche, Juden, Völkermord. Der Holocaust als Geschichte und Gegenwart*, ed. Jürgen Matthäus and Klaus M. Mallmann (Darmstadt: Wiss. Buchges., 2006), 87-102; Paweł Markiewicz, *Unlikely Allies: Nazi German and Ukrainian Nationalist Collaboration in the General Government During World War II* (West Lafayette, IN: Purdue University Press, 2021), 47-49.
131 Kubijovyč, *Meni 85*, 167. In his memoirs Kubijovyč wrote that Arlt's understanding of Ukrainian matters was influenced by Alfred Bisanz, a Galician German who knew Ukrainian well. See: Kubijovyč, *Meni 85*, 148. In his history of the UCC he credited Dmytro Paliiv for introducing Arlt to the "Ukrainian problem": Kubijovyč, *Ukraintsi v Heneralnii Hubernii*, 349.
132 Kubijovyč, *Meni 85*, 168.
133 Housden, *Hans Frank*, 142.
134 Ibidem, 148.
135 Ibidem, 198; Piotrowski, *Hans Frank's Diary*, 46.

conversations, usually after some alcohol intake ("whenever possible my glass was filled with water"), with administration and SS officials who were telling him: "You are such a sympathetic people and treat us [Germans] so well, but if you knew what awaits you ..."[136] Ironically, it was the Soviet victory, against which the Division *Galizien* fought, that prevented the realization of these genocidal plans against Ukrainians.

The Ukrainian Publishing House (*Ukrainske Vydavnytsvo*)

In 1939 Kubijovyč's vision of the UCC included an ambitious program of Ukrainian national revival in the Chełm, Lemko, Nadsanie and Podlasie regions for which he needed, among other things, a variety of books (from elementary school textbooks to more specialized literature) and periodicals that would also satisfy cultural needs of the Ukrainian colony in Cracow. In short, the UCC needed its own publishing center. On December 27, 1939 Kubijovyč with seven other Ukrainian activists registered in Cracow a limited company named *Ukrainischer Verlag* in German or *Ukrainske Vydavnytstvo* (Ukrainian Publishing House) in Ukrainian with a starting capital of ten thousand zloty, which Kubijovyč borrowed from one of the seven.[137] Formally the Ukrainian Publishing House (UPH) was not a part of the UCC's infrastructure. Instead, both organizations were tied through a personal connection: almost all shareholders of the UPH worked in the UCC's central apparatus. Kubijovyč personally held 65% shares (13 out of 20) of the company, though it did not pay dividends.[138] In Cracow, the UPH had two printing presses at its disposal, one of which the occupation authorities confiscated from the Polish Jewish newspaper *Nowy Dziennik* (New Daily).[139] In his history of the UCC Kubijovyč claimed that

---

136 Kubijovyč, *Meni 85*, 104.
137 The company's charter in Ukrainian translation is available in: Kubijovyč, *Ukraintsi v Heneralnii Hubernii*, 521-524. The Cracow District Court registered the company on January 16, 1940: Ibidem, 251.
138 Ibidem, 251.
139 Ibidem, 252, 257.

the UPH owed neither of the presses, though on the same page he mentioned buying a linotype (an expensive purchase) for one of them from Germany.[140] The first director of the UPH, Yevhen Yulii Pelenskyi (1908-1956), was also in charge of the confiscated press.[141]

German authorities never allowed the creation of another Ukrainian press, thus making the UPH a monopolist in printing Ukrainian-language publications in the General Government.[142] This status lasted until the incorporation of Galicia in summer 1941. At that point, the occupation regime set up a German publishing house in Lviv which began to print a Ukrainian-language newspaper *Lvivski Visti*, a competitor to *Krakivski Visti* in a sense.[143] The UPH even came under threat of being "bought" (read acquired) by Germans, now that the Ukrainian population of the General Government had increased significantly. Kubijovyč resisted this acquisition attempt and even threatened to resign from the UCC. Eventually, a compromise was reached: the German publishing house would continue to publish *Lvivski Visti*, but the UPH was allowed to operate in district Galicia and open a branch in Lviv.[144]

The UPH distributed most of its publications in the General Government and in the Third Reich.[145] In 1940-1941 the UPH faced a multitude of tough issues — lack of financial capital; limited production capability (two printing presses quickly proved to be not enough); unqualified and little qualified personnel, conflicts within

---

140 Ibidem, 257.
141 Ibidem, 252, 257, 260. It seems that Pelenskyi was appointed a *Treuhänder* (Ukrainians often referred to such people as "commissars") of the confiscated press by the occupation administration. After the war Kubijovyč complained that these lucrative positions, to manage expropriated Jewish businesses, attracted many "qualified professional" Ukrainians, whom he would have preferred to use in the UCC: Kubijovyč, *Ukraintsi v Heneralnii Hubernii*, 326. Ivan Kedryn also wrote about the phenomenon in his memoirs, describing it as a "clear and honest" way to earn money under the occupation: Kedryn, *Zhyttia — podii — liudy*, 348.
142 Kubijovyč, *Ukraintsi v Heneralnii Hubernii*, 253.
143 Ostap Tarnavskyi, *Literaturnyi Lviv, 1939-1944: Spomyny* (Lviv: Prosvita, 1995), 86-87.
144 Kubijovyč, *Meni 85*, 101.
145 Kubijovyč, *Ukraintsi v Heneralnii Hubernii*, 282. At one point, Kubijovyč even wanted to open a UPH branch in Berlin (this plan was not realized): Ibidem, 283.

the management; shortages of paper; difficulties with occupation censorship.[146] Nonetheless, the UPH turned out to be profitable already by the end of 1940. It would have earned even more had it not published periodicals. They were a financial loss in 1940-1941.[147] That said, Kubijovyč treated the UPH as a "public institution" rather than as a commercial enterprise, so profitability was not his key concern. To support the Ukrainian intelligentsia ("producers of spiritual values"), the UPH paid honoraria even for unpublished manuscripts, including those that it "had no intention to publish" in the first place. "But I thought it was a good investment of capital," wrote Kubijovyč after the war.[148]

The UPH's book catalog consisted mostly of school materials (primers, textbooks, readers), Ukrainian literary classics (Shevchenko was leading here) and popular literature.[149] This was not accidental. When the UPH wanted to publish more sophisticated literature, it usually received a flat rejection from the censors (typically under the pretext of paper shortage). Similarly to the racial hierarchy, it was important for German occupiers to maintain a hierarchy of cultures. The forms of higher cultural expressions were reserved primarily for them—Ukrainians needed to be educated, but only sufficiently to understand their German superiors and follow their orders. Any intellectual, cultural parity between the two groups—Germans and Ukrainians—was unthinkable for the German occupiers. For example, it took Kubijovyč's personal intervention, using his German connections, to get the censor's approval for the publication of a book by the Ukrainian archeologist Yaroslav Pasternak (1892-1969).[150] The whole affair highlighted for Kubijovyč that academic publications were "for Germans only."[151]

---

146 Ibidem, 255-262.
147 Ibidem, 262, 283-284.
148 Ibidem, 281-282.
149 Ibidem, 262-272.
150 Yaroslav Pasternak, *Staryi Halych: arkheolohichno-istorychni doslidy u 1850-1943 rr.* (Krakiv-Lviv: Ukrainske vydavnytstvo, 1944).
151 Kubijovyč, *Meni 85*, 170.

Krakivski Visti: origins, content and distribution

For its official news the UCC published *Visnyk Ukrainskoho Tsentralnoho Komitetu* (Herald of the Ukrainian Central Committee).[152] Kubijovyč's ambition, however, was greater: he wanted to have a major Ukrainian-language newspaper for the Ukrainian population of the General Government. This newspaper was to fill the vacuum left after *Dilo*, the best-known and most popular newspaper in Western Ukraine. The Soviets closed it down in September 1939 by confiscating its printing press and offices in Lviv, which they used for the newspaper that they decided to publish instead — *Vilna Ukraina* (Free Ukraine).[153] *Dilo* was founded in Lviv in 1880 making it one of the oldest Ukrainian newspapers. It was also the first Ukrainian daily newspaper (since 1888). In the history of the Ukrainian national project, newspapers played an important, though somewhat underappreciated role, which explains why they have been studied so poorly in historiography. Besides their primary function — news — they also focused on "awakening" and later affirming and spreading Ukrainianhood. By the beginning of the 20th Century *Dilo* had become more than just a leading Ukrainian newspaper, but the Ukrainian **national** newspaper, demonstrating that a high culture with its articulated, sophisticated expressions and forms was possible in Ukrainian too.[154]

The newspaper that Kubijovyč had in mind in 1939 was to play a similar nationalizing role. The guidelines that either the UCC or the UPH prepared for its editors stated unambiguously that the newspaper's primary ideology was "Ukrainian nationalism."[155] Commitment to the national cause was shown even in the smallest of details — for example, throughout the war all official correspondence within the UCC was signed not with *Heil Hitler!* but *Slava*

---

[152] Kubijovyč, *Ukraintsi v Heneralnii Hubernii,* 129, 138.
[153] Nimchuk, *595 dniv,* 24, 29.
[154] For a history of *Dilo* see: Yu. H. Shapoval, *I v Ukraini sviatylos te slovo* (Lviv: PAIS, 2003).
[155] "Pravylnyk dlia Redaktsiï shchodennyka 'Krakivski Visti.'" PAA, Michael Chomiak fonds, File PR1985.0191/28.

Ukraini (Glory to Ukraine).[156] Initially, even the newspaper's name was supposed to be either *Ukrainski Visty* (Ukrainian News) or *Ukrainskyi Holos* (Ukrainian Voice), but the occupation authorities did not allow ethnonyms in titles of periodicals.[157] The next name choice was *Yaroslavskyi Visnyk* (Yaroslav Herald), after the town of Yaroslav (Polish Jarosław), where the initial seat of the UCC was expected to be. But since it was decided that the Committee would instead have its headquarters in Cracow the name of the newspaper was changed to *Krakivski Visty* (Cracow News).[158] Due to an orthography reform that Ukrainian cultural activists and educators passed in the General Government in March 1940 *visty* now had to be spelled as *visti*. The newspaper changed its name from *Krakivski Visty* to *Krakivski Visti* on May 6, 1940.[159]

The newspaper's first issue was dated January 7, 1940.[160] At first, *Krakivski Visti* appeared two times per week, from May 1, 1940 three times per week and from November 1, 1940 daily. To expand the Committee's reach to the rural population of the General Government a weekly edition of *Krakivski Visti* was also established.[161] The two editions were supposed to differ in the selection of texts and in the sophistication of their presentation: at a higher level in the daily edition (for city dwellers) and lower in the weekly one (for peasants). In reality, the weekly edition often was used for those texts that were deemed publishable but, for various reasons, did not make it into a daily edition. A typical daily issue of *Krakivski Visti* looked as follows.

If there were any important speeches of Nazi leaders (Hitler, Goebbels, Göring, etc.) that the occupation administration deemed

---

156 For some reason, the slogan is mainly associated with one faction of the OUN, namely Banderites. In reality, it was ubiquitous among Ukrainian nationalists in the 1930s-1940s, even Hetmanites used it.
157 Ye. Yu. Pelenskyi, "Pered dvoma rokamy," *Krakivski Visti*, no 1 (448) January 2, 1942, 3.
158 Ibidem.
159 Ivan Zilynskyi, "Chomu zmineno nazvu 'Krakivskykh Vistei'?" *Krakivski Visti*, no. 38 May 6, 1940, 1-2.
160 According to Kubijovyč, it was printed on January 6: Kubijovyč, *Ukraintsi v Heneralnii Hubernii*, 253.
161 Himka, "*Krakivs'ki visti*: An Overview," 252.

necessary to publish, then they opened the issue. For some reason, the speeches were paraphrased rather than fully translated, typically with only two or three paragraphs being a direct translation. The next important block was reports on the course of the war. These were the largest and the most unoriginal content published in the *Krakivski Visti*, typically translated or paraphrased from German information bulletins. It was not rare for an issue to have up to half of its space filled with such war-related materials. Next in importance were political news and opinion pieces. There was a clear distinction in reporting on the Axis and the Allied powers. News about the former was purely informative (Minister Ciano arrived in Budapest on such a date, met with such officials, etc.). News about the latter, on the other hand, was always packaged with negative stamps borrowed from Nazi propaganda. Besides news political analysis was also frequent, and these entries were more original.

The next regular block of materials concerned identity politics: articles on national issues, religious affairs, language, and history of the Ukrainians. These were the most original and sophisticated pieces published in the newspaper. This cultural legacy, which remains mostly unknown in contemporary Ukraine, was written by the Ukrainian intellectual elite of the 20th century. They included the following: Dmytro Doroshenko, Panas Fedenko, Damian Horniatkevych, Myron Korduba, Yurii Kosach, Hryhorii Kostiuk, Ivan Krypiakevych, Zenon Kuzelia, Bohdan Lepkyi, Denys Lukiianovych, Yurii Lypa, Evhen Malaniuk, Vasyl Mudryi, Oleksander Ohloblyn, Yevhen Onatskyi, Sofiia Parfanovych, Yurii (George Y.) Shevelov, and Mykhailo Vozniak.[162] These three blocks—war, politics and culture—featured in the newspaper throughout its whole existence. In addition, the newspaper published articles on a wide variety of topics, from personal hygiene to Galician yoga. The last page of *Krakivski Visti* was usually reserved for advertisements, which are quite insightful about everyday life in the General Government.

Chronologically the history of *Krakivski Visti* can be split into four periods: 1) January 1940 – June 1941; 2) June 1941 – Spring

---

162 Himka, "*Krakivski visti* and the Jews," 84.

1943; 3) Spring 1943 – October 1944; 4) October 1944 – April 1945. This periodization reflects changes in Nazi press policy, in the quality of *Krakivski Visti* as a newspaper, and in its general ideological direction. During the first period *Krakivski Visti* focused mostly on local matters (Chełm, Lemko, Nadsanie and Podlasie regions) and was not allowed by the censorship to publish any negative materials about the Soviet Union which at that time was a quasi-ally of Nazi Germany. The second period started after the German invasion of the Soviet Union in June 1941 and the inclusion of Galicia in the General Government. The newspaper was now allowed to write on a larger variety of topics, it became engaged in intensive anti-Semitic and anti-Soviet propaganda and significantly expanded its readership after the incorporation of Galicia. Spring 1943 marked the beginning of the third period. Germany was losing the war, and the authorities made some steps to increase loyalty among the occupied population (except Jews, of course) and boost their participation in the war effort.[163] Ukrainians were allowed to create their own military formation, the Waffen-SS division *Galizien*, the campaign for which was widely reflected in *Krakivski Visti*. Anti-Soviet propaganda and praise for Nazi Germany as the only bulwark against "Judeo-Bolshevik hordes" became even more fervent. With the advance of the Red Army into Poland, the newspaper and its staff were transferred from Cracow to Vienna in October 1944, marking its fourth and last period. The weekly edition was terminated, but the daily one resumed after a short delay.[164]

Nonetheless, the move to Vienna proved to be a heavy blow to the newspaper's quality since it lost the majority of its authors — some stayed behind, some were determined to move as far West as possible, some started to write for other Ukrainian newspapers in the Third Reich. Within the General Government, *Krakivski Visti* was undoubtedly the main Ukrainian newspaper, which made its gravitational pull of authors the strongest. By moving to the Third

---

163 More on this change see: Dobroszycki, *Reptile Journalism*, 125-128.
164 The last daily Cracow issue no. 227 (1260) appeared with the date October 8, 1944, the first daily Vienna issue — no. 228 (1261) with the date October 10, 1944. The last weekly issue was dated October 15, 1944.

Reich, to Vienna, it became just one of dozens of Ukrainian newspapers and had to compete with other popular periodicals from Berlin and Prague. As a result, in terms of content, *Krakivski* Visti became a semi-official bulletin. As one of its last employees, Sviatoslav Hordynskyi, wrote in a letter to Arkadii Liubchenko from December 23, 1944: "I sit alone in the editorial office of *Kr. Visti*, where I am supposed to work as a copy editor, but in fact all I am doing is translating and correcting the language of government communiques."[165]

At the end of the war *Krakivski Visti* also changed affiliation: it became the official publication of the Ukrainian National Committee, a Ukrainian proto-government recognized by the German authorities as of March 1945. General Pavlo Shandruk (1889-1979) became its head, with Kubijovyč assuming the position of his deputy. The newspaper was renamed *Ukrainskyi Shliakh* (Ukrainian Path) on March 30, 1945. Despite adopting a new name, it continued its numeration from *Krakivski Visti*. The last, 1406th issue of *Krakivski Visti* (daily edition) or the fifth issue of *Ukrainskyi Shliakh* had appeared in Vienna on April 4, 1945.[166]

Before moving to Vienna copies of *Krakivski Visti* were mainly distributed inside the General Government. Despite significant inflation all issues published in Cracow—from no. 1 on January 7, 1940 to no. 1260 on October 8, 1944—had the same price of 30 *sotyky* (0.3 of one złoty) per issue.[167] The price of issues published in Vienna was 20 pfennigs per issue. The print run of the daily edition of *Krakivski Visti* initially was smaller than that of *Dilo* in 1939 (10,000 on average per issue) but it steadily increased throughout the war: its circulation was 7,177 in 1940, 10,350 in 1941, 10,210 in 1942, 15,000 in 1943, 17,000 in 1944 and 22,450 in 1945 on average per issue.[168] The print run of the weekly edition was 6,500 in 1940, 7,120 in 1941, 17,700 in 1942, 18,660 in 1943 and 26,950 in 1944 on average per issue.[169] This data should be considered carefully

---

165 Holovata, *Ukrainskyi legalnyi vydavnychyi rukh*, 318.
166 PAA, Michael Chomiak fonds, File PR1985.0191/184.
167 For comparison the price of *Dilo* in 1939 was 20 *sotyky* per issue.
168 PAA, Michael Chomiak fonds, File PR1985.0191/184.
169 PAA, Michael Chomiak fonds, File PR1985.0191/184.

because print runs of newspapers do not necessarily reflect their real (un)popularity, especially of newspapers published under Nazis (or Soviets). On the surface it seems that *Krakivski Visti* at the end became twice (or four times if one combines both daily and weekly editions) as popular as *Dilo*, but in reality it most likely meant that the UCC was spending more on *Krakivski Visti* than the UNDO on *Dilo* (in the interwar period *Dilo* was an unofficial organ of the UNDO).

Outside the General Government, *Krakivski Visti* was regularly received in the Third Reich, primarily in Berlin and Prague which after 1920 became the two largest centers of Ukrainian emigration in Europe. The distribution to other Axis countries — Croatia, Hungary, Italy, Slovakia, Romania — was irregular and often interrupted by censorship both of the General Government and of the receiving countries.[170] Remarkably, the most difficult Axis territory for *Krakivski Visti* to penetrate was the *Reichskommissariat* Ukraine, where Ukrainians constituted an absolute majority among an almost 17-million large population (according to the German census from January 1943).[171] In the spirit of the German policy of compartmentalizing information, newspapers from the General Government were banned from circulation in the *Reichskommissariat*. Kubijovyč and Khomiak attempted at least once, in March 1943, to convince the occupation authorities to change this policy in the case of *Krakivski Visti*, but they were not successful. As Emil Gassner, the General Government's press chief, explained to them, the ban was implemented both by the Reich Ministry for the Occupied Eastern Territories and by the authorities of the *Reichskommissariat*.[172]

Khomiak also attempted a different approach to circumvent the ban — he tried to get *Krakivski Visti* into the *Reichskommissariat* through a publication exchange with editors of Ukrainian

---

170 For example, in September 1943 Khomiak had to stop sending *Krakivski Visti* to Yuliian Revai because the Slovak authorities banned all legal press from the General Government from circulating in Slovakia. See: Letter from Mykhailo Khomiak to Yuliian Revai September 24, 1943. PAA, Michael Chomiak fonds, File PR1985.0191/41.
171 Karel C. Berkhoff, *Harvest of Despair: Life and Death in Ukraine under Nazi Rule* (Cambridge, MA: Belknap Press of Harvard University Press, 2004), 36-37.
172 Himka, "*Krakivs'ki visti*: An Overview," 253-254.

newspapers published there. Some of the editors did respond and sent issues of their newspapers to Khomiak in 1943, but it seems that such exchanges were short-lived.[173] Another Axis-occupied territory with a sizeable Ukrainian population inaccessible to *Krakivski Visti* was the Transnistria Governorate (*Guvernământul Transnistriei*), which during the war was administered by Romania in a similar manner as the Third Reich administered the General Government. The Russian-language press from the latter freely circulated in the Governorate, but newspapers in the Ukrainian language, including *Krakivski Visti*, had to be smuggled in.[174]

Initially, *Krakivski Visti* was also distributed to neutral countries—Portugal, Spain, Switzerland, Norway, Sweden, Turkey, Southern America (mainly Argentina), and even Manchukuo and China. A Ukrainian reader from Shanghai wrote to Khomiak in March 1941 asking whether he could subscribe to the newspaper by sending Lipton tea because paying for it in local currency was prohibitively expensive.[175] However, in 1942 the authorities of the General Government banned the UPH from distributing its publications, including *Krakivski Visti*, to neutral countries.[176] Apparently, the newspaper also reached the Soviet Union. At least Yaroslav Halan (1902-1949), the prominent Galician Ukrainian communist who ended up in the Soviet Union during the war, had access to some issues of *Krakivski Visti* as is evident from his invective "Smerdiakovy na dosuge" (1942). In the article, besides his usual epithets directed at Ukrainian nationalists ("yellow-blue mold"), he somehow, just through reading *Krakivski Visti*, had grasped that the newspaper was an attempt to revive *Dilo* with which he was familiar from his life in interwar Poland: "There [in Cracow] 'Dilo' from Lviv has been turned into 'Krakivski Visti.'"[177]

---

173 Ibidem, 254.
174 Lev Shankovskyi, *Pokhidni hrupy OUN: prychynky do istorii pokhidnykh hrup OUN na tsentralnykh zemliakh Ukrainy v 1941-1943 rr.* (Munich: Ukrainskyi samostiinyk, 1958), 238.
175 Letter from Mykyta Kvashenko to Mykhailo Khomiak March 26, 1941. PAA, Michael Chomiak fonds, File PR1985.0191/34.
176 PAA, Michael Chomiak fonds, File PR1985.0191/184.
177 Holovata, *Ukrainskyi legalnyi vydavnychyi rukh*, 296.

Editors

According to Kubijovyč and Khomiak, the first chief editor of *Krakivski Visti* was Borys Levytskyi (1915-1984), an Ounite intellectual.[178] The latter had some previous experience of editorial work: he edited the Lviv-based weekly newspaper *Nove Selo* (New Village) in 1938-1939.[179] During the breakup of the OUN in 1940-1941 Levytskyi sided with Banderite faction, in which he belonged to its left wing, specifically to the so-called Mitrynga group (it formally separated from Banderites in 1942).[180] It seems that Levytskyi lasted less than a month as chief editor, falling victim to his own assumptions. When *Krakivski Visti* featured a short article about the Soviet-Finnish War in January 1940, this led to the first big clash with occupation censorship. Since the article was composed from official German sources, Levytskyi assumed it required no censor's approval. He either missed or did not grasp that German press policy in the General Government was based on parcellation and control of information, no matter even if it came from the Third Reich. The issue was resolved by firing him.[181] His departure from the newspaper was publicly announced on January 17, 1940.[182]

He was replaced by Mykhailo Khomiak (1905-1984) who was listed as the newspaper's editor (on its last page) from the very first issue.[183] Khomiak studied jurisprudence at the Jan Kazimierz

---

178 Kubijovyč, *Ukraintsi v Heneralnii Hubernii*, 276; PAA, Michael Chomiak fonds, File PR1985.0191/184. Levytskyi spelled his last name as Lewytzkyj in German.
179 Vasyl Habor, "Nove Selo," *Ukrainski chasopysy Lvova 1848-1939 rr. Istoryko-bibliohrafichne doslidzhennia. Tom 3, Knyha 2: 1929-1939 rr.*, ed. M.M. Romaniuk and M.V. Halushko (Lviv: Svit, 2003), 136.
180 "Natsionalistychnyi rukh pid chas Druhoi svitovoi viiny: Interviu z B. Levytskym," *Diyaloh* no 2 (1979): 4-24; "Borys Levytskyi (1915-1984)," *Diyaloh* no. 10 (1984): 7-8; Bogumiła Berdychowska, "Od nacjonalisty do lewicowca (Przypadek Borysa Łewyckiego)," *Zeszyty Historyczne* 145 (524) 2003: 215-217. After the war Levytskyi settled in Munich. Throughout the Cold War he published extensively on Soviet affairs in German, earning him reputation of one of the leading Sovietologists in Western Germany.
181 Kubijovyč, *Ukraintsi v Heneralnii Hubernii*, 274.
182 "Zmina u provodi Redaktsii," *Krakivski Visti*, no. 4 January 17, 1940, 1. The announcement gave his first name's initial as R instead of B.
183 Issues no. 1-6 listed Khomiak as executive editor (*za Redaktsiiu vidpovidaie*), but from no. 7 and onwards he was named the chief editor (*nachalnyi redaktor*). His

University in 1926-1931 and graduated with a master's degree (*magister juris*) on July 9, 1931. He worked at courts in Bibrka and Lviv (*sudova praktyka*) in 1931-1932. Then he continued at a private law firm (one of its lawyers was a relative) in Sanok in 1932-1934. Besides a legal career, Khomiak also had journalistic ambitions and started to write for *Dilo* in 1928 as a court reporter, specializing in political cases. In April 1934 he accepted an invitation to join its editorial board where he worked until the newspaper's closure in September 1939.[184] It is unclear what his editorial duties were: maybe they needed a permanent editor with legal expertise to deal with the Polish censorship, or maybe he worked with court reporters (or both).[185]

In October 1939 Khomiak escaped the Soviet territory and arrived in the General Government, eventually settling in Cracow.[186] As a former *Dilo* editor, he was an attractive candidate for Kubijovyč's project of a major Ukrainian newspaper and joined *Krakivski Visti* as one of its three starting editors (Borys Levytskyi, Mykhailo Khomiak and Ivan Durbak).[187] After Levytskyi was fired, Khomiak was promoted to the chief editor which, according to him, he reluctantly accepted under strong pressure from Yevhen Yulii Pelenskyi (director of the UPH at that time).[188] In this reluctant position Khomiak worked until the very end of the newspaper in April 1945. For a brief period, he was also the chief editor of the weekly edition of *Krakivski Visti* until it received its own editorial staff and became essentially a separate newspaper under the same title. In addition,

---

first name's initial was often given as L instead of M for conspiratorial reasons (a common practice at that place and time).

184 "Fragebogen" October 2, 1946. PAA, Michael Chomiak fonds, File PR1985.0191/20; "Mii zhyttiepys." PAA, Michael Chomiak fonds, File PR1985.0191/96.

185 Two of *Dilo* editors, Ivan Kedryn and Ivan Nimchuk, left memoirs: Kedryn, *Zhyttia – podii – liudy*; Nimchuk, *595 dniv*. Nimchuk did not mention Mykhailo Khomiak at all, Kedryn only mentioned him as a "junior colleague" from *Dilo* without describing his duties (p. 349).

186 "Mii zhyttiepys." PAA, Michael Chomiak fonds, File PR1985.0191/96.

187 "Chleny Redaktsii 'Krakivskykh Vistei' i spivrobitnyky." PAA, Michael Chomiak fonds, File PR1985.0191/23.

188 Letter from Mykhailo Khomiak to Arkadii Zhukovskyi December 30, 1980. PAA, Michael Chomiak fonds, File PR1985.0191/172.

Khomiak worked as an executive (*vidpovidalnyi*) editor of monthly magazine *Iliustrovani Visti* (Illustrated News) and weekly newspaper *Kholmska Zemlia* (Kholm Land) published by the UPH in 1940-1941 and 1943-1944 respectively.

Mykhailo Khomiak, chief editor of *Krakivski Visti*. Early 1940s, Cracow. Copyright Provincial Archives of Alberta, Canada (Michael Chomiak Fonds PR1985.0191)

Three features distinguished Khomiak from Levytskyi. First, he knew well the business of running a daily, especially the purely technical, production aspects. Second, though he was a Ukrainian nationalist, he was not a member of any Ukrainian political party or organization (I have found no evidence that he was a UNDO member in the 1930s). Third, he was not an intellectual, which perhaps made him an ideal candidate for the position of chief editor at a legal newspaper published under German occupation during World War II. The editorial archive of *Krakivski Visti* fails to show Khomiak's intellectual imprint (if there was any) on the newspaper. People who knew Khomiak fairly well—such as Kubijovyč and

Kedryn—never wrote about him in intellectual terms.[189] Ukrainian historian Ivan L. Rudnytsky, who met Khomiak in February 1940, described him to Osyp Nazaruk as "a good guy, but completely without his own individuality."[190] Khomiak's widow, Alexandra Khomiak (1915-2005), in an interview with John-Paul Himka in 1999, described her husband as more of a courier between German censorship and the editorial office, rather than a real editor during his work at *Krakivski Visti*.[191]

It is worth noting that throughout all his time at *Krakivski Visti* Khomiak may had written only one article for the newspaper.[192] His private correspondence during and after the war reveals him as a man of simple, unsophisticated views who perceived much (if not all) of surrounding reality through the lenses of ethnic politics. After immigrating to Canada in 1948, he, like many Ukrainian emigres, continued to live in the past. He worried about preparing a documentary collection exposing interwar Poland's anti-Ukrainian policies (he never progressed beyond planning it) and feared that his daughters would not marry ethnic Ukrainians (two of them indeed married non-Ukrainians).[193] The danger of mixed, interethnic marriages for the Ukrainian nation was one of the important themes in *Krakivski Visti* (see chapter 3). My impression from

---

189 Besides Kedryn's and Kubijovyč's memoirs. see their correspondence with Khomiak in PAA, Michael Chomiak fonds, File PR1985.0191/177 (Kedryn) and File PR1985.0191/184 (Kubijovyč).
190 Letter from Ivan Rudnytskyi to Osyp Nazaruk, February 9, 1940. Central State Historical Archives of Ukraine in Lviv (TsDIAL of Ukraine), f. 359, op. 1, spr. 309, ark. 5-5 (zv.). I am grateful to Larysa Holovata for helping me to locate the letter.
191 John-Paul Himka, Email to author, November 18, 2015.
192 His name appears only once in the newspaper's honorarium files, in payments for April-May 1941. See: Letter from *Krakivski Visti* to the UPH June 12, 1941. PAA, Michael Chomiak fonds, File PR1985.0191/32. However, none of the articles in *Krakivski Visti* for April-May 1941 are signed with his name or initials.
193 About Khomiak's plans for the documentary collection see: Letter from Mykhailo Khomiak to Ivan Kedryn, January 29, 1976. PAA, Michael Chomiak fonds, File PR1985.0191/177. On his fears of mixed marriages see: Letter from Mykhailo Khomiak to Mykhailo Ostroverkha, November 20, 1968. PAA, Michael Chomiak fonds, File PR1985.0191/204; Letter from Mykhailo Khomiak to Kost Pankivskyi, November 30, 1966. PAA, Michael Chomiak fonds, File PR1985.0191/208; Letter from Mykhailo Khomiak to Sofiia Parfanovych, January 24, 1968. PAA, Michael Chomiak fonds, File PR1985.0191/209.

reading his postwar correspondence is that Khomiak belonged to those in the Ukrainian diaspora who were taken out of interwar Galicia but never took interwar Galicia out of themselves.[194]

Khomiak's primary concern in running the newspaper was to establish a good relationship with the German censorship and press officials (probably so he would not suffer the fate of his predecessor). Later Kubijovyč wrote that Khomiak had a useful ability "to sense how and what could be written under the strict German reality, and he gained some trust among the German officials, without which his [editorial] work would have been impossible."[195] This appraisal seems genuine: after the war, in 1946, Khomiak testified in favor of the press chief Emil Gassner, describing him as a reasonable and helpful individual, who helped Polish and Ukrainian journalists when they got into trouble with the Gestapo.[196] Nonetheless, after the war, both Khomiak and Kubijovyč complained about the heavy German censorship under the occupation. Kubijovyč, who also highly regarded Gassner for his "good understanding of Ukrainian issues," wrote in his history of the UCC that Gassner did not hesitate to ban a text from publication in *Krakivski Visti* even on suspicion of a hidden message.[197]

That said, one should also be careful not to exaggerate the severity of the censorship. Many German officials in the occupation administration, censors including, took bribes. "It was an open secret that corruption and profiteering were the order of the day in the German departments ... in the General Government," noted Diemut Majer, adding that Berlin officials were shocked by its widespread character and referred to it as the *Polish disease*.[198] In his history of the UCC, Kubijovyč mentioned that "discreet gifts to the censors or their superiors" were the quickest way to get the UPH publications approved.[199] Ivan Kedryn, a contributor to *Krakivski*

---

194 Most of the postwar correspondence is located at: PAA, Michael Chomiak fonds, Boxes 12-14.
195 Kubijovyč, *Ukraintsi v Heneralnii Hubernii*, 277.
196 See Khomiak's "Eidesstattliche Erklärung" (November 29, 1946) on Emil Gassner in: PAA, Michael Chomiak fonds, File PR1985.0191/3.
197 Kubijovyč, *Ukraintsi v Heneralnii Hubernii*, 273.
198 Majer, *"Non-Germans" under the Third Reich*, 282.
199 Kubijovyč, *Ukraintsi v Heneralnii Hubernii*, 256.

Visti and for some time its editor, wrote in his memoirs that you could get a *Druckgenehmigung* (permission to print) from a clerk in the Propaganda Office by bribing him with a bottle of vodka and a piece of *solonyna* (salted meat).[200] Ostap Tarnavskyi was one of those Ukrainian journalists who experienced both Soviet and German censorship during the war as he lived and worked in Lviv in 1939-1944. Similarly to Kubijovyč and Khomiak, he described German censorship as strict and often opaque. "But compared to the Soviet period, the [Ukrainian legal] press was in a better situation. It was edited by independent [Ukrainian] editors who only had to come up with ways to get independently written materials through censorship. In the Soviet press, everything was decided by the party ... there was no room for independent thought."[201]

Apparently, Khomiak did get into some trouble with the censorship during his work as the chief editor: in his history of the UCC Kubijovyč wrote that Germans threatened him with "re-education" or being replaced by a German editor.[202] But the most serious threat to Khomiak's position came from within, during his long-lasting conflict with Ivan Kotsur (1895-1971), one of the directors of the UPH. The details of their conflict are not entirely clear. It seems that in August 1940 Kostur faced a difficult situation: a group of his employees filed a complaint against him, later co-signed by *Krakivski Visti*'s editors, to the Supervisory Board (Nadzirna Rada) of the UPH. In support of the complaint, Khomiak submitted a personal memorandum to Kubijovyč on August 28, 1940 in which he accused Kotsur of excessive bureaucracy; lack of knowledge of the publishing business, especially its technical aspects; disrespectful behavior at the workplace, including toward the newspaper's editors; inability to represent the UPH at meetings with German officials; and finally attempts to curtail the editorial autonomy of *Krakivski Visti*.[203]

Kotsur somehow managed to weather the situation and remain in the directorial position. Apparently, his behavior toward

---

200 Kedryn, *Zhyttia – podii – liudy*, 363-364.
201 Tarnavskyi, *Literaturnyi Lviv*, 97.
202 Kubijovyč, *Ukraintsi v Heneralnii Hubernii*, 274.
203 "Do Nadzirnoi Rady Ukrainskoho Vydavnytsva" August 28, 1940. PAA, Michael Chomiak fonds, PR1985.0191/28.

the editors changed little since Khomiak continued complaining about him to Kubijovyč.[204] Kotsur even scored a short-lived victory: on April 28, 1941 Kubijovyč issued an order appointing Vasyl Mudryi (1893-1966), chief editor of *Dilo* in 1927-1935, as de facto chief editor of *Krakivski Visti*.[205] Khomiak was demoted to an executive editor and his duties were narrowed to dealing with German censorship. However, the same order also reaffirmed the editorial autonomy of the newspaper vis-à-vis the UPH directors. Their authority over the editorial board was limited to "administrative" matters. As for more important things, the editors were responsible only to Kubijovyč.[206] In the end, Khomiak emerged victorious from this episode of office politics. In less than a month Mudryi was gone from the office: according to the editorial chronicle, he transferred all editorial affairs, without any explanation, back to Khomiak on May 21, 1941.[207] Later Kubijovyč claimed that Germans removed Mudryi for "an article that mentioned the hostile attitude of Ukraine's Western neighbors toward Ukrainian people."[208] In June 1941 Kotsur "departed" (*vybuv*) from his directorial position and Ukrainian linguist Ivan Zilynskyi (1879-1952) became the sole director of the UPH.[209] It seems Khomiak had little to no issues in working with Zilynskyi. Kubijovyč and Khomiak never mentioned this episode in their personal postwar correspondence (it lasted until the early 1980s). The former did not mention the conflict either in his memoirs or in his history of the UCC in which he described their relationship as "harmonious cooperation" during the war.[210]

---

204 See: Letter from Mykhailo Khomiak to Volodymyr Kubijovyč November 26, 1940. PAA, Michael Chomiak fonds, PR1985.0191/28.
205 "U spravi redahuvannia 'Krakivskykh Vistei'" April 28, 1941. PAA, Michael Chomiak fonds, PR1985.0191/28.
206 Ibidem.
207 "Chleny Redaktsii 'Krakivskykh Vistei' i spivrobitnyky." PAA, Michael Chomiak fonds, PR1985.0191/23.
208 Kubijovyč, *Ukraintsi v Heneralnii Hubernii*, 274. I suspect that the article mentioned by Kubijovyč provided Germans with a convenient excuse to remove Mudryi and reinstate Khomiak, who was a lesser (and thus more preferred) figure, in charge of *Krakivski Visti*. According to Khomiak, the idea of Mudryi's appointment to the newspaper was resisted by German officials from the beginning: Letter from Mykhailo Khomiak to Ivan Kotsur April 14, 1941. PAA, Michael Chomiak fonds, PR1985.0191/28.
209 Kubijovyč, *Ukraintsi v Heneralnii Hubernii*, 260.
210 Kubijovyč, *Ukraintsi v Heneralnii Hubernii*, 277.

The editorial staff of *Krakivski Visti* suffered from a rapid turnover of personnel throughout the war. Many editors quit the newspaper after working months, some—even after mere weeks. The majority of the editors were little-known figures at the time. In chronological order of beginning of their employment they were (according to Khomiak): Ivan Durbak, Vasyl Kachmar, Vasyl Ryvak, Lev Lepkyi, Roman Holian, Mariian Kozak, Petro Sahaidachnyi, Ivan Kedryn, Ivan Nimchuk, Bohdan Nyzhankivskyi, Ostap Tarnavskyi, Mykola Tvorydlo, Fedir Dudtko, Bohdan Halaichuk, Oleksander Mokh, Vitalii Levytskyi, Ya. Zaremba, Ihor Shkrumeliak, Kost Kuzyk, Fedir Kovshyk, Damian Horniatkevych, Denys Savaryn, Borys Kriukov, V. Chaikivskyi, Bohdan Hoshovskyi, Sviatoslav Hordynskyi, Omelian Masikevych, Mstyslav Dolnytskyi.[211]

Editors of *Krakivski Visti* (from left to right): Ivan Durbak, Lev Lepkyi, Mykhailo Khomiak, Vasyl Kachmar. Early 1940s, Cracow. Copyright Provincial Archives of Alberta, Canada (Michael Chomiak Fonds PR1985.0191)

Besides Khomiak, one of the longest-serving editors was Mariian Kozak, who worked at the newspaper from November 1, 1940 until

---

211 Established on the basis of: PAA, Michael Chomiak fonds, File PR1985. 0191/184.

August 4, 1944. He belongs to that category of Ukrainian intellectuals, who were clearly people of considerable talent but never got a chance to develop and shine because they had the misfortune of living in one of the bloodiest places and periods in European history. Very little is known about Kozak. According to his brief CV, he was born on May 7, 1906 in Krzeszowice near Cracow. His editorial career started in 1927. By the time the war began, he had experience working for Ukrainian periodicals such as *Nova Zoria, Meta, Dzvony, Postup,* and *Dilo*.[212] One of his main intellectual interests was Ukrainian political thinker and historian Viacheslav Lypynskyi.[213] He was also interested in the writings of Oswald Spengler[214] and the biography of Swedish king Gustaf V.[215] Unlike Khomiak, Kozak regularly wrote for *Krakivski Visti*—most of its editorials were written by him—and some of them are interesting to read even today.[216] With the approach of the Red Army in the summer of 1944, Kozak, like most Ukrainians in Cracow, was preparing for a major life change. In his short history of *Krakivski Visti,* Khomiak dryly wrote that Kozak "departed" from his job on August 4th.[217] Kubijovyč was more expressive and implied that Kozak became a national renegade and stayed in postwar Poland: "You were asking me about the fate of Kozak. In the summer of 1944, he

---

212 "Schriftleiter Kosak [sic] Marian" April 16, 1941. PAA, Michael Chomiak fonds, File PR1985.0191/28.
213 Mariian Kozak, "Z zhyttia i dialnosti Viacheslava Lypysnkoho," *Dzvony* no. 6 (1932): 420-428; Mariian Kozak, "Za zrozuminnia ukrainskoi diisnosty. V 13-ti rokovyny smerty Viacheslava Lypynskoho (14 chervnia 1931 r.)," *Krakivski Visti,* no. 128 (1161) June 15, 1944, 3.
214 Letter from Mariian Kozak to Ivan L. Rudnytsky July 14, 1943. UAA, Ivan L. Rudnytsky fonds, Accession no. 1984-155, File 742. A copy of the letter can be found at: PAA, Michael Chomiak fonds, File PR1985.0191/41.
215 Letter from Mariian Kozak to Anatol Kurdydyk June 21, 1943. PAA, Michael Chomiak fonds, File PR1985.0191/40.
216 See a selection of his texts at: https://zbruc.eu/taxonomy/term/27946 (accessed July 29, 2024).
217 PAA, Michael Chomiak fonds, File PR1985.0191/184. The editorial chronicle gives a much more convoluted story of Kozak's departure from *Krakivski Visti* in 1944—it also mentions that he quit the newspaper on August 4 (after "a misunderstanding"), but then it writes about his trips between Cracow and Vienna in September-October as if he was still an employee. See: "Chleny Redaktsii 'Krakivskykh Vistei' i spivrobitnyky." PAA, Michael Chomiak fonds, File PR1985.0191/23.

left the editorial staff of 'KRAKIVSKI VISTI,' severed [contacts] with Ukrainians, and stayed among Poles in Cracow. It is a pity because he was a talented and smart man but a coward in life."[218] Another important editor, though not as influential as Kozak in my opinion, was Lev Lepkyi (1888-1971), officially the only deputy editor that Khomiak ever had.[219] Lev was seventeen years older than Khomiak and the most famous thing about him was his brother, prominent Ukrainian writer Bohdan Lepkyi (1872-1941). It seems from the editorial correspondence that these three men—chief editor Khomiak, deputy editor Lepkyi, and editor Kozak—were the triumvirate that ran the newspaper and defined its character (within the limits of their power).

After the German invasion of the Soviet Union and the creation of the district Galicia, the UPH kept its headquarters in Cracow and also created a large branch in Lviv, the center of the new district. *Krakivski Visti* soon followed suit and also created its own editorial branch in Lviv. Ivan Nimchuk (1891-1956), the last chief editor (1935-1939) of *Dilo*, became head of the branch and ran it until the end of its existence in 1944. Besides him, Bohdan Nyzhankivskyi, Ostap Tarnavskyi, Mykola Shlemkevych and Roman Kupchynskyi (all-prominent figures of the Galician Ukrainian cultural scene) worked at the branch.[220]

Contributors

The factor that influenced the quantity and availability of contributors to *Krakivski Visti* the most was the war. In this regard, the newspaper's history can be divided into four periods. In the first, from

---

218 Letter from Volodymyr Kubijovyč to Ivan L. Rudnytsky, September 23, 1960. UAA, Ivan L. Rudnytsky fonds, Accession no. 1984-155, File 768.
219 Himka, "*Krakivs'ki visti*: An Overview," 255. According to the editorial chronicle Lev Lepkyi joined the editorial board of *Krakivski Visti* on May 1, 1940 and became the deputy editor by November 1, 1940: "Chleny Redaktsii 'Krakivskykh Vistei' i spivrobitnyky." PAA, Michael Chomiak fonds, File PR1985.0191/23.
220 PAA, Michael Chomiak fonds, File PR1985.0191/184. For some reason, in his memoirs Tarnavskyi made no mention of working for *Krakivski Visti*, see: Tarnavskyi, *Literaturnyi Lviv*.

January 1940 to June 1941, the pool of potential authors was mainly limited to those who lived in the General Government. During this period many contributors, though they were available and willing to write, were afraid to work with the legal press in the General Government, fearing that their texts might endanger their relatives in Galicia under Soviet rule, which is ironic because during this time *Krakivski Visti* was barred from publishing any anti-Soviet materials.[221] In the second period, from June 1941 to summer 1943, the newspaper received a significant boost of contributors both in terms of quantity and quality due to the German occupation of Galicia and its subsequent incorporation into the General Government.

The third period, from summer 1943 till October 1944, saw another boost as many *skhidniaky* (literally "Easterners," meaning Ukrainians who came into the General Government from the East) arrived from the *Reichskommissariat* Ukraine, fleeing the advancing Red Army. Among the arrivals were people regarded as the leading Ukrainian intellectual and cultural figures of the 20th Century. Galicians, many of whom believed that the purges of the 1930s erased most of the Soviet Ukrainian intelligentsia, were amazed by the new arrivals. Mariia Strutynska, a journalist working for *Lvivski Visti* and *Nashi Dni*, wondered in her diary on November 7, 1943 how could it be possible that Soviet Ukraine after "all the Bolshevik purges and deportations" still had so many "worthy people"? She wrote: "they were so different! Reserved, very European, Shevelov with a note of self-irony, dynamic Bahrianyi, purebred [*rasova*] Kovalenko, Humenna, who resembles a Kalmyk: she has quite a character! Modest, with intelligent eyes Hr. Kostiuk."[222] Most of them became contributors to *Krakivski Visti* which now could claim an all-Ukrainian character thanks to them. In the fourth period, from October 1944 until April 1945, the newspaper lost the majority of its pre-evacuation contributors due to relocation to Vienna. As a result,

---

221 Ye. Yu. Pelenskyi, "Pered dvoma rokamy," *Krakivski Visti*, no 1 (448) January 2, 1942, 3.
222 Strutynska, *Daleke zblyzka*, 191. Tarnavskyi's impressions of *skhidniaky* were also quite positive, though his experiences with one of them—Todos Osmachka—were rather awkward: Tarnavskyi, *Literaturnyi Lviv*, 89-95.

its content suffered immensely and the newspaper lost much of the intellectual and cultural character it had managed to acquire before the evacuation. During 1940-1944, besides authors from within the General Government, *Krakivski Visti* always had a number of contributors from the Protectorate of Bohemia and Moravia and Germany proper, but they were a minor group and for most of its content the newspaper relied on "internal" contributors. *Krakivski Visti* never had any authors who were residents of the *Reichskommissariat* Ukraine.

Besides a basic human need to express themselves (somewhat more intense among intellectuals) there were at least three more specific reasons to write for *Krakivski Visti*. The first, and perhaps the most important, was the severe narrowing of the periodical scene by the occupation authorities.[223] In 1940-1941 *Krakivski Visti* was the only major Ukrainian-language publication in the General Government. The situation improved after June 1941 when the Germans created *Lvivski Visti* (Lviv News), which became the second largest Ukrainian legal newspaper under the occupation, and allowed the UPH to publish *Nashi Dni* (Our Days), the only journal, though a thin one, in Ukrainian.[224] There was also a weak underground Ukrainian press run by the Banderites—it was intellectually primitive in its discourse, poorly circulated, paid nothing and could result in a very unpleasant time with the Gestapo.[225] Thus, for anyone living in the General Government and looking for a printed organ to express him/herself in Ukrainian, *Krakivski Visti* became often the first and only consideration.

---

223 "It turns out that before the war the annual demand for paper [to print periodicals] in Poland was over 37,000 tons and in the GG [General Government] some three thousand tons. The number of newspaper copies per capita before the war came to twenty-two; in the GG the number was only eight." See: Dobroszycki, *Reptile Journalism*, 67.
224 In his memoirs Tarnavskyi claimed that *Lvivski Visti* was more popular in Galicia and had a print run of over 70 thousand (I was not able to verify this number): Tarnavskyi, *Literaturnyi Lviv*, 88. But on the same page, he recognized that *Krakivski Visti* enjoyed more editorial freedom.
225 On the OUN's underground press see: Oleksandra Stasiuk, *Vydavnycho-propahadyvna diialnist OUN (1941-1953 rr.)* (Lviv: Tsentr doslidzhen vyzvolnoho rukhu, Instytut ukrainoznavstva im. I. Krypiakevycha, 2006).

The second reason was income. In general, the economic conditions in the General Government were intentionally worsened compared to the prewar situation in Poland, which was hardly a prosperous country, with even further economic pressure applied on the non-German population, primarily Jews but also Poles.[226] The occupiers' exploitative and rigid economic policies quickly led to rapid inflation, high prices, shortage of goods and a "massive" black market economy (which was blamed on Jews, naturally, even after their ghettoization).[227] As a result, many life choices in the General Government, even for Ukrainians, became about everyday basic survival in the environment with very limited economic opportunities. Sooner or later, nearly anyone from the Ukrainian educated class had to face the possibility of either working for the occupiers directly or indirectly (in the UCC), or engage in shady business activities, or simply starve.[228] As Ukrainian journalist Ivan Kedryn (who lived in Cracow in 1940-1944) wrote in his memoirs, "it is no surprise that under such exceptionally difficult and challenging conditions [of the occupation], people sought ways to survive better. You cannot demand from everyone to be heroes and have steel characters."[229] Writing for the legal press in this situation was not enough to cover living expenses (with some rare exceptions), but nonetheless, it was an income. Ostap Tarnavskyi wrote in his memoirs that under the German occupation "the honorarium was ... the main reason to write for a newspaper."[230] The same

---

226 In July 1940 Hitler instructed Frank to keep living standards for Poles as low as possible: Majer, *"Non-Germans" under the Third Reich*, 765.
227 "A massive black market developed [in the General Government], which not only was tolerated by the German authorities but evolved into an indispensable feature of life, as food supplies could not have been maintained without it." See: Majer, *"Non-Germans" under the Third Reich*, 273. The police reports blaming black markets on the Jews are quoted in: Ibidem, 807.
228 In his memoirs Kedryn gives an example of such a shady business operation that he himself was part of. It involved bribing a German official in Cracow to get a permit for printing one thousand copies of a popular title from Polish fiction. Then making a deal with a printing press to print ten thousand copies, of which one thousand were sold legally but the rest were sold wholesale to bookstores in Warsaw. See: Kedryn, *Zhyttia – podii – liudy*, 347-348.
229 Kedryn, *Zhyttia – podii – liudy*, 360.
230 Tarnavskyi, *Literaturnyi Lviv*, 126.

Kedryn, despite his dislike of Nazi propaganda (Kedryn was half-Jewish), had to seek, in his own words, "additional income" and decided to write for *Krakivski Visti* "partly due to [financial] necessity, partly due to a real desire [to write]."[231] The newspaper paid relatively well, on average 15 zloty for an article in 1940 (due to inflation, it rose to 100 zloty in 1943).[232]

The third reason was identification. The occupied learned quickly that under German rule, having an ID and even more, having a certain kind of ID could make a crucial difference in life (and in death). For example, freedom of movement was severely restricted under the German occupation, especially by train — an ID of a correspondent could be used to alleviate most of these difficulties. *Krakivski Visti* was bombarded by unknown Ukrainians claiming to be journalists who wanted to become the newspaper's correspondents, which, of course, would lead to their accreditation through either the Ministry of Propaganda and Public Enlightenment in Berlin or the respective occupation authorities. Some of these ID seekers did not even hide their motives. A certain Vasyl Veresh-Sirmianskyi from Slovakia begged Khomiak to issue him a correspondent ID, promising in return to write for free "about the political and cultural life of Slovakia and its Ukrainian emigration."[233]

Besides external factors of occupation and censorship, the editors of *Krakivski Visti* also had other difficulties with their contributors. A significant problem plaguing the existence of the newspaper throughout its history was that some authors intentionally put little effort into writing their texts, considering them as acceptable or good enough for the newspaper. At least one author did not even conceal that she was going to produce compilations from German publications. Olena Kysilevska, a contributor to the rubric "Zhinocha storinka" (Women's Page) in *Krakivski Visti*, openly wrote to Khomiak that she was going to write for the rubric on the basis of

---

231 Kedryn, *Zhyttia — podii — liudy*, 349.
232 See honoraria in: PAA, Michael Chomiak fonds, File PR1985.0191/32.
233 Letter from Vasyl Veresh-Sirmianskyi to Mykhailo Khomiak December 9, 1942. PAA, Michael Chomiak fonds, File PR1985.0191/31.

two German women journals to which she subscribed.[234] Apparently, Khomiak had to accept her offer because Kysilevska became one of the most prolific authors of the newspaper, mainly writing about women's issues and general hygiene.

In their turn, some contributors were displeased with the low professional level of the newspaper's editors and technical staff. They believed their submissions were hastily and poorly edited, frequently leading to factual errors and awkward style. Historian Myron Korduba complained to Khomiak about errors and especially ("made me very angry") textual changes introduced in his series of articles on Bolesław-Yurii II.[235] Another historian, Mykola Andrusiak, voiced identical grievances to Khomiak and the UPH when the newspaper published his series.[236] Prominent journalist Yevhen Onatskyi was offended by stylistic changes made to his articles: "The editorial board treats me, an old experienced journalist, as some newcomer who does not know what is he writing about, who does not know the Ukrainian language enough."[237] Such complaints were routine in the editorial correspondence throughout the newspaper's existence. Another frequent complaint was the editors' poor communication with the contributors and readers. A certain Oleksander Nedilko, after Khomiak ignored his letters, wrote to him again, lecturing the chief editor on the ethics of correspondence (based on German culture) and scolding him for the lack of

---

[234] Letter from Olena Kysilevska to Mykhailo Khomiak July 20, 1940. PAA, Michael Chomiak fonds, File PR1985.0191/33.

[235] Letter from Myron Korduba to Mykhailo Khomiak June 17, 1940; Letter from Myron Korduba to Mykhailo Khomiak June 22, 1940. PAA, Michael Chomiak fonds, File PR1985.0191/33.

[236] Letter from Mykola Andrusiak to the UPH May 13, 1940; Letter from Mykola Andrusiak to Mykhailo Khomiak May 17, 1940; Letter from Mykola Andrusiak to Mykhailo Khomiak May 20, 1940; Letter from Mykola Andrusiak to the UPH June 1, 1940; Letter from Mykola Andrusiak to Mykhailo Khomiak June 4, 1940. PAA, Michael Chomiak fonds, PR1985.0191/33.

[237] Letter from Yevhen Onatskyi to Mykhailo Khomiak August 26, 1942. PAA, Michael Chomiak fonds, PR1985.0191/37.

any.²³⁸ Writer and journalist Vasyl Grendzha-Donskyi asked Khomiak "to give even a negative response" to his letters.²³⁹

Reception

The reception of *Krakivski Visti* throughout the war was mostly a negative one. The majority of its readers compared the newspaper unfavorably either to the pre-war Ukrainian press (*Dilo* in most cases) or to the current German-language press such as *Krakauer Zeitung*, which the occupation authorities published for Germans in the General Government. Most criticisms were expressed privately, in letters and diaries. Milena Rudnytska described the first issues of the newspaper as "very miserable" in her letter to Osyp Nazaruk from January 12, 1940.²⁴⁰ Metropolitan Andrei (Sheptytskyi) in his meeting with a certain "Dr. Frédéric" (allegedly it was the French historian and journalist René Martel) in September 1943, was more descriptive, giving his opinion on the whole Ukrainian legal press in the General Government: "Our newspapers are German [newspapers], translated into Ukrainian. They write about Southern America, about Paraguay, about Australia, [but] this does not interest our peasants, one cannot find in them anything about our provincial life, and only topics about the latter would be of interest to the average [Ukrainian] reader."²⁴¹ The metropolitan told "Dr. Frédéric" that he would like the Ukrainian press in the General Government to be more like the current "French newspapers, edited by the French for the French, having a clear European direction, but with national framing."²⁴²

Another important cleric critical of the Ukrainian legal press was Ilarion (secular name Ivan Ohiienko), the Orthodox

---

238 Letter from Oleksander Nedilko to Mykhailo Khomiak January 26, 1941. PAA, Michael Chomiak fonds, PR1985.0191/34.
239 Letter from Vasyl Grendzha-Donskyi to Mykhailo Khomiak April 24, 1940. PAA, Michael Chomiak fonds, PR1985.0191/File 34.
240 Milena Rudnytska, *Statti, Lysty, Dokumenty* (Lviv: Misioner,1998), 592.
241 Liliana Hentosh, "Pro stavlennia mytropolyta Sheptytskoho do nimetskoho okupatsiinoho rezhymu v kontekstsi dokumenta z kantseliarii Alfreda Rozenberga," *Ukraina Moderna* no. 20 (2013): 311.
242 Hentosh, "Pro stavlennia mytropolyta Sheptytskoho," 311.

Archbishop of Chełm and Podlasie regions. The archbishop believed that the UCC and Kubijovyč personally were biased in favor of Greek Catholicism and hostile to the Ukrainian Orthodox faith and church. Ilarion complained in his letters to Metropolitan Andrei (Sheptytskyi) that his church had not been allowed to have its own newspaper. Meanwhile, the region in his ecclesiastical jurisdiction, Chełm, had been "flooded" by the "Greek-Catholic" *Krakivski Visti*, which "stubbornly" failed to report on the region, its Orthodox church and hierarchy, while writing at lengths about "Greek-Catholic" hierarchs and their activities. This whole situation of under-representation wrote Ilarion, could lead to "very bitter thoughts" about Greek Catholics among the Orthodox intelligentsia of the Chełm region.[243] Ilarion also voiced his grievances to the occupation administration, which eventually led to a direct meeting supervised by Gassner between him and Kubijovyč, Khomiak and Ostap Tarnavskyi (representing the UCC, *Krakivski Visti*, and the UPH) on March 9, 1943. The meeting did not resolve the situation; some of Ilarion's demands, such as receiving fifty percent of the UPH's shares, were simply unacceptable, so his complaints continued.[244] In his history of the UCC, Kubijovyč praised Ilarion for his role in "the [Ukrainian] national revival" of the Chełm region but added that he suffered from "an overabundance of ambition and sensitivity" and meddled in "purely secular matters" that were in the UCC's competence.[245]

Besides these critical opinions expressed in private exchanges, there was no lack of criticisms of *Krakivski Visti* addressed to Khomiak and Kubijovyč directly. For example, Hennadii Kotorovych, a Ukrainian journalist and contributor to *Krakivski Visti*,

---

243 See two letters from Ilarion to Andrei—from January 20, 1942 and from November 17, 1942—in the special issue of journal *Pamiatky: Pamiatky* no. 2: Epistoliarna spadshchyna Ivana Ohiienka (mytropolyta Ilariona) (1907-1968) (2001): 300, 307. Ironically, almost a year before the first letter, the newspaper felt a need to publish an editorial explaining why it had been writing so much about the Orthodox Church but so little about the Greek Catholic Church in the General Government: "Chomu pro odnykh bahato—pro druhykh malo?" *Krakivski Visti* no. 21 (177) February 1, 1941, 1-2.
244 Himka, "*Krakivs'ki visti*: An Overview," 257-258.
245 Kubijovyč, *Ukraintsi v Heneralnii Hubernii*, 316.

wrote somewhat diplomatically to Khomiak in November 1940 that the first issues of the newspaper made a very poor impression on the Ukrainian colony in Berlin.[246] Another journalist and contributor, Anatol Kurdydyk, writing to Khomiak in May 1941, was blunter and characterized *Krakivski Visti* as an intellectually underperforming publication considering the role it should have been playing in Ukrainian national life as the main Ukrainian newspaper of the General Government.[247] Eventually, these criticisms from the newspaper's own correspondents came to Kubijovyč's attention. Rather than downplay or reject them, he fully acknowledged their validity. On August 8, 1941 he issued an internal memorandum for the UCC staff with the following statement: "*Krakivski Visti* has received various wishes [of change] from everywhere. These reproaches are more or less justified. But the correspondents need to realize existing conditions. Thus, our only periodical on this side of the [river] San needs to be valued and not undermined."[248]

The newspaper was also criticized publicly, at least in the first years of its existence. Galician Ukrainian historian Mykola Andrusiak in an article that appeared in Prague-based weekly *Nastup* in November 1940, claimed that *Krakivski Visti* carried "alien poisonous cargo" by publishing "nonsense" that its chief editor ("khlopets-terminator") was incapable to catch and correct even though he was mentored by such an experienced editor as Ivan Kedryn ("dark spirit of *Dilo*").[249] Most likely, "khlopets" (boy) alluded not only to Khomiak's inexperience as a chief editor but also to his height (159 cm). "Terminator" has no relation to the killer robots of Canadian filmmaker James Cameron. In pre-war Galicia, the term meant "apprentice," usually of master artisans. In response to the article, Khomiak wrote a denouncing letter to the chief editor of

---

246 Letter from Hennadii Kotorovych to Mykhailo Khomiak, November 13, 1940. PAA, Michael Chomiak fonds, File PR1985.0191/33.

247 Letter from Anatol Kurdydyk to Mykhailo Khomiak, May 18, 1941. PAA, Michael Chomiak fonds, File PR1985.0191/34.

248 Holovata, *Ukrainskyi legalnyi vydavnychyi rukh*, 314. The newspaper also addressed criticisms in an editorial: "Gazeta prosyt u Chytachiv zrozuminnia," *Krakivski Visti*, no. 71 (227) April 2, 1941, 1-2.

249 Mykola Andrusiak, "Problema pravdyvykh informatsiï," *Nastup*, no. 44 (64) November 1, 1940, 5.

Nastup, accusing Andrusiak of disloyal and quarrelsome behavior vis-à-vis Ukrainian national institutions and figures in the interwar period.[250] Almost half a year later, Khomiak was happy to publish an article that attacked Andrusiak.[251]

Another example of public criticism was an anonymous letter "Odvertyi lyst do ukrainskykh pysmennykiv" (An open letter to Ukrainian writers), published by the Prague-based journal *Proboiem* in its November 1941 issue.[252] Its author (most likely a Ukrainian émigré), hiding behind the pseudonym "Ukrainian writer," called people working at the UPH and *Krakivski Visti* Galician "parvenus" who imagine themselves "giants."[253] *Krakivski Visti*, the letter claimed, had been playing a destructive role in Ukrainian national life and had continuously engaged in a campaign of "self-spitting, self-shaming, self-abasement." Its short feuilletons were "stupid" and its editorials were nothing but "disparagement" of Ukrainians.[254]

But while Galicians and Ukrainian interwar émigrés compared *Krakivski Visti* to their pre-war press, *skhidniaky* had a different frame of reference. Before his arrival into the General Government in February 1943, Yurii Shevelov had read only Soviet press and legal Ukrainian newspapers of the *Reichskommissariat* Ukraine.[255] Upon his arrival, he devoured local newspapers and formed a remarkably different impression about the Ukrainian legal press in the General Government. He found *Lvivski Visti* a "factually German organ" and as much *pustoporozhnia* (literally "double

---

250 Letter from Mykola Khomiak to Stepan Rosokha November 28, 1940. PAA, Michael Chomiak fonds, PR1985.0191/28.
251 Hanna Nakonechna, "U spravi kulturno-naukovykh informatsiï chuzhyntsiv," *Krakivski Visti*, no. 63 (219) March 23, 1941, 7. See correspondence between Khomiak and Nakonechna regarding Andrusiak: Letter from Hanna Nakonechna to Mykhailo Khomiak March 13, 1941; Letter from Mykhailo Khomiak to Hanna Nakonechna March 17, 1941; Letter from Hanna Nakonechna to Mykhailo Khomiak April 14, 1941. PAA, Michael Chomiak fonds, PR1985.0191/34.
252 Ukr. pysmennyk, "Odvertyi lyst do ukrainskykh pysmennykiv," *Proboiem* 8, no. 11 (November 1941): 658-662.
253 Ibidem, 659.
254 Ibidem, 660.
255 Shevelov, *Ya – mene – meni… (i dovkruhy)* vol. 1, 506.

empty") as legal newspapers in the *Reichskommissariat*, though "slightly more liberal since the [German] regime in Galicia was somewhat more liberal."[256] On the other hand, *Krakivski Visti* had made upon him a much more favorable impression: "[the newspaper] was edited by Mykhailo Khomiak. I have never met him in person. The newspaper was in Ukrainian hands. It gave general information from German sources, [but] its Ukrainian material was honest, though completely not suitable for a newspaper and entirely accidental ... The newspaper could not become a center attracting [Ukrainian] intellectual forces (and, perhaps, did not even want to) because it was based in Cracow and even more importantly due to its general objectively-indifferent character."[257] After reading the Soviet press for two decades Shevelov's main criticism of *Krakivski Visti* was its uncontemporary character reflected in "long articles, often with continuation in subsequent issues, many of them had scholarly value, but they were far from [current] problems, lively discussion and painful [questions]. Quite often these articles were typical *prychynky* — an old Galician word, describing publications reflecting reality factually, but without any living thought behind them."[258]

The many criticisms of *Krakivski Visti* prove, among other things, that it was widely read, thus supporting the observation that Dobroszycki made about the Polish legal press of the General Government.[259] The newspaper is frequently mentioned in the Ukrainian intelligentsia's wartime correspondence and diaries. The same Milena Rudnytska, who in 1940 berated the newspaper, in 1943 instructed her son to visit the editorial office of *Krakivski Visti* and make sure that they send her the newspaper, which she had not received for two months.[260] The reception of the newspaper changed drastically soon after the war. People then saw in it less of a polluting Nazi influence and the service of German interests and

---

256 Ibidem, 522.
257 Ibidem, 522-523.
258 Ibidem.
259 Dobroszycki, *Reptile Journalism*, ix.
260 Letter from Milena Rudnytska to Ivan L. Rudnytsky November 2, 1943. UAA, Ivan L. Rudnytsky fonds, Accession no. 1984-155, File 742.

more of a survival of Ukrainian thought and culture in difficult times. As early as 1947 Khomiak started to receive praise for his work at *Krakivski Visti* and requests to borrow its issues.[261] With time these requests, which continued until the end of Khomiak's life, only multiplied. Ironically, the war had to end for people to appreciate him and the newspaper.

---

261 See for example a letter from Stepan Baran to Mykhailo Khomiak November 20, 1947. PAA, Michael Chomiak fonds, File PR1985.0191/9.

II A School of Hate: Images of Poles, Russians/Soviets and Jews in *Krakivski Visti*

After conquering Poland, the first ideological campaign of the German occupation authorities was directed at the defeated state. It had to be portrayed as unjust, corrupt and ineffective. The campaign's main goal was to present the Polish state as an unviable and artificial creation of the Versailles system and to frame the German occupation as part of the natural course of history.[262] One of the issues highlighted in the propaganda was the interwar Polish treatment of national minorities, primarily Germans, but also Belarusians, Lithuanians and Ukrainians. The Ukrainian case was somewhat special, as from their point of view, they were the only minority in Poland that lost their statehood, the short-lived Western Ukrainian People's Republic (WURP) of November 1918 – July 1919, because of the reborn Polish state which won the war against the WURP with Western (mainly French) help.[263] Most Ukrainian memoirs describe their experience of living under the interwar Polish regime as that of second-class citizens, especially after the Polish "pacification" of Galicia in 1930, which was an attempt to intimidate Ukrainians en masse in response to the OUN's Sabotage Action in summer 1930.[264] One of the childhood memories that Lev Bilas carried through his life was how a Polish policeman humiliated his aunt when she asked him in Ukrainian for directions in

---

262 Dobroszycki, *Reptile Journalism*, 97-98, 102.
263 For a history of the Western Ukrainian People's Republic see: Vasyl Kuchabsky, *Western Ukraine in Conflict with Poland and Bolshevism, 1918-1923* (Toronto: Canadian Institute of Ukrainian Studies Press, 2009). Though the book originally appeared in German in 1934 and its factual material is somewhat outdated, it remains one of the best works on the subject. Another important history of the WURP is: Torsten Wehrhahn, *Die Westukrainische Volksrepublik: zu den polnisch-ukrainischen Beziehungen und dem Problem der ukrainischen Staatlichkeit in den Jahren 1918 bis 1923* (Berlin: Weissensee, 2004).
264 There is an excellent study of the "pacification": Roman Skakun, *"Patsyfikatsiia": polski represii 1930 roku v Halychyni* (Lviv: Vydavnytstvo Ukrainskoho katolytskoho universytetu, 2012).

Lviv in the 1930s: the policeman took offense at the very language in which he was asked the question and started shouting that this (Lviv) is Poland so how dare she address a representative of "the authority" in that language.[265] In the 1930s, Ukrainian nationalists looked at Poles with a mixture of hatred, fear and envy, considering them, unlike the Ukrainian masses, a "complete" nation.[266] The anti-Polish feelings were the strongest among the Galician Ukrainian youth: "all of us truly hated the Polish regime," wrote Roman Volchuk (1922-2014) in his memoirs.[267] It is worth noting that neither Bilas nor Volchuk were members of the OUN. The latter's rise in influence and popularity among young Western Ukrainians in the 1930s was deeply tied to the Polish-Ukrainian national antagonism, which the OUN also nurtured by its terrorist actions.

The Polish state's policies against Ukrainian national life in the interwar period were discriminatory (with the exception of Volhynia to a degree): measures of assimilation and denationalization as well as limitation in civil rights.[268] The nationalist segment of Polish society mostly supported the state's anti-Ukrainian policies and the atmosphere of ethnic intimidation. The same Volchuk recalled gangs of Polish students from Lviv Polytechnic (*Politechnika Lwowska*) running on the streets of Lviv, armed with sticks, and shouting: "Beat up Jews and Rusyns!" in the late 1930s.[269] On a political level, attempts to reach a Polish-Ukrainian compromise repeatedly failed. Even Ukrainian politicians from the UNDO, who tried the most to find a modus vivendi with the Polish state in the 1930s, admitted in 1938 that their policy of normalization resulted in a fiasco.[270] By the end of the 1930s Polish-Ukrainian

---

265 Bilas, *Ohliadaiuchys nazad*, 18.
266 Ibidem, 71.
267 Roman Volchuk, *Spomyny z peredvoiennoho Lvova ta voiennoho Vidnia* (Kyiv: Krytyka, 2002), 35.
268 John-Paul Himka, "Western Ukraine between the Wars," *Canadian Slavonic Papers* 34, no. 4 (December 1992), 398-400.
269 Volchuk, *Spomyny z peredvoiennoho Lvova*, 82. Volchuk contrasted this prewar atmosphere with living in Lviv under the first Soviet occupation of 1939-1941, which made him feel as a "full-fledged citizen."
270 K. K. Fedevych, *Halytski ukraintsi u Polshchi. 1920 – 1939 rr. (Intehratsiia halytskykh ukraintsiv do Polskoi derzhavy u 1920 – 1930-ti rr.)* (Kyiv: Osnova, 2009), 251.

relations had become deeply antagonistic (partly due to the international situation, i.e. the rise of Nazi Germany) and the very existence of the Ukrainian minority in Galicia and Volhynia was now seen as a security risk by the Polish government and military officials.[271] When German occupiers arrived in this environment in September 1939, they did not have to plant seeds of ethnic hatred between Ukrainians and Poles. That tree had been growing for at least a decade. The Polish government-in-exile continued to have a strong anti-Ukrainian bias and regarded its Ukrainian subjects at best as disloyal and at worst as hostile.[272]

Poles

When *Krakivski Visti* was started in January 1940 it received strong encouragement from the occupation authorities to pursue Polish-Ukrainian relations or any other Polish topics as long as their depiction would cast a negative light on the defeated state and nation. In seeking potential authors for articles on these subjects on January 28, 1940 Khomiak wrote to one of the most renowned Ukrainian journalists of the time, Osyp Nazaruk (1883-1940), who similarly to thousands of other Galician Ukrainians fled into the German-occupied part of Poland from the advancing Red Army in September

---

271 Fedevych, *Halytski ukraintsi u Polshchi*, 248-268. This book also claims that the majority of Ukrainian national activists, including Ounites, "remained loyal to the Polish state up until the second half of September 1939, when Poland's defeat became evident": Ibidem, 267. In my opinion, it infers too much from a passive position of "let's wait and see" masked with public declarations of loyalty.

272 Anti-Ukrainian sentiment dominated Polish émigré officials as evident from various memoranda on the Ukrainian question they submitted to the Polish government-in-exile. The majority of them called not for abandoning the prewar policies—denationalization, assimilation and limitation in civic rights—against Ukrainians in Poland, but for their intensification. One memo debated the very name "Ukrainian" and argued for its suppression in favor of "Rusyn." The most radical memo offered to solve the Ukrainian question in Poland once and for all through a program of forcible resettlement of all Ukrainians from prewar Polish borders into "Soviet Russia" after victory over the Nazi Germany. See: I. I. Iliushyn, *OUN-UPA i ukrainske pytannia v roky Druhoi svitovoi viiny (v svitli polskykh dokumentiv)* (Kyiv: Instytut Istorii Ukrainy NAN Ukrainy, 2000), 144-145, 159, 194.

1939 and ended up eventually in Cracow.²⁷³ Nazaruk was a conservative and clerical journalist, famous in Ukrainian circles for his literary talent and eccentric views.²⁷⁴ Khomiak asked Nazaruk to write a series of articles on "what was the main reason for the decline of Poland," paying principal attention to "the whole politics of the [former] Polish government against our [Ukrainian] people in the past 20 years." The series had to showcase what lessons Ukrainians could draw from the experience of the Second Polish Republic. On the one hand, Khomiak expected Nazaruk to show "how we have to act in establishing our state in the near future," that is, how in the aftermath of World War I, Poland had succeeded in gaining independence while Western Ukraine failed. On the other hand, Nazaruk was to show how "not to undermine our own state from within and push our nation to the brink." At the end of his letter, Khomiak hinted that *Krakivski Visti*, at least for the time being, was quite limited in the topics it may pursue but on Polish subjects the newspaper has been allowed to publish an "infinite" number of texts.²⁷⁵

It is not clear how Nazaruk responded to Khomiak's offer. In any case, he died soon afterward, on March 31, 1940.²⁷⁶ By that time, the task of writing an anti-Polish series was picked up by Khomiak's colleague from *Dilo* and a member of the UNDO establishment—Ivan Rudnytskyi (pen name Ivan Kedryn, 1896-1995). In terms of journalistic fame and talent, Kedryn was Nazaruk's closest rival at the time. In a sense, Kedryn was better prepared to write about the Second Polish Republic and its Ukrainian question than

---

273 Nazaruk left a short memoir about his escape from the Soviets: Osyp Nazaruk, *Zi Lvova do Varshavy: utecha pered sovitamy v pamiatnykh dniakh 2-13 zhovtnia 1939 roku* (Lviv: Naukove t-vo imeni Shevchenka, 1995).
274 Ivan L. Rudnytsky's study of Nazaruk's friendship and conflict with Lypynskyi remains the best biography of the former: Ivan Lysiak-Rudnytskyi, "Nazaruk i Lypynskyi: istoriia ikhnoi druzhby ta konfliktu," in *Lysty Osypa Nazaruka do Viacheslava Lypynskoho*, ed. Ivan Lysiak-Rudnytskyi (Philadelphia: W. K. Lypynsky East European Research Institute, 1976), xv-xcvii.
275 Letter from Mykhailo Khomiak to Osyp Nazaruk January 28, 1940. Central State Historical Archives of Ukraine in Lviv (TsDIAL of Ukraine), f. 359, op.1, spr. 333, ark 5-5zv.
276 "D-r Osyp Nazaruk," *Krakivski Visti*, no. 26 April 7, 1940, 1, 7; "Pokhoron d-ra O. Nazaruka," *Krakivski Visti*, no. 27 April 11, 1940, 7.

Nazaruk. Among Ukrainian journalists of interwar Poland Kedryn was a unique figure. He was not only a journalist and editor who observed and analyzed political life but also a known political insider privy to the inner workings of the Polish state, especially in the 1930s during the so-called normalization that his party, the UNDO, had facilitated.[277] In September 1939 Kedryn fled from Lviv to Cracow, rightfully fearing that the Soviets would arrest him.[278] Looking for sources of additional income, he turned to *Krakivski Visti* and eventually joined its editorial board. However, after "exactly one month," he was dismissed from the newspaper "on the Gestapo's demand (Prof. Kubijovyč officially told me this)."[279] Kedryn believed that the reason for the dismissal was his Jewish background, which, according to him, was revealed to the occupation authorities by his Ukrainian enemies already in fall 1939.[280]

---

277 The most important, though also flawed, biography of Kedryn is: Mariusz Sawa, *Ukraiński emigrant: działalność i myśl Iwana Kedryna-Rudnyckiego (1896-1995)* (Lublin: Instytut Pamięci Narodowej - Komisja Ścigania Zbrodni przeciwko Narodowi Polskiemu, Oddział w Lublinie, 2016). See Ola Hnatiuk's review where she points out some of the issues with the book: Ola Hnatiuk, "Conditio sine qua non," *East/West: Journal of Ukrainian Studies* IV, No. 2 (2017): 275-290, http://dx.doi.org/10.21226/T20D1V
278 Kedryn, *Zhyttia – podii – liudy*, 343-344.
279 See Ivan Kedryn's letter to Jerzy Giedroyc from May 11, 1952 published in: Bogumila Berdykhovska, ed., *Yezhy Gedroits ta ukrainska emigratsiia: lystuvannia 1950-1982 rokiv* (Kyiv: Krytyka, 2008): 706. According to the editorial chronicle, Kedryn worked as an editor at *Krakivski Visti* from January to April 1941: "Chleny Redaktsii 'Krakivskykh Vistei' i spivrobitnyky." PAA, Michael Chomiak fonds, File PR1985.0191/23.
280 Berdykhovska, ed., *Yezhy Gedroits ta ukrainska emigratsiia*, 705. The files of the NSDAP's Office of Foreign Affairs at the German Federal Archives (Bundesarchiv, NS43/32) contain an anonymous report titled "Kurze Angaben uber die Ukrainische Frage in den fruheren poln. Gebieten" (Brief information on the Ukrainian question in the former Polish territories) dated November 1939. Its author most likely was a Ukrainian or at least someone well-informed about Ukrainian affairs. The document mentions that Kedryn's mother was Jewish and that she raised him and his three brothers as Ukrainians. Strangely, it omitted their sister Milena Rudnytska. The report described Kedryn as a valuable pro-German (*deutschfreundliche*) journalist and suggested using him. "[On] Kedryn-Rudnickij: I could imagine the case where a half-Jew is tolerated in German newspapers because of his merits. Perhaps this exception could also be made for Rudnickij and he could be allowed to work in the Ukrainian newspaper."

Under the pseudonym *Homo politicus* (political human), he wrote a series of twenty-seven articles titled "Prychyny upadku Polshchi" (Causes of Poland's Fall), which appeared in *Krakivski Visti* from March 27 to August 7, 1940.[281] The series reads like an indictment of Polish society and its political class. It started with a strong claim that the quick breakdown ("a couple of days") of the Polish state after the German invasion was "unprecedented" in world history. But it would be false to explain this "downfall," Kedryn claimed, only by the German military triumph over the Polish army.[282] The Polish state was rotten from the inside, beginning from its re-emergence in 1918. It was Poles—"not Germans, not Ukrainians and not Russians [*moskali*]" — who "prepared the destruction of their own state by their own hands." The state's faulty domestic, foreign and military policies resulted in the rule of greed, corruption, nepotism and incompetence. This "house of cards" only needed a slight external blow—the German invasion—to fall apart.[283]

By giving us a story of the "real" Poland, continued Kedryn, he was not trying to treat Poles in the same hurtful way that they treated Ukrainians for two decades of the interwar period, taking pleasure in their suffering and the impotence of "Ukrainian fury." On the contrary, the goal of the series was twofold: first, to establish historical truth, since the occupied Polish society had already started to construct myths about what happened in their state from 1919 to 1939; second, "to show how *not* to govern a state!"[284] That

---

281 Homo politicus [Ivan Kedryn], "Prychyny upadku Polshchi," *Krakivski Visti*, no. 23 March 27, 1940, 3; no. 24 March 31, 1940, 3-4: no. 25 April 4, 1940, 3-4; no. 26 April 7, 1940, 3; no. 27 April 11, 1940, 3-4; no. 28 April 14, 1940, 3; no. 29 April 17, 1940, 3-4; no. 30 April 21, 1940, 3-4; no. 32 April 28, 1940, 8-9; no. 34 May 6, 1940, 3; no. 38 May 15, 1940, 3-4; no. 39 May 17, 1940, 3-4; no. 41 May 22, 1940, 3-4; no. 43 May 27, 1940, 8; no. 45 May 31, 1940, 3-4; no. 48 June 9, 1940, 3-4; no. 49 June 11, 1940, 3-4; no. 51 June 15, 1940, 3-4; no. 54 June 21, 1940, 3-4; no. 56 June 26, 1940, 3-4; no. 61 July 8, 1940, 3-4; no. 62 July 10, 1940, 3-4; no. 65 July 17, 1940, 3-4; no. 67 July 22, 1940, 3-4; no. 70 July 29, 1940, 3-4; no. 73 August 5, 1940, 3-4; no. 74 August 7, 1940, 3-4.
282 Homo politicus [Ivan Kedryn], "Prychyny upadku Polshchi," *Krakivski Visti*, no. 23 March 27, 1940, 3.
283 Ibidem.
284 Ibidem.

does not mean, continued Kedryn, that he was interested in "lecturing" Poles so that they could avoid repeating their past mistakes in the future. "I do not believe," he wrote, that the famous Polish proverb "mądry Polak po szkodzie" (a Pole is wise after harm has been done) is "true." For "even if fate would smile on the Poles once more" and they would regain their state in the prewar borders— they would commit the same, if not worse, mistakes again.[285]

After this passionate introduction Kedryn proceeded to look at specific subjects in support of his claims: the Polish mentality; the political structure of the Polish state; the role of Józef Piłsudski in Polish politics; Polish political parties; internal Polish political anarchy; the political roles of Wincenty Witos, Ignacy Mościcki, Edward Rydz-Śmigły, Kazimierz Bartel and Walery Sławek; the authoritarian and chauvinistic character of the interwar Polish state; attempts to reach a Polish-Ukrainian compromise in 1918-1939; Polish pacification, normalization and lost opportunities of Polish-Ukrainian relations; Polish policies against other national minorities—Germans, Belarusians, Lithuanians, Jews and Russians; Polish foreign policy, Poland's relationship with Germany, "Russia" (the Soviet Union) and Britain; the role of the Polish military in the Polish state and political life; the press in interwar Poland and state censorship; the corruption and financial machinations of Polish state officials; the German-Polish war in September 1939; the disintegration of the Polish state during the war and the Polish legend of "Ukrainian betrayal."

The last, twenty-eighth article—the conclusions—did not appear in *Krakivski Visti*. Instead, it appeared with the rest of the series republished as a book (297 pages of text plus illustrations and maps) by the UPH in fall 1940.[286] In the conclusions, Kedryn charged "Polish society" with the inability to accept the hard lessons of history, which in his opinion were two in regards to the interwar Polish state: 1) in foreign policy, it should have followed "Great Germany" since a strong Germany would have reemerged

---

285 Ibidem.
286 Homo politicus [Ivan Kedryn], *Prychyny upadku Polshchi* (Krakiv: Ukrainske Vydavnytstvo, 1940).

in any case and Poland would never have been able to prevent it; 2) from the very outset the Polish state should have recognized its multinational character and, instead of doomed attempts to absorb a population of 10 million members of national minorities, it should have offered them autonomy and adopted federalism as its political foundation. But the Poles, he wrote, would not have been able to grasp these lessons because "99.9%" of them believe in the ideal of "a great and mighty Poland." This belief and the Polish propensity to act upon it rather than on the basis of political reality, concludes Kedryn, is proof that the Poles are politically immature as a nation.[287]

According to Kedryn's memoir, a Polish translation of the book was also prepared with an introduction by the Polish conservative politician Piotr Dunin-Borkowski (1890-1949), his good personal acquaintance.[288] However, German censorship did not allow its publication because the book constituted "political literature," and Poles were allowed to have none.[289] In his memoirs, Kedryn denied that the series was, as some Poles claimed, an "anti-Polish diatribe." His counterargument — "I wrote it under fresh impressions ... using rich source materials" — did not really address the accusation.[290] Besides the series, Kedryn published several more articles in *Krakivski Visti*, but none of them contained as strong an anti-Polish message as the series.[291] In the Ukrainian corpus of anti-Polish writings, Kedryn's "Prychyny upadku Polshchi" to this day remains one of the most sophisticated and well-written texts.

Incidentally, the most substantial critique of the series/book was provided by his sister, Milena Rudnytska. It seems that at some point in the early 1960s, Kedryn entertained the idea to republish "Prychyny upadku Polshchi" because Milena sent him three pages

---

287 Ibidem, 286-297.
288 Kedryn, *Zhyttia – podii – liudy*, 349. On Dunin-Borkowski see: Ola Hnatiuk, "Piotr Dunin-Borkowski," *Zeszyty Historyczne* no. 155 (2006): 188-225.
289 Kedryn, *Zhyttia – podii – liudy*, 349.
290 Ibidem.
291 For example: I. Kedryn, "Bilshe sertsia dlia zemliakiv," *Krakivski Visti*, no. 4 (472) Rizdvo Khrystove (January 6?), 1943, 13.

of her comments and corrections.[292] She praised the book for its factual material and encouraged her brother to republish it, but with two substantial revisions. First, "change or omit everything pro-Hitlerite" from the text, especially praises of "Hitlerite" foreign policy and military aggression against Poland. She recommended to rework or omit entirely the chapter on foreign policy and adjust the conclusions accordingly. Second, eliminate passages that "offend Poles, question their honesty and patriotism, remove all reproaches of moral character directed against the entire Polish people [narodu]."[293] She defended Poles against some of such passages. In response to Kedryn's criticisms of the eighteenth-century Polish state and society, their internal decline and the *szlachta*'s role in it, she wrote that it is not the Ukrainians' place to judge: "in attempts to build a state our people [Ukrainians] showed themselves even less capable than the Poles." She disagreed with Kedryn's charge that the Polish democratic camp produced only mediocre politicians in the interwar period: "What about Witos, Daszyński, Lieberman, Rataj, Hołówko, Sławek, from the *endecja* [National Democrats] Stanisław Stroński, Trąmpczyński? ... Those were very gifted people."[294]

Finally, Milena challenged the book's argument that Poland should have granted autonomy to its national minorities and adopted a federal state structure. In her opinion, even a "liberal national policy" would have failed in Poland because "the centrifugal force of the minorities was too strong" due to their large percentage of the total population. Federalism would not have worked either: "the idea of federation was alien and unacceptable not only to the Poles, but also to the national minorities." However, she did agree with the thought that the Second Polish Republic was doomed because it acquired too many minorities during the establishment of

---

292 See: Milena Rudnytska, "Zauvazhennia do knyzhky Kedryna." UAA, Ivan L. Rudnytsky fonds, Accession no. 1991-138, Box 6. The typescript is undated but on its last page it mentions that the Ukrainian language has changed a lot in the twenty years since the book's appearance. So it is safe to assume that it was written in the early 1960s.
293 Rudnytska, "Zauvazhennia," 1.
294 Ibidem, 2.

its borders in 1919-1921: "the seeds of death were already planted at Poland's [re]birth, it could not pursue a healthy policy while almost 40% of its population was non-Polish."[295]

Another important figure who contributed anti-Polish material to *Krakivski Visti* was the Galician Ukrainian Stepan Baran (1879-1953). Like Kedryn, Baran belonged to the UNDO establishment and also knew Polish political life from the inside, having served as an MP in the Polish parliament in 1928-1939. By education Baran was a lawyer (Ph.D. in law, 1909), but his intellectual interests were primarily in Ukrainian church affairs.[296] A series of eight articles, which he published under his real name, dealt with the situation of the Orthodox Church in Poland.[297] The series provided a sober and strong critique of the interwar Polish political elites and their domestic policies against Orthodox Ukrainians. Legally, Baran reminded his readers that, by its two constitutions of 1921 and 1935 respectively, Poland guaranteed equal rights to all of its citizens, notwithstanding their national, religious or racial identity. But in practice, this legal norm was routinely and intentionally violated. The Second Polish Republic, wrote Baran, was founded on "self-deception": around 40% of its population was non-Polish and yet not only Polish "national extremists" but even governing circles regarded "Poland [as] a Polish nation[-state]." This self-deception and policies of ignoring the national needs of minorities prevented the "internal consolidation" of the country and made the national

---

295 Ibidem, 3.
296 Baran was one of the first biographers of Metropolitan Andrei (Sheptytskyi), see: Stepan Baran, *Mytropolyt Andrei Sheptytskyi: zhyttia i dialnist* (Munich: Vernyhora, 1947).
297 The titles of articles were different, but it was one continuous series: Stepan Baran, "Tserkovne pytannia u b. Polshchi," *Krakivski Visti*, no. 30 April 21, 1940, 4-5; "Avtokefaliia Pravoslavnoi Tserkvy u b. Polshchi," *Krakivski Visti*, no. 31 April 24, 1940, 4; "Pravni osnovy Pravoslavnoi Tserkvy u b. Polshchi," *Krakivski Visti*, no. 33 May 4, 1940, 3-4; "Z tserkovnoi istorii Kholmshchyny i Pidliashsha," *Krakivski Visti*, no. 34 May 6, 1940, 5-6; "Kholmskyi tserkovnyi zizd ta ioho postanovy," *Krakivski Visti*, no. 39 May 17, 1940, 4; "Za unormuvannia vidnosyn Pravoslavnoi Tserkvy," *Krakivski Visti*, no. 40 May 19, 1940, 3-4; "Statut pro tymchasovu upravu pravoslavnykh parokhii zatverdzhenyi," *Krakivski Visti*, no. 47 June 6, 1940, 3-4; "Vykhidna tochka do dalshoi organizatsii Pravoslavnoi Tserkvy u General-Gubernatorstvi," *Krakivski Visti*, no. 49 June 11, 1940, 5-6.

question the weakest link of Polish statehood. For Baran this served as proof of the Polish inability to maintain a viable state: Poland once again showed that it had "neither prominent strategists, nor prominent politicians." Polish statesmen were *mirnoty* — petty people — who were not worthy to be called *derzhavni muzhi* (statesmen). "They learned nothing from their own history" and could not even learn from the surrounding reality because their own "megalomania and self-deception" obscured it from them.[298]

Baran argued that all Ukrainians suffered in interwar Poland because of their nationality, but some Ukrainians suffered more than others because of their Orthodox faith. Officially, Orthodox believers were the second largest religious group (11.8%) in the Second Republic, but both in terms of Polish law and Polish reality, they fared worse than Greek Catholics, Protestants, followers of Judaism, and even Muslims. No other group of believers suffered so much persecution in interwar Poland, which "took away and destroyed Orthodox churches, turned them into Roman Catholic *kościoły*, illegally seized church lands and transferred them to Polish colonists."[299] In addition, the Polish state forcibly Polonized Orthodox educational institutions and pushed for linguistic Polonization of the Orthodox church, including the liturgy, despite the fact that there were almost no ethnic Poles among the Orthodox faithful. Some Poles did convert to Orthodoxy, but in most cases, according to Baran, they did so only to get a divorce when the Polish Roman Catholic church had refused them. The Polish army chaplains were the vanguard of this Polonization. In 1938 two Poles were ordained as Orthodox bishops — both of them were army chaplains. If the war did not start in 1939 and things continued in the same way, then it was only a matter of time, wrote Baran, that the next Orthodox metropolitan would be a Pole as well. This campaign of linguistic Polonization of the Orthodox church, Baran concluded, had a far-

---

298 Stepan Baran, "Tserkovne pytannia u b. Polshchi," *Krakivski Visti*, no. 30 April 21, 1940, 4.
299 Ibidem.

reaching goal of national Polonization of its faithful, most of whom were ethnic Ukrainians.[300]

The main shortcoming of Baran's series was a lack of data. For example, he could not provide even an approximate number of Ukrainian Orthodox churches that were closed down by the Polish state or turned into *kościoły*. This task was accomplished by other articles. The article, which listed no author, "Kilko tserkov znyshchyly poliaky na Kholmshchyni?" (How many churches did the Poles destroy in the Chełm region?) estimated that in 1919 the Chełm and Podlasie regions had 383 Orthodox churches. By spring and summer of 1938 115 of the churches had been destroyed (one dating to the 12th century) by Polish "vandalism." By September 1, 1939 out of 383 only 51 were still in Orthodox hands (13,47%), 149 were turned into *kościoły* (38,9%), and 183 were completely destroyed or burned down (47,73%). The number of Orthodox parishes dropped from about 250 to 51 (an 80% decline).[301]

An important event in the history of the Orthodox faith in the Chełm region — the transfer of the Chełm cathedral back to the Orthodox church in May 1940 — was also used as an opportunity for the anti-Polish campaign. The cathedral's history encapsulated the development of Christianity in these parts of Europe. The first Chełm cathedral was allegedly built in the time of Volodymyr the Great, who Christianized Kyivan Rus in 988.[302] After the Union of Brest (1596), the cathedral was changed from Orthodox to Greek Catholic. In 1875 the Russian imperial authorities returned it to the Orthodox. In 1918, after the occupation of the Chełm region by the reemerged Poland, the Orthodox cathedral was turned into a Roman Catholic *kościół*.[303]

Hans Frank announced his decision to return the cathedral to the Orthodox faithful again on April 19, 1940 during his meeting with a Ukrainian delegation headed by Kubijovyč. Such April visits

---

300 Stepan Baran, "Pravni osnovy Pravoslavnoi Tserkvy u b. Polshchi," *Krakivski Visti*, no. 33 May 4, 1940, 3-4.
301 "Kilko tserkov znyshchyly poliaky na Kholmshchyni?" *Krakivski Visti*, no. 31 April 24, 1940, 2-3.
302 "Peredacha soboru v Kholmi," *Krakivski Visti*, no. 31 April 24, 1940, 1.
303 "Velychave sviato v Kholmi," *Krakivski Visti*, no. 43 May 27, 1940, 3.

to Frank became a yearly tradition for the UCC leadership. The delegation arrived on the eve of Hitler's birthday (April 20) to congratulate Frank as the personification of "the Führer of Great Germany" in these lands and to thank him (Hitler) for "taking under his care" the Ukrainian population in the General Government.[304] The ceremony of the cathedral's return occurred a month later, on May 19.[305]

Krakivski Visti devoted almost an entire issue (no. 43 May 27, 1940) to the event. Reports and articles in the issue, on the one hand, praised the German occupation authorities for their just and orderly rule, and on the other hand, framed Poland and Poles as antithetical to values of justice and order. The event was attended by many Ukrainian notables and high-ranking German officials (though not by Frank), including Kubijovyč, who echoed this contrast of German justice and order versus "Polish barbarians" in his speech at the transfer ceremony.[306] A short piece "Polska protyaktsiia" (Polish counter-action) in the same issue of Krakivski Visti complained that the event was not attended by many Ukrainians because of heavy rain and "the criminal agitation of Poles." The latter, claimed the article, spread rumors and leaflets (in Ukrainian and Polish) in neighboring villages that the Germans planned to seize attending peasants and ship them as laborers to Germany or to confiscate their horses.[307]

Besides sophisticated and well-written articles by Kedryn and Baran, there were numerous shorter pieces filled with anti-Polish rhetoric and statements in Krakivski Visti. Quite often, these articles were devoted to a variety of mundane topics, such as reporting about local developments and Ukrainian celebrations in villages and towns of the General Government, but they were also used for an anti-Polish message to contrast the difference between Polish and German rule. Such articles were regularly published in Krakivski Visti from its second issue until June 1941, when the newspaper made an important ideological turn from an anti-Polish to an

---

304 "Peredacha soboru v Kholmi," Krakivski Visti, no. 31 April 24, 1940, 1.
305 "Peredacha soboru," Krakivski Visti, no. 43 May 27, 1940, 4.
306 "Promova prof. d-ra V. Kubijovyča," Krakivski Visti, no. 43 May 27, 1940, 5.
307 "Polska protyaktsiia," Krakivski Visti, no. 43 May 27, 1940, 3.

anti-Soviet direction. The first article to set this pattern was "Pevnym krokom vperid!" (March ahead in confidence!) by a certain V. Nemyrych. Though the main theme of his piece was the future potential of Ukrainian national development in the General Government (Nemyrych advocated looking up to the Germans and their culture in this regard), he also made negative comments about Poland and Poles, ridiculing the Second Polish Republic as an "artificial" country and claiming that Polish culture amounted to nothing more than *khamstvo* (boorishness). For him, the Polish belief in their "cultural and civilizational superiority [*vyshchist*]" was a manifestation of their "true [national] infantilism."[308]

The main themes of these short anti-Polish pieces were the following. First, the most important and widespread theme was the Polish national oppression of Ukrainians in the Second Polish Republic expressed primarily in the Polonization of Ukrainian education and children,[309] the persecution and destruction of Ukrainian national institutions and churches,[310] and Polish brutality against

---

308 V. Nemyrych, "Pevnym krokom vperid!" *Krakivski Visti*, no. 2 January 11, 1940, 2.
309 See: M. Slavych, "'Uchitesia—braty moi' ... Perelomove znachinnia v zhytti narodu—vidkryttia narodnikh shkil," *Krakivski Visti*, no. 2 January 11, 1940, 4; "Vistky z poludnevoi Kholmshchyny," *Krakivski Visti*, no. 2 January 11, 1940, 5; "Veselishe stalo zhyty," *Krakivski Visti*, no. 5 January 21, 1940, 3; Batko, "Naimenshi dity svoim batkam," *Krakivski Visti*, no. 8 February 4, 1940, 2; R. Samota, "Yaki oboviazky maie zhinka selianka?," *Krakivski Visti*, no. 10 February 11, 1940, 3; M. D., "Nikomu ne vbyty dushi narodu," *Krakivski Visti*, no. 12 February 18, 1940, 2; St. Var., "Khochemo ukrainskoi shkoly," *Krakivski Visti*, no. 23 March 27, 1940, 2; Yurii Tarkovych, "'Liubliu ia ditei i liubliu ikh uchyty,'" *Krakivski Visti*, no. 32 April 28, 1940, 12; Andrii Kachor, "Kladim tverdi osnovy," *Krakivski Visti*, no. 42 May 24, 1940, 5.
310 M. L., "Teperishnii stan i vymohy nashoho hospodarskoho zhyttia," *Krakivski Visti*, no. 5 January 21, 1940, 2-3; H. Ya., "Yak Yaroslavshchyna pratsiuie," *Krakivski Visti*, no. 6 January 25, 1940, 3; Svii, "Naselennia Volodavshchyny znovu u svoii tserkvi," *Krakivski Visti*, no. 12 February 18, 1940, 4; V. Ostrovskyi, "Dvi vesny natsionalnoho vidrodzhennia Kholmshchyny," *Krakivski Visti*, no. 25 April 4, 1940, 1; Bohorodchanyn, "Molod sela Bohorodytsi pratsiuie," *Krakivski Visti*, no. 25 April 4, 1940, 2; S., "Nas ne zlomyv teror!," *Krakivski Visti*, no. 28 April 14, 1940, 2; Iza, "Pratsiuimo vperto i poslidovno," *Krakivski Visti*, no. 34 May 6, 1940, 10; Roman Huchvanovych [Hennadii Kotorovych], "Rozdumalysia liudy dobri," *Krakivski Visti*, no. 35 May 9, 1940, 3-4; "Literaturno-mystetskyi vechir z nahody vidkryttia biblioteky «Prosvity» u Krakovi," *Krakivski Visti*, no. 38 May 15, 1940, 7; "Pobut arkhyiep. Serafyma v Liublyni i v Kholmi," *Krakivski Visti*, no. 36 May 11, 1940, 3-4.

Ukrainians.[311] Virtually any problem experienced by Ukrainians in interwar Poland was blamed on the Polish authorities or Polish society. For example, one anonymous article blamed the Polish state for the massive unemployment of Ukrainians before the war.[312] Special attention was given to crimes allegedly committed by the Polish state, army and police against Ukrainians on the eve of the war or during its course. Among the topics were the executions of Galician Ukrainians who served in the "Carpathian Sich,"[313] the physical extermination of Ukrainian prisoners in the first days of the war,[314] the ethnic cleansing of Ukrainian villages in the Stryi region,[315] and the murder of innocent Ukrainian civilians by retreating Polish troops.[316] In addition, *Krakivski Visti* published short memoirs of those Ukrainians who survived Polish arrests and imprisonment in the 1930s.[317]

The second theme was the portrayal of Polish culture, the Polish state and Poles in a ridiculing, demeaning manner, as a historically inferior phenomenon: incompetence is in the Polish nature,[318] Poles are incapable of creating anything lasting and they

---

311 S. Nukvyt, "Viter iz Volodavshchyny," *Krakivski Visti*, no. 7 January 31, 1940, 5; Yaroslav Naddnistrianskyi, "Na storozhi zakhidnioi mezhi (reportazh z Lemkivshchyny)," *Krakivski Visti*, no. 13 February 21, 1940, 2; M.B., "Nas ne rozbyv polskyi piastuk," *Krakivski Visti*, no. 19 March 13, 1940, 2; "Polska vulytsia huliaie," *Krakivski Visti*, no. 22 March 24, 1940, 2; Ya. H., "Selo Krasivka ne darmuie," *Krakivski Visti*, no. 21 March 20, 1940, 2; "Kulturno-osvitnia pratsia v seli Poturzhyni," *Krakivski Visti*, no. 35 May 9, 1940, 4; "Pidliashshia ide vpered," *Krakivski Visti*, no. 40 May 19, 1940, 6.
312 "Zapomohy dlia bezrobitnykh," *Krakivski Visti*, no. 4 January 17, 1940, 6.
313 Oles Bystrenko, "Oprychnyky z 'KOP'-u," *Krakivski Visti*, no. 37 May 13, 1940, 5. There is an important study of these extrajudicial killings: Oleksandr Pahiria, "Polska storinka teroru v Karpatskii Ukraini (1938-1939 rokiv)," *in Ukrainophobia yak iavyshche ta polittekhnolohiia*, ed. Ya. Harasym et al. Vyp. 1 (Lviv, 2014), 34-59.
314 "Vbyvstva na sygnal," *Krakivski Visti*, no. 11 February 14, 1940, 4.
315 Ivan Pakhal, "Strashni zvirstva poliakiv u Stryishchyni," *Krakivski Visti*, no. 26 April 7, 1940, 4; no. 29 April 17, 1940, 4.
316 o. T., "Kryvavyi veresen u Starosambirshchyni," *Krakivski Visti*, no. 40 May 19, 1940, 4-5; H. S. D., "Koly rozlitalosia 'motsartvo' ...," *Krakivski Visti*, no. 49 June 11, 1940, 4-5.
317 M. Kholodnyi, "Dopyty na stanytsi 'KOP-'u," *Krakivski Visti*, no. 16 March 3, 1940, 4; no. 17 March 7, 1940, 4-5; no. 19 March 13, 1940, 4-5.
318 H. R., "Yak khliborob povynen pryity do hospodarskoi rivnovahy?" *Krakivski Visti*, no. 6 January 25, 1940, 4; Petro Stelmashenko, "Rozbudovuimo hospodarsku kulturu," *Krakivski Visti*, no. 26 April 7, 1940, 1-2.

possess no stable values,[319] Poles never fight fairly,[320] the Polish Roman Catholic church is chauvinistic,[321] the Polish obsession with titles (*tytulomaniia*) shows their mental emptiness and so on.[322] It was not uncommon for these articles to describe Poles with nasty epithets ("scum")[323] and to overdramatize the conditions of Polish rule, calling it a "yoke."[324] A certain Kost Shumoskyi even wrote a play "Pid hnetom Polshchi" (Under Poland's yoke), which dramatized life in a Ukrainian village in the Chełm region on the eve of the war.[325] The majority of these texts ascribed permanent negative features to the Polish identity. For example, Mykhailo Ostroverkha in his article with a telling title "Nevylikuvalna neduha" (Incurable disease) argued, that on one hand, there are nations destined to produce culture and heroes and on the other hand, there is the Polish nation—a nation of loud self-promoters, worthless, dirty and destructive *Hochstapler* (German for fraudsters). Throughout its history the Polish state was never able to sustain itself; it survived only as long as it managed to sap the vitality of neighboring peoples.[326] Another article compared Poland's war against Germany with Finland's war against the Soviet Union. In both cases, smaller nations lost, but the Finns demonstrated exemplary valor while the Poles once again showed how dishonorable they are.[327]

Some articles carried not only accusations about Polish behavior in the past but also warnings about Poles in the present and the future. For example, an anonymous piece "Za hlybynu zhyttia" (For depth of life) wrote that the collapse of Poland in 1939 was a

---

319 "Miska spozhyvcha kooperatsiia," *Krakivski Visti*, no. 4 January 17, 1940, 4.
320 Yu. Tarnovych, "Kult poliahlykh," *Krakivski Visti*, no. 52 June 17, 1940, 4-5.
321 "Polskyi manastyr hnizdom nenavysty ta brudu," *Krakivski Visti*, no. 10 February 11, 1940, 3; "Oraty i siiaty musymo perelih," *Krakivski Visti*, no. 40 May 19, 1940, 6.
322 Mamai, "Tytulomaniia," *Krakivski Visti*, no. 16 March 3, 1940, 7.
323 "Shkilnyi kontsert v Lubni," *Krakivski Visti*, no. 43 May 27, 1940, 9.
324 "Selo Horky pratsiuie," *Krakivski Visti*, no. 20 March 17, 1940, 2.
325 Teo, "Kholmshchyna vidrodyliasia i pratsiuie!" *Krakivski Visti*, no. 31 April 24, 1940, 7.
326 M. Tybrskyi [Mykhailo Ostroverkha], "Nevylikuvalna neduha," *Krakivski Visti*, no. 19 March 13, 1940, 1-2.
327 Skat, "Finlandiia zderla masku z Anglii," *Krakivski Visti*, no. 23 March 27, 1940, 1-2.

triumph of historical justice, but the author called for vigilance: Poland is gone, but its legacy is not. Ukrainians still need to get rid of Polish influences and habits they acquired during the interwar period.[328] This view of Ukrainians and Poles as two antithetical sides locked in some sort of existential struggle was present in many texts in *Krakivski Visti*. O. Ottokar, in his piece, wrote that the "wind of history" blew Poland away, but "Poles still remain." And Ukrainians need to continue to fight them "at every step."[329] Another article wrote that to deal with those Poles who remained (*nedobytky*) in the Ukrainian villages and towns after 1939 Ukrainians need to have their own police force which would keep this Polish threat in check.[330] The other author advocated for increased representation of Ukrainians in the occupation administration, which at lower levels was almost fully staffed by Poles. These Polish officials were attempting to drive a wedge between the German regime and the local Ukrainian population, continuing their pre-1939 chauvinistic treatment of Ukrainians. The author called on Ukrainians to apply for positions in the occupation administration.[331] The subject of the Polish officials who stayed in their positions after September 1939 and continued to behave as if little had changed was also raised in the anonymous piece against S. Barna, *soltys* (elder) of the village Voroblyk. The article accused the *soltys*, a Pole, of "terrorizing" the Ukrainian population of the village before the war and continuing his anti-Ukrainian sabotage after the German arrival.[332]

Yet another article essentially advocated for extending to Polish businesses the measures that occupation authorities had already placed on Jewish ones: it argued that for the benefit of Ukrainian credit and cooperative organizations Polish "elements" must be removed from trade in the General Government and large Polish firms should receive Ukrainian commissars (alluding to

---

328 "Za hlybynu zhyttia," *Krakivski Visti*, no. 3 January 14, 1940, 5.
329 O. Ottokar, "Vyprostuimo kryzhi!" *Krakivski Visti*, no. 3 January 14, 1940, 5-6.
330 "Volodavshchyna vidrodzhuietsia," *Krakivski Visti*, no. 5 January 21, 1940, 3.
331 B. Halit, "Ukrainskyi viit v ukrainskii volosti," *Krakivski Visti*, no. 54 June 21, 1940, 5-6.
332 "Chomu Voroblyk ne mozhe rozvyvatysia?" *Krakivski Visti*, no. 55 June 24, 1940, 11.

Ukrainian commissars already appointed by the Germans to run former Jewish businesses). As to the Polish colonists, the author favored their resettlement back into ethnic Polish lands because they had shown themselves to be poor proprietors (*hospodari*). Some articles pointed out that the Ukrainian population still lives in fear of Poles, so deeply two decades of Polish rule affected their psyche.[333] The article "Polske dykunstvo" (Polish savagery) warned that Poles were still attempting to treat Ukrainians in the same manner as before the war and pointed to an incident in the village of Horbiv where a group of Poles armed with axes and pitchforks tried to intimidate a Ukrainian procession to the local cemetery. The Polish mistake was, according to the article, to also call on the local police, which was staffed by Germans. The latter arrived accompanied by a Gestapo officer who took the Ukrainian side in the incident and ordered policemen to disperse the Polish *shumovynnia* (mob).[334]

Poles were portrayed not only as a dangerous national or religious element but also as a criminal one. Reports about criminal activities in the General Government often emphasized the Polish ethnicity of their perpetrators and implied a link between the Polish identity and crime/disorder. Other ethnicities were not named in crime reports. One report wrote about a Polish criminal who committed an armed robbery in October 1939 but was eventually caught and sentenced to death by a German court in Cracow. The report concluded: "Perhaps he [the criminal] forgot that this is no longer Poland and that German authorities punish thievery and robbery severely."[335] The article "Spadshchyna polskoi demoralizatsii" (The legacy of Polish demoralization) happily reported about a series of recent German trials over "Polish" criminal gangs and praised the trials as triumphs of order. The eliminated gangs were the "sad legacy of Polish rule, under which honest people were persecuted, but bandits could walk around without fear of punishment."[336] The article "Liubartiv uvilnenyi vid bandytiv"

---

333 "Pratsia v seli Bonchi," *Krakivski Visti*, no. 23 March 27, 1940, 2; Mistsevyi, "Chesanivshchyna klyche," *Krakivski Visti*, no. 23 March 27, 1940, 2.
334 "Polske dykunstvo," *Krakivski Visti*, no. 45 May 31, 1940, 6.
335 "Novynky," *Krakivski Visti*, no. 11 Feb 14, 1940, 11.
336 "Spadshchyna polskoi demoralizatsii," *Krakivski Visti*, no. 13 February 21, 1940, 7.

(Lubartów liberated from bandits) wrote that before the war the town of Lubartów was ruled by criminal gangs but thankfully the Germans had cleared them out.[337] The article "Vbyv matir svoiei liubky" (He killed his lover's mother) reported about a Masurian (Polish subethnic group) who killed his lover's mother. "Obviously, only a Masurian could commit such a crime," explained the article, which concluded that this crime proved a "lack of culture among Poles-Masurians."[338]

The newspaper also republished fully or summarized articles critical of Poland and Poles from the foreign press, primarily German and Italian.[339] Some articles were also taken from the Allied press if they fit the anti-Polish message. For example, "Tvereza dumka pro poliakiv" (A sober opinion on Poles) from May 1940 was a summary of an article from a French periodical. Its author argued that Polish politicians (meaning the Polish government-in-exile) should base their political goals on reality rather than history: they dream of restoring prewar Poland, but their chances of achieving it were as realistic as France's chances of restoring Charlemagne's empire.[340]

It is interesting to see how Ukrainians who were directly or indirectly involved in the anti-Polish campaign changed their attitude toward Poles and Poland after the war. Their milieu and political conditions changed: they became émigrés, settling in Western Europe and North America. After 1948 Poland was under firm communist rule and became a Soviet satellite. Western Ukrainian lands were now a part of Soviet Ukraine, formally a Ukrainian state, but the Ukrainian émigrés considered it to be under Soviet control just as Polish émigrés regarded their own country. A common enemy is a good recipe for reconciliation. All this, plus the natural flow of time, soothed whatever wounds life in interwar Poland inflicted upon their souls. Some of them forgave. Some of them forgot. Both

---

337 "Liubartiv uvilnenyi vid bandytiv," *Krakivski Visti*, no. 21 March 20, 1940, 7.
338 "Vbyv matir svoiei liubky," *Krakivski Visti*, no. 54 June 21, 1940, 7.
339 "Italiiska presa pro peresliduvannia ukraintsiv u b. Polshchi," *Krakivski Visti*, no. 27 April 11, 1940, 7; "Stattia pro ukraintsiv v nimetskomu shchodennyku," *Krakivski Visti*, no. 34 May 6, 1940, 11.
340 "Tvereza dumka pro poliakiv," *Krakivski Visti*, no. 36 May 11, 1940, 5.

Kedryn and Kubijovyč wrote memoirs critical of the interwar Polish *state* (but not of Polish *people*) and its policies toward Ukrainians.[341] Both developed contacts with Polish émigrés (the *Kultura* circle foremost) and pursued rapprochement between the two nations.[342]

But there was one who neither forgave nor forgot—Mykhailo Khomiak. In the 1960s-70s he became an amateur historian with the ambition of several book projects. He realized none of them, one of which was a collection of secret Polish documents exposing the anti-Ukrainian policies of the interwar Polish regime. Khomiak claimed that he came into possession of secret Polish documents in 1940. Both Kedryn and Kubijovyč were quite skeptical about this project because of their lack of faith in Khomiak's academic abilities. The latter took on faith any anti-Polish information if it was coming from a Ukrainian source. For example, Khomiak firmly believed in the typhus conspiracy—the theory that Poles spread typhus among soldiers of the Ukrainian Galician Army in 1919 and that this was the first use of a bacteriological weapon in the 20th century.[343] In 1971 Kubijovyč asked Khomiak to review drafts of two articles for *Entsyklopediia Ukrainoznavstva*—"Poliaky" (Poles) and "Poliaky na Ukraini" (Poles in Ukraine). Khomiak's review showed that his anti-Polish feelings were still strong, which Kubijovyč noted in his reply. "Your valuable remarks show a combative attitude toward Poles and Poland. [You are] Correct: they buried us and buried themselves. ... But a lot of blame was on Ukrainians too. ... There was no lack of mutual killings in 1943-44. *Now [all] this is ash* [Emphasis is mine]. There are almost no Poles in Ukraine and

---

341 Volodymyr Kubijovyč, *Meni 70* (Munich: Logos, 1970); Volodymyr Kubijovyč, *Meni 85* (Munich: Molode zhyttia, 1985); Ivan Kedryn, *Zhyttia – podii – liudy. Spomyny i komentari* (New York: Chervona Kalyna, 1976).
342 See the correspondence between Ivan Kedryn and Jerzy Giedroyc: Bogumila Berdykhovska, ed., *Yezhy Gedroits ta ukrainska emigratsiia: lystuvannia 1950-1982 rokiv* (Kyiv: Krytyka, 2008): 705-717.
343 Letter from Mykhailo Khomiak to Ivan Yarema July 9, 1963. PAA, Michael Chomiak fonds, File PR1985.0191/170.

no Ukrainians in Poland: political border aligns with ethnic and ... both peoples are part of the Sov[iet] Empire."[344]

The Soviets/Russians

When Polish rule over Western Ukraine was liquidated in September 1939 by invading German and Soviet armies, both invaders were welcomed by the local Ukrainian population, though in the German case that welcome was undoubtedly warmer and more sincere. The two occupiers—Nazi Germany and the Soviet Union— occupied very different places in the Western Ukrainian imagination, both in general terms and vis-à-vis their relationship with Ukrainians. Nazi Germany was perceived in a far more positive light and was considered a power friendlier to Ukrainians. The Soviets enjoyed a similar reputation with many Western Ukrainians in the 1920s during their policy of indigenization (*korenizatsiia*) within the Soviet Union, which, in the Ukrainian case, translated into Ukrainianization (*ukrainizatsiia*) in Soviet Ukraine. However, that positive image was shattered and reversed in the 1930s as Soviet Ukraine endured Stalinist policies: forced collectivization, Holodomor, purges and Russification, which resulted in significant demographic, intellectual and cultural losses for Ukrainians as an ethnic group. All of those developments were reported in the Ukrainian press of interwar Poland, foremost by *Dilo*. So, when the Western Ukrainian population welcomed the Soviet troops in September 1939, it was for their liberation from Polish rule, not because of some pro-Soviet sympathies in Western Ukrainian society, which at that time were extremely rare (limited to a few individuals like Yaroslav Halan). The Soviet occupation of Western Ukraine in September 1939 – June 1941 reinforced anti-Soviet attitudes among the local Ukrainian population: the General Government received a steady influx of Ukrainian refugees from the Soviet-occupied territories, even after January 1940 when the Soviets tightened the border control. No Ukrainians were fleeing in the opposite direction.

---

344 Letter from Volodymyr Kubijovyč to Mykhailo Khomiak, February 26, 1971. PAA, Michael Chomiak fonds, File PR1985.0191/184.

Before the German attack on the Soviet Union on June 22, 1941 *Krakivski Visti* did not pay much attention to the Soviet Union and carefully avoided expressing any (especially negative) opinion on it: most of the texts were dry reports about the course of the Soviet-Finnish war, visits and statements of Soviet leaders, etc. The one exception was an article by Andrii Turskyi (pseudonym of Atanas Mylianych) "Pid znamenem hospodarstva" (Under the banner of the economy) which compared the economic development of Nazi Germany and the Soviet Union in the 1930s.[345] One can easily construe the article as unfavorable to the Soviets or Stalin: it gave all of its praise to Hitler, whose measures, in the author's opinion, rejuvenated the German economy and improved the well-being of German citizens. Stalin's industrialization, on the other hand, led to an unprecedented drop in living standards for the people of the Soviet Union. This veiled criticism was the only negative statement about the Soviet Union published between January 7, 1940 (first issue) and June 22, 1941.

Openly anti-Soviet materials started to appear in the newspaper from June 23, 1941, beginning with the Ukrainian translation of Adolf Hitler's speech from the previous day in which he declared Germany's war on the Soviet Union.[346] In contrast to the newspaper's anti-Polish articles and their discourse of Polish transgressions against justice and order, anti-Soviet content was about civilization or, to steal the title of a famous book, of the "clash of civilizations." Poles and Poland, despite their portrayal as disorderly and unjust, were never othered as non- or anti-European entities. The Soviet Union, on the other hand, was described precisely in such terms. Interestingly, German propaganda reflected quite accurately the inner views of the Nazi leadership on the Soviet Union as an archenemy of European civilization, Western tradition and the Aryan race. In the Nazi view, the Soviets were a completely

---

345 Andrii Turskyi [Atanas Mylianych], "Pid znamenem hospodarstva," *Krakivski Visti*, no. 32 April 28, 1940, 18. Authorship established on the basis of honoraria records. PAA, Michael Chomiak fonds, File PR1985.0191/32.
346 Adolf Hitler, "Viina z Moskvoiu! Prokliamatsiia Firera do nimetskoho narodu," *Krakivski Visti*, no. 133 (288) June 23, 1941, 1-2.

alien entity capable of inhuman levels of cruelty and criminality.[347] Hence, focus on the abominable nature of the Soviet regime and its crimes (which were indeed horrific) dominated Nazi propaganda after June 22, 1941. *Krakivski Visti* followed these two themes, but its authors, even when they used Nazi tropes, did so for specific Ukrainian reasons, as the Soviet Union by 1941 already had a record of crimes against its Ukrainian population: forced collectivization and the famine of 1929-33, Stalinist purges and Russification of the 1930s, imprisonment and deportations of thousands of Western Ukrainians in 1939-41 and most recently mass murder of Western Ukrainian prisoners in summer 1941.

There was also a significant point of divergence between Nazi anti-Soviet discourse and that of *Krakivski Visti*. In Nazi discourse the Russian Empire and the Soviet Union were two separate, quite distinct historical entities: the former in their view experienced strong Germanizing influences through its German elite and settlers, while the latter was heavily Jewified (in Nazi eyes the Bolshevik revolution was a Jewish reversal of this Germanic Westernization that began with Peter the Great). But the Ukrainian anti-Soviet discourse of *Krakivski Visti* regarded both polities as essentially the same with different façades. Hence, the newspaper did not distinguish between the Russian Empire and the Soviet Union, as both were oppressive toward Ukrainians and in both cases the identity and language of the oppressors were primarily Russian. Thus, editors and authors of *Krakivski Visti* made no distinction between *Russian* and *Soviet*. Initially, the newspaper used a Ukrainian derogatory term for Russians—*moskali* to describe the Soviets, their armed forces, etc. However, already by the second week of its existence it dropped *moskali* and *moskalskyi* and began to use *rosiiskyi* (Russian) and *sovitskyi* (Soviet) instead.[348] This practice continued until late June 1941 when *moskali* and its derivatives made a return, and all of

---

[347] The issue of the Nazi leadership's views on the Soviet Union has a rich historiography. One of the most recent works discussing it is: Stephen G. Fritz, *Ostkrieg: Hitler's War of Extermination in the East* (Lexington, KY: University Press of Kentucky, 2011), 7-11.
[348] See: "Sovity peresterihaiut Shvetsiiu i Norvehiiu," *Krakivski Visti*, no. 4 January 17, 1940, 8.

the above terms were used interchangeably afterward. Statements like the following were commonplace in the newspaper: "the Muscovite [tsarist] imperialism is factually equal to Bolshevism."[349] This was also the view of many Ukrainian émigrés in the West after the war, including Kubijovyč, who regarded both the Treaty of Perpetual Peace (1686) between Muscovite Tsardom and the Polish-Lithuanian Commonwealth and the Riga Treaty between Soviet Russia and Poland (1921) as "building stages of the Russian Empire— white [tsarist] or red."[350]

An opportunity to expose the murderous nature of the Soviet regime from both Nazi and Ukrainian perspectives presented itself immediately after the German invasion of the Soviet Union in June 1941. By then, the Soviet regime had ruled over former eastern Poland for nearly 22 months. Ukrainians in Soviet Galicia and Volhynia, similarly to Ukrainians of the General Government, were on the receiving end of positive discrimination. These lands were now a part of Soviet Ukraine; hence, public space, healthcare, local administration, press, and education were Ukrainianized and de-Polonized.[351] For example, the dream of several generations of Galician Ukrainians to have a Ukrainian university in Lviv was finally realized by the Soviet authorities in 1940: they renamed Jan Kazimierz University after the Ukrainian writer Ivan Franko and steadily increased the percentage of ethnic Ukrainians among its students and faculty.[352] This process was stopped by the German arrival in June 1941, which resulted in the closure of the university. But those 22 months of Soviet rule were also a period of speedy Stalinization with all its hallmarks: liquidation of the public sphere and ideological diversity, the introduction of communal apartments, fake elections, deportations and arrests of thousands.[353]

---

349 M. Danko, "Nevtralni derzhavy i bolshevyzm," *Krakivski Visti*, no. 9 (747) January 19, 1943, 1.
350 Letter from Volodymyr Kubijovyč to Mykhailo Khomiak, February 26, 1971. PAA, Michael Chomiak fonds, File PR1985.0191/184.
351 Christoph Mick, *Lemberg, Lwów, L'viv, 1914-1947: Violence and Ethnicity in a Contested City* (West Lafayette, IN: Purdue University Press, 2016), 264-265.
352 Mick, *Lemberg, Lwów, L'viv*, 266.
353 Oleksandr Lutskyi, "Lviv pid radianskoiu okupatsiieiu 1939 – 1941 rr.," *Ukrainskyi vyzvolnyi rukh* no. 7 (2006): 89-119.

The exact number and ethnic composition of inmates in prisons in Soviet Western Ukraine at the time of the German invasion is still debated.[354] Ukrainians constituted a majority among prisoners, which, for many contemporary Ukrainians and later for Ukrainian scholars, was a clear indication of the anti-Ukrainian agenda of the Soviets. Other prisoners were Poles and Jews, who, in terms of percentages of the total population, were overrepresented. Politically, the largest groups of prisoners were Polish and Ukrainian nationalists—by early 1941 the NKVD had infiltrated and dismantled both the Polish and Ukrainian nationalist underground in Galicia and Volhynia.[355] But there were also non-Soviet Leftists (Trotskyists etc.) in the prisons as well. In the situation of the German rapid advance and hectic Soviet evacuation, the NKVD had to decide what to do with the political prisoners. On the one hand, it could not evacuate them. On the other hand, it considered it too dangerous just to leave them in prisons for eventual German liberation. Unsurprisingly, it decided to kill them. Estimates of murdered prisoners range from 10,000 to 40,000, with Ukrainians comprising up to two-thirds of the victims.[356] Their bodies were usually discovered in the very first days of the Germans' arrival into Western Ukrainian cities and towns in June-July 1941.

The legal Ukrainian press started to report on these findings almost immediately. German troops reached Lviv on June 30, 1941 and the reports about the murdered prisoners appeared in the very first issue of the Lviv daily *Ukrainski Shchodenni Visti* (Ukrainian Daily News) on July 5, 1941.[357] *Krakivski Visti* reported on the matter

---

354 By one estimate the Soviets arrested 66,653 people from September 1939 to May 1941. Mick, *Lemberg, Lwów, L'viv*, 271.
355 I. I. Iliushyn, *Protystoiannia UPA i AK (Armii Kraiovoi) v roky Druhoi svitovoi viiny na tli diialnosti polskoho pidpillia v Zakhidnii Ukraini* (Kyiv: Instytut Istorii Ukrainy NAN Ukrainy, 2001), 5-46.
356 Ksenya Kiebuzinski and Alexander Motyl, eds., *The Great West Ukrainian Prison Massacre of 1941: A Sourcebook* (Amsterdam: Amsterdam University Press, 2017), 31.
357 "U lvivskykh tiurmakh NKVD," *Ukrainski Shchodenni Visti*, no. 1 July 5, 1941, 3; "Muchenytstvo ukrainskoho dukhovenstva," *Ukrainski Shchodenni Visti*, no. 1 July 5, 1941, 3; "Velyka zhaloba ukrainskoho narodu," *Ukrainski Shchodenni Visti*, no. 1 July 5, 1941, 3; I. Hrytsynenko, "Kryvavi dni Lvova," *Ukrainski Shchodenni Visti*, no. 1 July 5, 1941, 3. The occupation authorities closed down

the following day with three articles.[358] It continued to publish materials on the murdered prisoners in almost every issue until early August 1941. The last item on this subject appeared in August 24 issue.[359] Besides texts, the newspaper featured photos of the victims, prisons and grieving relatives.[360] The majority of these articles were original materials (twenty six pieces);[361] others were

---

Ukrainski Shchodenni Visti on August 24, 1941 and transferred its editors and staff to the newspaper which they created instead — *Lvivski Visti* (Lviv News).
358 KTV [Hennadii Kotorovych], "Zhakhlyvi bolshevytski masakry u Lvovi," *Krakivski Visti*, no. 146 (301) July 6, 1941, 1; "Podii na zakhidno-ukrainskykh zemliakh (Interviu z dots. d-rom H.I. Baierom)," *Krakivski Visti*, no. 146 (301) July 6, 1941, 2-3; "Bolshevytskyi pohrom u Lvovi," *Krakivski Visti*, no. 146 (301) July 6, 1941, 6.
359 Lvovianyn [Ivan Nimchuk], "Zi Lvova i z kraiu," *Krakivski Visti*, no. 186 (341) August 24, 1941, 3-4.
360 "Yak skazhenily katy," *Krakivski Visti*, no. 148 (303) July 9, 1941, 3; "Yak skazhenily katy v Dubni. Ponad 1500 zhertv," *Krakivski Visti*, no. 149 (304) July 10, 1941, 3; "Bezimenni muchenyky," *Krakivski Visti*, no. 150 (305) July 11, 1941, 6; "Zhertvy kryvavoi masakry u Lvovi," *Krakivski Visti*, no. 151 (306) July 12, 1941, 5.
361 KTV [Hennadii Kotorovych], "Zhakhlyvi bolshevytski masakry u Lvovi," *Krakivski Visti*, no. 146 (301) July 6, 1941, 1; "Podii na zakhidno-ukrainskykh zemliakh (Interviu z dots. d-rom H.I. Baierom)," *Krakivski Visti*, no. 146 (301) July 6, 1941, 2-3; Volodymyr Kubijovyč, "Pered maiestatom nepovynnoi krovy," *Krakivski Visti*, no. 147 (302) July 8, 1941, 1-2; KTV [Hennadii Kotorovych], "Svit klonyt holovu pered trahediieiu Ukrainy (vid nashoho korespondenta)," *Krakivski Visti*, no. 149 (304) July 10, 1941, 2-3; M. K. [Mariian Kozak], "Peklo bolshevytskykh viaznyts. Ochevydets pro kryvavu masakru ukraintsiv u Lutsku," *Krakivski Visti*, no. 152 (307) July 15, 1941, 2-3; "Uryvky z lystiv," *Krakivski Visti*, no. 155 (310) July 18, 1941, 5; "Muchenyky Zhovkivshchyny," *Krakivski Visti*, no. 155 (310) July 18, 1941, 5; "Ukrainski hekatomby," *Krakivski Visti*, no. 156 (311) July 19, 1941, 2; "Nema porivnan," *Krakivski Visti*, no. 156 (311) July 19, 1941, 2; "Ochevydets iz Sambora pro dni zhakhu," *Krakivski Visti*, no. 157 (312) July 20, 1941, 3; Anatol Kurdydyk, "Kryvava propahanda Ukrainy," *Krakivski Visti*, no. 159 (314) July 23, 1941, 1-2; "700 muchenykiv u Dobromylshchyni," *Krakivski Visti*, no. 159 (314) July 23, 1941, 2; "Uryvky z lystiv," *Krakivski Visti*, no. 160 (315) July 24, 1941, 2; "Pravdyve oblychchia Moskvy," *Krakivski Visti*, no. 160 (315) July 24, 1941, 3; "Zhertvy NKVD," *Krakivski Visti*, no. 163 (318) July 27, 1941, 2; "Zalishchyky i Stanyslaviv," *Krakivski Visti*, no. 163 (318) July 27, 1941, 4; B. Halit, "Ne rydai, a zdobuvai," *Krakivski Visti*, no. 164 (319) July 29, 1941, 1-2; "Zhertvy NKVD v Drohobychi," *Krakivski Visti*, no. 169 (324) August 3, 1941, 4; "Bolshevytskyi pohrom u Dobromylshchyni," *Krakivski Visti*, no. 171 (326) August 6, 1941, 2; "Vistky z kraiu," *Krakivski Visti*, no. 171 (326) August 6, 1941, 3; "1500 ukraintsiv zamorduvaly bolshevyky u Kremiantsi," *Krakivski Visti*, no. 171 (326) August 6, 1941, 5; "Rikamy plyly trupy," *Krakivski Visti*, no. 173 (328) August 8, 1941, 5; "Zhertvy bolshevytskoho teroru v Horodku," *Krakivski Visti*, no. 173 (328) August 8, 1941, 5; "Z kraiu," *Krakivski Visti*, no. 179 (334) August 15, 1941, 3; "Bolshevytski strakhittia v Halychyni," *Krakivski Visti*,

A SCHOOL OF HATE 101

translations from foreign, primarily Axis press (fifteen pieces)[362] or republished from *Ukrainski Shchodenni Visti* (three pieces).[363] After the 1941 campaign *Krakivski Visti* kept returning to the June 1941 murders with commemorative pieces in 1942[364] and 1943,[365] but for some reason not in 1944.

Descriptions of the prisons and victims in the 1941 texts were quite graphic—"blood splattered up to the ceiling"—if one gives rein to the imagination.[366] Many articles stressed that corpses showed signs of gruesome torture and missing body parts. Most of the texts went beyond reporting on murders per se (locations,

---

no. 183 (338) August 21, 1941, 5; Lvovianyn [Ivan Nimchuk], "Zi Lvova i z kraiu," *Krakivski Visti*, no. 186 (341) August 24, 1941, 3-4.

362 "Bolshevytskyi pohrom u Lvovi," *Krakivski Visti*, no. 146 (301) July 6, 1941, 6; "Zhakhlyvyi pohrom ukraintsiv," *Krakivski Visti*, no. 147 (302) July 8, 1941, 2; "Masakra u viaznytsi NKVD v Dubni," *Krakivski Visti*, no. 147 (302) July 8, 1941, 2-3; "Kryvavi bolshevytski zvirstva u Lvovi," *Krakivski Visti*, no. 148 (303) July 9, 1941, 2; "Zhakhlyva masakra 1500 ukraintsiv u Lutsku," *Krakivski Visti*, no. 148 (303) July 9, 1941, 2; "Zakord. zhurnalisty pro bolshevytskyi teror u Lvovi," *Krakivski Visti*, no. 148 (303) July 9, 1941, 4; "Z bolshevytskoho pekla u Lvovi," *Krakivski Visti*, no. 148 (303) July 9, 1941, 6; "Taki potvory ie soiuznykamy Anglii," *Krakivski Visti*, no. 149 (304) July 10, 1941, 1; "Zaslona opadaie," *Krakivski Visti*, no. 149 (304) July 10, 1941, 4; "Kryvavyi teror na ukrainskykh zemliakh. Ukrainske naselennia vitaie nimetske viisko," *Krakivski Visti*, no. 149 (304) July 10, 1941, 6; "Chervonyi teror liutuie i nad ukrainskymy selamy. Nimetska presa ne vmovkaie pro zhakhlyvi zvirstva bolshevykiv," *Krakivski Visti*, no. 150 (305) July 11, 1941, 2; "Strakhittia zolochivskoi tsytadeli," *Krakivski Visti*, no. 154 (309), July 17, 1941, 4; "Zhakhlyvi bolshevytski zlochyny v Zakh. Ukraini," *Krakivski Visti*, no. 160 (315) July 24, 1941, 4; V. Grendzha-Donskyi, "Slovatska ta khorvatska presa pro bolshevytski zvirstva nad ukraintsiamy," *Krakivski Visti*, no. 164 (319) July 29, 1941, 4; KTV [Hennadii Kotorovych], "Pid shkaralushcheiu rosiiskoho imperializmu. Prof. d-r Pavlo Rorbakh ta inshi nimetski publitsysty pro znachchinnia Ukrainy," *Krakivski Visti*, no. 165 (320) July 30, 1941, 2.

363 "Vistky zi Lvova," *Krakivski Visti*, no. 148 (303) July 9, 1941, 2; "Vistky zi Lvova," *Krakivski Visti*, no. 151 (306) July 12, 1941, 6; "Vistky z kraiu," *Krakivski Visti*, no. 172 (327), August 7, 1941, 2-3.

364 MK [Mariian Kozak], "Naibilsha zahroza. U rokovyny bolshevytskykh zvirstv," *Krakivski Visti*, no. 137 (584) June 26, 1942, 1-2.

365 P. B. [Bohdan Halaichuk], "Tsina krovy," *Krakivski Visti*, no. 138 (876) June 30, 1943, 1-2; (N), "Pered dvoma rokamy," *Krakivski Visti*, no. 138 (876) June 30, 1943, 2; Sv., "Yak masakruvaly viazniv," *Krakivski Visti*, no. 138 (876) June 30, 1943, 3; "Panakhydy po zhertvakh bolshevytskoho teroru," *Krakivski Visti*, no. 140 (878) July 2, 1943, 3; "Pomynky zhertv NKVD u Berezhanakh," *Krakivski Visti*, no. 156 (894) July 21, 1943, 3.

366 "Kryvavi bolshevytski zvirstva u Lvovi," *Krakivski Visti*, no. 148 (303) July 9, 1941, 2.

numbers, names, etc.) and were dominated by two trends. The first was to represent the crimes as revealing the true nature of the "Judeo-Bolshevik" state. These inhuman acts were its natural behavior rather than an aberration: "The massacre in Lutsk prison is not something exceptional. It shows the diabolical methods of Bolshevism, which have not changed since the revolution of 1917. It proves what kind of ENEMY AND MONSTER is fighting against an orderly and clean Europe."[367] The second trend, as John-Paul Himka noted in his article about the campaign, was to ethnicize both the victims and the perpetrators, who in reality were ethnically diverse—Jews, Poles, and Ukrainians among the former and Jews, Russians and Ukrainians among the latter.[368] But in *Krakivski Visti*, this diversity was erased. Whenever reports mentioned the ethnicity of victims, they declared it to be Ukrainian, creating an image of a purely anti-Ukrainian crime: "they ... perished only because they were conscious Ukrainians and loved Ukraine above all else."[369] However, at least one-third of those murdered were non-Ukrainians.[370]

The perpetrators were initially characterized as "Bolshevik," "Judeo-Bolshevik," or by some other generic names such as *zviri* (beasts).[371] The very first article about the murders blamed them on "NKVD sadists" and "the bestial Jewish-Polish mob."[372] This was the only time when Poles were explicitly identified among perpetrators. Volodymyr Kubijovyč himself contributed a piece early on

---

367 "Zhakhlyva masakra 1500 ukraintsiv u Lutsku," *Krakivski Visti*, no. 148 (303) July 9, 1941, 2. Capitalization in the original.
368 John-Paul Himka, "Ethnicity and the Reporting of Mass Murder: *Krakivs'ki visti*, the NKVD Murders of 1941, and the Vinnytsia Exhumation," *Shatterzone of Empires: Coexistence and Violence in the German, Habsburg, Russian, and Ottoman Borderlands*, ed. Omer Bartov and Eric D. Weitz (Bloomington, IN: Indiana University Press, 2013), 378-98.
369 B. Halit, "Ne rydai, a zdobuvai," *Krakivski Visti*, no. 164 (319) July 29, 1941, 1.
370 Kiebuzinski and Motyl, eds., *The Great West Ukrainian Prison Massacre of 1941*, 31. On Lviv specifically see: Mick, *Lemberg, Lwów, L'viv*, 288.
371 One article argued against comparing Bolshevik murderers to "beasts": the former were "apocalyptic monsters" and calling them "beasts" is offensive to animals, who are incapable of such cruelty. See: "Nema porivnan," *Krakivski Visti*, no. 156 (311) July 19, 1941, 2.
372 KTV [Hennadii Kotorovych], "Zhakhlyvi bolshevytski masakry u Lvovi," *Krakivski Visti*, no. 146 (301) July 6, 1941, 1.

titled "Pered maiestatom nepovynnoi krovy" (Facing the majesty of innocent blood).[373] He also avoided specifying the ethnicity of the perpetrators, simply referring to them as "the eternal enemies of the Ukrainian people" and "a whole league of our eternal enemies" and called for "resolute ruthlessness" against them in the future. John-Paul Himka believes that by "the eternal enemies" Kubijovyč meant "the Russians, Jews, and Poles."[374]

Beginning from July 15, the articles started to focus more on the identity of perpetrators, identifying them to the larger extent as Russians, to the lesser — as Jews, or as a mixture of both ("Muscovite-Jewish executioners"), which was actually a term directly borrowed from Nazi propaganda. There was only one mention of a Ukrainian perpetrator, a Galician Ukrainian from the Sambir district.[375] But there must have been more than one Ukrainian among the perpetrators. Most of the Soviet administration, especially at lower levels, arrived in Western Ukraine from the rest of Soviet Ukraine in 1939-41.[376] They were referred to by locals as *skhidniaky* (Easterners) and appear in diaries and letters of the time and later memoirs of Western Ukrainians, but in *Krakivski Visti*, as John-Paul Himka rightfully pointed out, they were "invisible."[377]

This narrative of ethnic Ukrainians as martyrs and Russians/Jews as perpetrators was repeated two years later when *Krakivski Visti* ran a series of articles on the Vinnytsia murders. In 1937-1938, during the Great Terror in the Soviet Union, the NKVD executed around ten thousand people in Vinnytsia, a city in Central Ukraine.[378] Their bodies were buried in almost one hundred mass

---

373 Volodymyr Kubijovyč, "Pered maiestatom nepovynnoi krovy," *Krakivski Visti*, no. 147 (302) July 8, 1941, 1-2.
374 Himka, "Ethnicity and the Reporting," 386.
375 "Ochevydets iz Sambora pro dni zhakhu," *Krakivski Visti*, no. 157 (312) July 20, 1941, 3.
376 Hrynevch, *Nepryborkane riznoholossia*, 238-263.
377 Himka, "Ethnicity and the Reporting," 387.
378 On the Vinnytsia murders see: Ihor Kamenetsky, ed., *The Tragedy of Vinnytsia: Materials on Stalin's Policy of Extermination in Ukraine during the Great Purge 1936-1938* (Toronto-New York: Ukrainian Historical Association in cooperation with Bahriany Foundation Inc. and Ukrainian Research and Documentation Center, 1989); Oleh Romaniv, ed., *Narodovbyvstvo v Ukraini: ofitsiini materialy pro masovi vbyvstva u Vinnytsi* (Lviv: Lvivska oblasna istoryko-kulturolohichna

graves within the city. Vinnytsia was occupied by Germans from July 1941 to March 1944. Locals started to ask for the exhumation of mass grave sites immediately after the Germans established their administration in the city, but it was allowed only in May 1943 when Nazi Germany began one of its most famous (and quite successful) propaganda campaigns against the Soviet Union with regards to the Katyn murder site. The Nazi campaign on the Katyn murders was directed both at internal and international consumption. Internationally, its primary goal was to drive a wedge between the Allies and the Soviet Union, and to some extent, it was achieved. Though the anti-Hitler coalition did not fall apart, the campaign led to the severing of diplomatic relations between the Soviet Union and the Polish government-in-exile, on the one hand, and strengthened those in the British and American political establishment who believed in a tough stance toward the Soviet Union—the future Cold War warriors—on the other hand.

Krakivski Visti started to report on the Vinnytsia murders and its international investigation (invited by the Germans to the site) rather late—the first article on the murders appeared on June 23, 1943.[379] By that time the Ukrainian legal press of the *Reichskommissariat* Ukraine had been writing on the matter for almost a month.[380] The exact reason for such a delay is not known. In the case of the June 1941 prison murders in Western Ukraine, *Krakivski Visti* began reporting on them *after* the subject was picked first by the Reich's German newspapers (*Berliner Börsen-Zeitung* and *Berliner Illustrierte Nachtausgabe*). Perhaps the expectations were the same in 1943 and the editors of *Krakivski Visti* (and maybe even their superiors—the press authorities of the General Government) waited for the German press in the Third Reich to initiate the campaign on the Vinnytsia murders. The letters of *Krakivski Visti*'s two most important

---

orhanizatsiia "Memorial," 1995); Irina Paperno, "Exhuming the Bodies of Soviet Terror," *Representations* 75, no. 1 (2001), 89–118; Valerii Vasyliev and Roman Podkur, *Radianski karateli. Spivrobitnyky NKVS – vykonavtsi "Velykoho teroru" na Podilli* (Kyiv: Vydavets V. Zakharenko, 2017).

379 "Masove vbyvstvo ukraintsiv bilia Vynnytsi," *Krakivski Visti*, no. 132 (870) June 23, 1943, 1.
380 Himka, "Ethnicity and the Reporting," 380.

contributors from the Third Reich—Hennadii Kotorovych (a letter from July 1, 1943) and Anatol Kurdydyk (a letter from July 10, 1943)—to the newspaper's editors suggest that the Vinnytsia murders' campaign was initially delayed in the Reich's press to avoid overlapping with or coming out so soon after the Katyn murders' campaign.[381] Eventually, *Krakivski Visti* received the green light, and it ran its own series of articles appearing in almost every issue between July 9 and August 10, 1943, after which the number dropped significantly, with only a few appearing before September 29 when the last item on Vinnytsia murders was published.

But unlike with the June 1941 murders in Western Ukraine, which the newspaper's correspondents were able to investigate themselves by visiting the murder sites and interviewing locals, *Krakivski Visti* had no direct access to Vinnytsia, as the *Reichskommissariat* authorities were much stricter than those of the General Government and restricted not only physical travel between two occupied territories but also the travel of information between them.[382] Apparently, one of the reasons was the unfriendly relationship between Hans Frank and Erich Koch (head of the *Reichskommissariat*): the former despised the latter, who once used to be his subordinate, and privately referred to him as a *Schweinehund* ("pig dog").[383] Due to this information curtain, *Krakivski Visti* had to rely on articles from other newspapers in running its own campaign on the Vinnytsia murders. As a result, unlike in 1941, original submissions were in the minority (twelve pieces)[384] against texts from

---

381 Ibidem. The letters are located in: PAA, Michael Chomiak fonds, File PR1985.0191/41.
382 In his memoirs Ostap Tarnavskyi wrote that initially he was included, as a correspondent of *Lvivski Visti*, into a group of journalists that the Germans organized for a trip to Vinnytsia in summer 1943. However, on the night before his flight "superior authorities" decided that he would not go. He speculated that "the occupation regime, which had various crimes on its conscience, did not want the local Ukrainian press [in the General Government] to write about this tragedy, and therefore the investigation of the Vinnytsia tragedy was conducted according to the interests of Germany." See: Tarnavskyi, *Literaturnyi Lviv*, 122.
383 Kubijovyč, *Meni 70*, 56.
384 MK [Mariian Kozak], "Holovna prychyna," *Krakivski Visti*, no. 135 (873) June 26, 1943, 1-2; MK [Mariian Kozak], "Bez niiakykh oman," *Krakivski Visti*, no. 136

other newspapers (thirty-one pieces).[385] Despite such a disproportion of original and borrowed materials, the pattern of reporting

---

(874) June 27, 1943, 1-2; P. H., "Nad vidkrytymy mohylamy u Vynnytsi," *Krakivski Visti*, no. 149 (887) July 13, 1943, 1-2; D. S. [Denys Savaryn], "Pidstava bolshevytskoho teroru," *Krakivski Visti*, no. 151 (889) July 15, 1943, 1-2; P-ia-k, "Poklin vynnytskym zhertvam," *Krakivski Visti*, no. 159 (897) July 24, 1943, 2; V. Osadchuk [Bohdan Osadchuk], "«Bolshevyzm — smert narodam» Opovidannia d-ra Stefanovicha, serbskoho pysmennyka j polityka. (Vid nashoho korespondenta)," *Krakivski Visti*, no. 163 (901) July 29, 1943, 3-4; H. K., "Na mistsi zlochynu," *Krakivski Visti*, no. 164 (902) July 30, 1943, 4; A. Kurdydyk, "Vynnytsia i chuzhozemna presa," *Krakivski Visti*, no. 165 (903) July 31, 1943, 1; Yevhen Onatskyi, "Vynnytski strakhittia v italiiskii presi," *Krakivski Visti*, no. 167 (905) August 3, 1943, 3; E. M. [Evhen Malaniuk], "Z istorii bolshevytskoho teroru v Ukraini," *Krakivski Visti*, no. 168 (906) August 4, 1943, 3; Kent [Bohdan Kentrzhynskyi], "Finskyi uchenyi pro vynnytski vbyvstva. Interviu z profesorom Niilo Pesonenom," *Krakivski Visti*, no. 170 (908) August 6, 1943, 2-3; B. O. [Bohdan Osadchuk], "Kryvava propahanda Ukrainy. Vynnytsia v evropeiskii presi," *Krakivski Visti*, no. 171 (909) August 7, 1943, 2;

385 "Masove vbyvstvo ukraintsiv bilia Vynnytsi," *Krakivski Visti*, no. 132 (870) June 23, 1943, 1; "30 masovykh hrobiv bilia Vynnytsi," *Krakivski Visti*, no. 146 (884) July 9, 1943, 1; "Dokumenty bolshevytskoi zhadoby nyshchennia," *Krakivski Visti*, no. 147 (885) July 10, 1943, 1; "Vynnytski mohyly," *Krakivski Visti*, no. 148 (886) July 11, 1943, 1; "Dalshi podrobytsi zvirstva NKVD bilia Vynnytsi," *Krakivski Visti*, no. 148 (886) July 11, 1943, 1, 4; "Oburennia i vidraza u vsikh ukraintsiv," *Krakivski Visti*, no. 148 (886) July 11, 1943, 4; "Dalshi podrobytsi pro masovi mohyly u Vynnytsi," *Krakivski Visti*, no. 149 (887) July 13, 1943, 5; "Masovi mohyly pid hoidalkamy," *Krakivski Visti*, no. 150 (888) July 14, 1943, 2; "Belhiiets pro Vynnytsiu," *Krakivski Visti*, no. 151 (889) July 15, 1943, 2; "Vynnytski zhertvy," *Krakivski Visti*, no. 152 (890) July 16, 1943, 2; "'Vyna' vynnytskykh zhertv," *Krakivski Visti*, no. 153 (891) July 17, 1943, 2; "U vsikh ukrainskykh sertsiakh palaie sviatyi vohon pomsty (Holos ukrainskoi presy)," *Krakivski Visti*, no. 154 (892) July 18, 1943, 2; "Pratsia komisii dlia rozslidu vynnytskoho dushehubstva," *Krakivski Visti*, no. 155 (893) July 20, 1943, 2; "Frantsuzki holosy pro Vynnytsiu," *Krakivski Visti*, no. 156 (894) July 21, 1943, 2; "Finskyi professor pro vyslidy rozslidiv u Vynnytsi," *Krakivski Visti*, no. 156 (894) July 21, 1943, 2; "Reporter rumunskoho radiia pro Vynnytsiu," *Krakivski Visti*, no. 156 (894) July 21, 1943, 2; "Mizhnarodna likarska komisiia u Vynnytsi," *Krakivski Visti*, no. 159 (897) July 24, 1943, 2; "Kamera tortur NKVD u Vynnytsi," *Krakivski Visti*, no. 161 (899) July 27, 1943, 2; "Predstavnyky bolharskoho j danskoho uriady u Vynnytsi," *Krakivski Visti*, no. 161 (899) July 27, 1943, 2; "Tserkovni dostoinyky Rumunii pro svoi vrazhennia z Vynnytsi," *Krakivski Visti*, no. 162 (900) July 28, 1943, 2; "Mizhnarodni komisii u Vynnytsi," *Krakivski Visti*, no. 164 (902) July 30, 1943, 2; "Nimetski robitnyky nad masovymy mohylamy u Vynnytsi," *Krakivski Visti*, no. 167 (905) August 3, 1943, 2; Pier Sone, "Valonets pro Vynnytsiu. Shcho ia pobachyv u Vynnytsi, novomu Katyni," *Krakivski Visti*, no. 173 (911) August 10, 1943, 2; "Bolharyn pro vrazhinnia z Vynnytsi," *Krakivski Visti*, no. 178 (916) August 15, 1943, 5; "Hretskyi zhurnalist pro svoi vrazhinnia z Vynnytsi," *Krakivski Visti*, no. 185 (923) August 24, 1943, 5; "Mistse zhakhu ta smerty,"

was almost identical to the 1941 campaign. Just as then, the 1943 articles in *Krakivski Visti* provided its readers with gruesome details about how prisoners were murdered, some of which were claimed to have been buried alive. Female victims were often emphasized to underscore Bolshevik inhumanity: their bodies were found "completely naked, without underwear. ... We can say with certainty that the chekists, before murdering these unfortunate women, threw macabre orgies with them."[386]

Similarly to the 1941 articles, victims and perpetrators were ethnicized. The German forensic investigation could not identify all victims, but its findings sufficiently demonstrated that one-third of them were not Ukrainians. The newspaper, however, presented the victims as almost exclusively Ukrainian (one article mentioned an ethnic German). Perpetrators, following Nazi propaganda, were once again identified as either Russian or Jewish, and their deeds were a testament to the murderous nature of the Bolshevik regime: "The mass graves in Vinnytsia are a new, frightful proof of the system of methodical physical destruction to which Muscovite Bolshevism adheres. Jewish Bolsheviks and their lackeys introduced this policy of ruthless physical destruction in Ukraine from the first moment they came to power."[387]

For Mariian Kozak, the Vinnytsia murders proved continuity between tsarist Russia and the Bolshevik regime: the latter absorbed Russian imperialism but at the same time unshackled it from the constraints of Christian morality, thus unleashing a

---

Krakivski Visti, no. 187 (925) August 26, 1943, 3; I. Zhurlyvyi, "Z taiemnyts Vynnytsi," *Krakivski Visti*, no. 188 (926) August 27, 1943, 3; "Shvedskyi profesor medytsyny pro Vynnytsiu," *Krakivski Visti*, no. 197 (935) September 7, 1943, 5; "Pamiatnyk na bratskykh mohylakh u Vynnytsi," *Krakivski Visti*, no. 198 (936) September 8, 1943, 4; "Masovi bolshevytski vbyvstva v Ukraini," *Krakivski Visti*, no. 207 (945) September 18, 1943, 2; "Serby vidvidaly mistsia masovykh vbyvstv u Vynnytsi," *Krakivski Visti*, no. 208 (946) September 19, 1943, 5; "Vynnytski pokhorony," *Krakivski Visti*, no. 216 (954) September 29, 1943, 4.

386 Kent [Bohdan Kentrzhynskyi], "Finskyi uchenyi pro vynnytski vbyvstva. Interviu z profesorom Niilo Pesonenom," *Krakivski Visti*, no. 170 (908) August 6, 1943, 2. Translation by John-Paul Himka.

387 "Vynnytski mohyly," *Krakivski Visti*, no. 148 (886) July 11, 1943, 1. Translation by John-Paul Himka.

brutality that the tsars could not even imagine.[388] Another author, in the article "Nad vidkrytymy mohylamy u Vynnytsi" (Over the open graves in Vinnytsia), blamed the whole Russian people: "The Russian people is responsible for sheltering and handing over power to a gang of international killers. Other peoples will never forgive the Russians [moskaliam] for this. The third year of gigantic struggles with the wild Bolshevik beast in the East makes it clear what a terrible threat will continue to hang over Europe until the monster is broken. If Bolshevism were to triumph, all of Europe would turn into one great Vinnytsia or Katyn. Whoever does not want to see that moment come must stand up on the side of Germany, which has gone alone into this great historical battle."[389]

The identity of this author, hiding behind the initials P. H., is an important question. John-Paul Himka believes that it was written by Ivan L. Rudnytsky, establishing the authorship "on the basis of the Michael Chomiak papers, items 32 (honorarium) and 41 (letter of Mariian Kozak to Ivan Lysiak, 14 July 1943)."[390] Normally I would agree that being paid for an article proves authorship, but this case warrants a closer look at the archival evidence. According to the honoraria list Rudnytsky was paid for two articles published in *Krakivski Visti* — the first entry is for "Nad vidkrytymy mohylamy u Vynnytsi" and the second one is for "Voeinne znyshchennia ta vidbudova" (War destruction and reconstruction). He was paid 48 and 57 złoty, respectively. Both entries provide his Berlin address but give slightly different names — "Lysiak" (first entry) and "Lysiak Yu." (second entry).[391] Legally, "Lysiak" was Rudnytsky's last name after his father, Pavlo Lysiak (1887-1948), under whose name the second article had appeared in the newspaper.[392] In 1940-

---

388 MK [Mariian Kozak], "Bez niiakykh oman," *Krakivski Visti*, no. 136 (874) June 27, 1943, 1-2.
389 P. H., "Nad vidkrytymy mohylamy u Vynnytsi," *Krakivski Visti*, no. 149 (887) July 13, 1943, 2. Translation by Marco Carynnyk.
390 Himka, "Ethnicity and the Reporting," 387-388, 397 n. 106.
391 PAA, Michael Chomiak fonds, File PR1985.0191/32.
392 Pavlo Lysiak, "Voienne znyshchennia ta vidbudova," *Krakivski Visti*, no. 271 (1009) December 2, 1943, 1-2.

1944 Pavlo Lysiak resided in Cracow. During the war, he supported his son financially by sending him money.[393]

Himka's second proof is a letter from Mariian Kozak to Ivan Lysiak (Ivan L. Rudnytsky) from July 14, 1943, that is one day after the publication of "Nad vidkrytymy mohylamy u Vynnytsi." The letter does mention an article that Rudnytsky wrote for *Krakivski Visti*, but also makes it clear that it could not be "Nad vidkrytymy mohylamy u Vynnytsi." In this brief letter Kozak thanked Rudnytsky for sending an article written in response to one of his pieces, complimented his "interesting thoughts," but unfortunately had to inform him that *Krakivski Visti* cannot publish it.[394] This rejected article can be found in the Rudnytsky papers at the University of Alberta Archives.[395] Titled "Prohainovani nahody?" (Lost opportunities?), it was written in late May 1943 and polemicized with Kozak's article "Idealizm i realism," specifically with one of its points about Ukrainian national life in interwar Poland.[396] One should also be aware that "Nad vidkrytymy mohylamy u Vynnytsi" does not appear in the meticulous bibliography of Rudnytsky's publications that he kept for himself, nor is the article ever mentioned in his published diaries or archival correspondence (which I read in their entirety).[397] Considering all this, I believe that the weight of evidence points to the conclusion that "Nad vidkrytymy mohylamy u Vynnytsi," just as "Voienne znyshchennia ta vidbudova," was written by Lysiak-father who asked the newspaper to send his honorarium for each article to Lysiak-son. That said, ultimately, only one thing is certain—whoever compiled the honoraria list was not thinking about future historians.

---

393 In his diary Rudnytsky frequently mentions receiving money from his father, see: Ivan Lysiak-Rudnytskyi, *Shchodennyky* ed. Yaroslav Hrytsak and Frank Sysyn (Kyiv: Dukh i Litera, 2019), 116, 148, 153, 161, 166, 168, 195.
394 Himka consulted a copy of the letter. The original is found here: Letter from Mariian Kozak to Ivan L. Rudnytsky July 14, 1943. UAA, Ivan L. Rudnytsky fonds, Accession no. 1984-155, File 742.
395 UAA, Ivan L. Rudnytsky fonds, Accession no. 1984-155, File 517.
396 MK [Mariian Kozak], "Idealizm i realizm," *Krakivski Visti*, no. 103 (841) May 18, 1943, 1-2.
397 The bibliography is located here: UAA, Ivan L. Rudnytsky fonds, Accession no. 1984-155, Box 73.

It is hard to assess the effectiveness of the 1941 and 1943 propaganda campaigns about Soviet murders. The former happened in Western Ukraine, the home of most of the staff of the UCC and *Krakivski Visti*. The 1941 tragedy hit them and the rest of the Western Ukrainian population hard: they lost either relatives or people whom they knew in the massacre. Two years later, when the UCC campaigned for the Waffen-SS Division *Galizien*, which was reflected in *Krakivski Visti*, many young Galician Ukrainian men enlisted because images of the prison murders from summer 1941 — which was their first exposure to Soviet mass brutality — became entrenched in their minds.[398]

On the other hand, the Vinnytsia massacre happened in a region rather distant from Galicia, which already had been living for two years under war conditions and exposure to anti-Soviet propaganda, so news about a new Soviet crime, even such a massive one as Vinnytsia, may have been a product delivered to an oversaturated market. Human emotions have limits. After a certain amount of exposure to horrors, we are no longer horrified by them, not because they have become less horrific but because our capacity to be horrified has been exhausted. Judging by the editorial correspondence between Khomiak and Kozak, both of them in summer 1943 were more concerned with news of the ethnic massacres between Poles and Ukrainians in Volhynia than with the investigation of the murders in distant Vinnytsia.[399] Kozak even wrote to Anatol Kurdydyk that the newspaper would continue to accept materials on the Vinnytsia murders, but he could not guarantee that they would be published because "people are already fed up with the

---

398 A Galician Ukrainian, Bohdan Stasiv, in his short memoir about why he enlisted for the Waffen-SS Division *Galizien* mentioned among the reasons: "The horrifying images of our innocent (and unsentenced!) people murdered in prisons by chekists during their flight in June-July 1941 were still fresh in our memory [in 1943]." See: Bohdan Stasiv, "Chomu my ishly do dyvyzii 'Halychyna'?" in *Persha Ukrainska dyviziia Ukrainskoi natsionalnoii armii: istoriia stvorennia ta natsionalno-politychne znachennia. Materialy naukovo-praktychnoi konferentsii. Dopovidi ta povidomlennia*, ed. Yaroslav Dashkevych (Lviv: Novyi chas, 2002), 56.
399 PAA, Michael Chomiak fonds, File PR1985.0191/41.

subject."[400] The article Kurdydyk submitted did appear eventually. Ironically, it celebrated coverage of the Vinnytsia tragedy in the foreign press: the news about the crime put Ukraine and Ukrainians on the mental map of many foreigners who had never heard about them before.[401]

Naturally, the Western Ukrainian murders of 1941 and the Vinnytsia tragedy of 1937-1938 were not the only anti-Russian/Soviet materials in *Krakivski Visti*, which published hundreds of such texts after June 22, 1941. However, the articles about those two events stand out because they were a result of organized campaigns with specific goals about how to portray victims and perpetrators. Among other articles — on the Bolshevik conquest of Ukraine in 1918-1920; the famine of 1921-1922; collectivization of 1928-1933 and the Holodomor; purges and Russification of the 1930s — one series was remarkable not because it was the first to tie all those events into one narrative martyrology, but because it did so superbly. Its author was the brilliant Ukrainian poet and essayist Evhen Malaniuk (1897-1968).[402] The series was one of the original submissions for the newspaper's campaign on the Vinnytsia murders in 1943, but Malaniuk used the murders as a departure point for a wider topic — the Bolshevik terror against the Ukrainian nation.[403]

The European press, wrote Malaniuk, reported with shock about the uncovering of mass graves in Vinnytsia, but for

---

400 Letter from Mariian Kozak to Anatol Kurdydyk July 29, 1943. PAA, Michael Chomiak fonds, File PR1985.0191/41.
401 A. Kurdydyk, "Vynnytsia i chuzhozemna presa," *Krakivski Visti*, no. 165 (903) July 31, 1943, 1.
402 Malaniuk has been studied mostly as a literary figure, though in terms of intellectual value his essays rival his literary legacy. However, there is not a single study on Malaniuk which looks in detail at his life (and writings) during World War II. See: Taras Salyha, *Vohon, shcho ne zhasa...* (Kyiv: Lybid, 2017); Leonid Kutsenko, *Kniaz dukhu: statti pro zhyttia i tvorchist Yevhena Malaniuka* (Kirovohrad: [s.n.], 2003). Note that Malaniuk spelled his first name as Evhen, not as Yevhen, a choice that this book respects.
403 E. M. [Evhen Malaniuk], "Z istorii bolshevytskoho teroru v Ukraini," *Krakivski Visti*, no. 168 (906) August 4, 1943, 3; no. 169 (907) August 5, 1943, 4; no. 170 (908) August 6, 1943, 4. The series was not included in the two volumes of Malaniuk's selected essays published in the 1960s: Evhen Malaniuk, *Knyha sposterezhen* vols. 1-2 (Toronto: Homin Ukrainy, 1962-1966).

Ukrainians this news was "not surprising" since they had been suffering under the Soviets from the very beginning of their "acquaintance" in 1917. The first Ukrainian encounter with Bolshevik terror in 1917-1918 appeared as random killings of Ukrainian intelligentsia. Some Ukrainians naively considered them "misunderstandings," but in Malaniuk's opinion they clearly followed a pattern: systemic elimination of the "nation's most important sons" whom Ukrainian culture and the Ukrainian state so desperately needed. The Bolshevik war against Ukraine in 1918-1920 unleashed this terror openly accompanied by the "loud Jewish ... Soviet propaganda." Already back then, Soviet terror showed that it was not an excess, but a normal practice, without which the functioning of the "Soviet state machinery" would be hard to imagine.[404]

The Bolshevik victory in the Civil War in 1920 did not stop the terror. It continued until the end of the Bolshevik policy of war communism in 1923. By then, the terror had claimed "hundreds of thousands" of Ukrainian lives, whom "post-Versailles Europe wanted neither to see nor to know."[405] Malaniuk believed that Ukrainians made up 70-75% of the so-called "victims of Bolshevism in Russia" since they fought against Bolshevism in the White forces as well. But the "Kremlin Sanhedrin" was still not satisfied with "rivers of [Ukrainian] blood" because 30 million Ukrainians not only continued to reject Bolshevization but also served as a "living wall" against "spreading the communist revolution to the West—first of all to Poland, to Romania, to Hungary, then to Germany and Italy."[406] To break this wall, to undermine the Ukrainian people biologically, Bolshevism through "the Jewish mind of its leadership" arrived at the idea of man-made famine, which it organized in Ukraine in 1921-1922. A decade later, the Bolsheviks repeated this "experiment ... in a much improved and wider form."[407]

---

404 E. M. [Evhen Malaniuk], "Z istorii bolshevytskoho teroru v Ukraini," *Krakivski Visti*, no. 168 (906) August 4, 1943, 3.
405 E. M. [Evhen Malaniuk], "Z istorii bolshevytskoho teroru v Ukraini," *Krakivski Visti*, no. 169 (907) August 5, 1943, 4.
406 Ibidem.
407 Ibidem.

Malaniuk believed that whereas during the first famine in 1921-1922 the Soviets officially recognized that Ukraine had 3 million starving people, during the second famine of 1932-1933 that figure, "according to experts," must had been six-seven million, all of whom "certainly died from hunger."[408] The period between the two famines, accompanied by the NEP and Ukrainization (a Bolshevik provocation in Malaniuk's opinion) in Ukraine, was just an "armistice" that the Bolsheviks used for the "stabilization" of their power and accumulation of wealth. The Bolsheviks broke the "armistice" in 1929 and unleashed their "terror apparatus" again because they feared the "organic growth of a defeated but unbroken" Ukraine.[409]

According to Malaniuk, the source of this growth was the Ukrainian peasantry. It was the only Ukrainian social group strong enough to cause "stress" for the Bolsheviks, who had already eliminated whatever tiny Ukrainian aristocracy and bourgeoisie existed before 1917 during the Ukrainian "Liberation War" of 1918-1920.[410] But the peasantry continued to be the source from which the Ukrainian working class and national intelligentsia continued to regenerate. Malaniuk implied that the preventive Bolshevik terror in Ukraine after 1929 targeted these three Ukrainian social groups — peasantry, workers and intelligentsia — because the Soviets feared that if they were allowed to develop unchecked, they would eventually lead to the ascent of the Ukrainian nation.

Terror was not the only crime committed by the Bolsheviks in Ukraine. "Let's admit to ourselves," wrote Malaniuk, that through their propaganda "the enemy demoralized our masses." Ukrainians should not be ashamed of this fact because "the enemy deceived the whole world."[411] But after June 22, 1941 when Germany broke into the Soviet Union through its Western gate "rusted from Ukrainian blood," Europe and the whole world were finally able to see that what a handful of Ukrainian émigrés were saying about

---

408 Ibidem.
409 Ibidem.
410 E. M. [Evhen Malaniuk], "Z istorii bolshevytskoho teroru v Ukraini," *Krakivski Visti*, no. 170 (908) August 6, 1943, 4.
411 Ibidem.

Bolshevik terror and the "organized famine" of the 1930s was true. After revelations about the Katyn and Vinnytsia murders, "nobody has a moral right to say" that it was an "émigré fantasy" and "now the whole of Europe has seen with what a monster our people were left one on one ... for a long quarter century [1918-1943]."[412] It is remarkable how the main themes from Malaniuk's series in 1943 — Ukrainians shielded Europe from Bolshevism; terror is the essence of Bolshevism; the famines of 1921-1922 and 1932-1933 were manmade; Bolshevik actions against various Ukrainian social groups were part of a single anti-Ukrainian policy — became cornerstones of Ukrainian martyrology developed in the Ukrainian diaspora in the West during the Cold War.

Jews

In the Nazi discourse, Jews were the most dangerous and mortal enemy to the Aryan race because of their deeply subversive nature: on the surface, they appeared unthreatening and even useful, yet underneath, they were so alien and corrupting.[413] Nazi propaganda of anti-Semitism attacked both the liberal West and the Stalinist Soviet Union as incarnations of the same enemy — "world Jewry." The term "Judeo-Bolshevism" was ubiquitous in Nazi ideology and propaganda in which "Jews" and "Bolshevik/Soviet" were overlapping terms.[414] However, for *Krakivski Visti* the term "Soviet" overlapped primarily with "Russian," not "Jewish." Judeo-Bolshevism appeared in the newspaper as well, but mostly in those materials that were taken from the foreign, primarily Axis press. At the

---

412 Ibidem.
413 The literature on Nazi views on Jews is immense. For a concise treatment of the subject see: Doris Bergen, *War and Genocide: A Concise History of the Holocaust* 3rd ed. (Lanham, MD: Rowman & Littlefield, 2016), 52-56. For a book-length: Alon Confino, *A World Without Jews: The Nazi Imagination from Persecution to Genocide* (New Haven, CT: Yale University Press, 2014).
414 The term itself was not a Nazi invention, but of the Russian Whites during the Civil War of 1918-1920. On their anti-Semitism see: Peter Kenez, "The Ideology of the White Movement," *Soviet Studies* 32, no. 1 (1980): 77-80; Peter Kenez, "Pogroms and White Ideology in the Russian Civil War," in *Pogroms: Anti-Jewish Violence in Modern Russian History* ed. John D. Klier and Shlomo Lambroza (Cambridge, UK: Cambridge University Press, 1992), 293-313.

ideological core of original anti-Semitic texts written for *Krakivski Visti*, or at least most of them, was nativism (or to be more specific — the nativist component of Ukrainian nationalism), not biological racism. Even those original texts that used Nazi terminology should not be assumed to have been just a Ukrainian variation of Nazi propaganda, as one could engage with the topic of Jews using Nazi phraseology but for different (i.e. not racial) reasons. Another general reservation is that one also must be aware of the context in which this anti-Semitic content was produced: all of the legal newspapers in the General Government had to dive into anti-Semitism, but some went deeper than others. For example, *Lvivski Visti*, controlled more tightly by the occupation authorities, was much more vehemently anti-Semitic than *Krakivski Visti*.[415]

The anti-Semitic texts of *Krakivski Visti* may be split into three groups based on how they originated. First, there were materials that the newspaper received for publication from the Propaganda Office of the occupation regime — speeches of Nazi leaders, various information materials and selected articles from the Axis press, primarily German and Italian. Second, there were original Ukrainian articles that were commissioned by the occupation authorities in summer 1943 for an anti-Semitic campaign. Third, there were original Ukrainian texts that were not solicited by the editors: they were submitted by Ukrainian authors of their own volition. In terms of content, the anti-Semitic pieces in *Krakivski Visti* again may be divided into three groups: first, Jews as allies or beneficiaries of interwar Poland and its policies to denationalize Ukrainians; second, Jews as carriers of Bolshevism and agents of its crimes against Ukrainians; and third, Jews as the embodiment of values or features inimical to either European, or Christian or Ukrainian identity and interests (in the authors' understanding of those identities and interests).

---

415 On *Lvivski Visti* see: Henry Abramson, "*This is the Way it Was!*" Textual and Iconographic Images of Jews in the Nazi-sponsored Ukrainian Press of Distrikt Galizien," *Why Didn't the Press Shout? American & International Journalism and the Holocaust*, ed. Robert Moses Shapiro (New York: Yeshiva University Press, 2003), 537-556.

The anti-Semitic content from the Axis press appeared in *Krakivski Visti* frequently. The newspaper, following the example of *Krakauer Zeitung*, the main legal newspaper of the General Government, regularly republished or summarized speeches (often peppered with anti-Semitism) of leading Nazi figures from the Reich and the General Government.[416] Besides the speeches, *Krakivski Visti* also featured articles and news pieces from the Axis press— German, Italian, Bulgarian, Hungarian, Croatian and even Japanese. Typically, these were short texts, translations or summaries with self-explanatory titles. The following three examples were typical. "Na zhydiv spadaie vidpovidalnist za viinu" (Responsibility for the war falls on the Jews) was a summary of an article from the leading Italian newspaper *Il Regime Fascista*, which argued that the current war was to be blamed primarily on Jews, as they benefited the most from it.[417] "Nova mova Evropy" (New Language of Europe) was a summary of an article by Alfred Rosenberg, one of the most important Nazi ideologues, from *Völkischer Beobachter*, in which he argued that one of the ways in which Jews controlled the press and academia was through introducing terminological ambivalences and provided three examples of such terms which according to him Jews stripped of their true meaning—Europe, morality and peace.[418] "Zhydivski pliany panuvannia nad svitom" (Jewish plans to dominate the world) was a summary of an article from *Völkischer Beobachter* which "exposed" the Jewish conspiracy to achieve global dominance.[419] Finally, anti-Semitic messages appeared in materials that were presented as purely informational or educational. For example, an official announcement about the exchange of banknotes (100 and 500 zloty) made no mention of Jews in the text but was accompanied by an anti-Semitic cartoon.[420] A series of articles on typhus singled out Jews as the primary carriers

---

416 For example: "Istorychna promova Hitliera v raikhstagu," *Krakivski Visti*, no. 68 July 24, 1940, 1-3.
417 "Na zhydiv spadaie vidpovidalnist za viinu," *Krakivski Visti*, no. 6 January 25, 1940, 5.
418 "Nova mova Evropy," *Krakivski Visti*, no. 55 June 24, 1940, 5-6.
419 "Zhydivski pliany panuvannia nad svitom," *Krakivski Visti*, no. 160 (898) July 25, 1943, 2.
420 "Vymina 100 i 500 zol. u povnomu khodi," *Krakivski Visti*, no. 6 January 25, 1940, 1.

("90%") of the disease and warned against any physical contact with them.[421]

Anti-Semitic cartoon in *Krakivski Visti* (no. 6 January 25, 1940) under an official announcement about the exchange of banknotes. The cartoon depicts a working-class man going to a bank and saying to the four men trying to stop him: "No, speculators, you won't profit off my money."

In May 1943 *Krakivski Visti* received an order from the occupation authorities to publish a series of original anti-Semitic articles. The exact reasons and intentions behind the order are unknown. John-Paul Himka speculated that the occupation regime might have had several goals in mind: distraction from the situation of Ukrainians in the *Reichskommissariat* Ukraine; preventing Ukrainians from sympathizing with Jews in the ghettos; bolstering Ukrainian loyalty toward the Germans; change of policies toward local population

---

421 "Nuzhda, holod i brud—vyklykuiut tyf," *Krakivski Visti*, no. 113 (269) May 27, 1941, 5; "Berezhitsia zhebrakiv, zhydiv i volotsiuh!" *Krakivski Visti*, no. 115 (271) May 29, 1941, 7; "Vidokremlennia khvorykh i chystota—tse zbroia proty tyfu," *Krakivski Visti*, no. 116 (272) May 31, 1941, 5.

after Stalingrad, etc.[422] Any of these speculations might be correct (they are not mutually exclusive), but Stalingrad seems the most likely explanation—in the aftermath of their defeat in that city, the Germans intensified their anti-Semitic propaganda. So perhaps the legal press of the General Government, including *Krakivski Visti*, was ordered to add its voice to this anti-Semitic chorus.

How did the editors at *Krakivski Visti* react to this German order? There is evidence for only one editor's reaction, Mariian Kozak. In his letter to Ukrainian poet and essayist Yurii Lypa, he wrote: "The Jewish issue has had and continues to have its significance for us, but I understand very well that if we are to write about it today, it is primarily to divert attention from other matters. Obviously, I do not want that. However, when there is an opportunity to remind people [liudiam] of the harmful effects of Jewish influence, it must be done to maintain the understanding that Jews remain an important factor in international life. They will probably find ways to continue to harm us. Not many racial Jews were active in our cultural and civic life, but just recall what was going on in Lviv before September 1, 1939! You can imagine what would have happened to us if Jews had overwhelmed us like they did other nations [narody]."[423] The letter proves that Kozak was not a blind tool of German propaganda but someone who used the ideological space allotted within the propaganda to advance Ukrainian interests (as he understood them).

Kozak solicited articles for the campaign from at least ten authors, promising a higher honorarium than usual. Six of them were Galician Ukrainians (Stepan Baran,[424] Anatol Kurdydyk,[425] Kost

---

422 John-Paul Himka, "*Krakivski visti* and the Jews, 1943: A Contribution to the History of Ukrainian-Jewish Relations during the Second World War," *Journal of Ukrainian Studies* 21, no. 1-2 (Summer-Winter 1996): 85-86.
423 Letter from Mariian Kozak to Yurii Lypa May 26, 1943. PAA, Michael Chomiak fonds, File PR1985.0191/40.
424 Baran was asked to write about "Jews in Galicia during the serfdom and after the serfdom." See: Letter from Mariian Kozak to Stepan Baran May 15, 1943. PAA, Michael Chomiak fonds, File PR1985.0191/40. Baran wrote a large article about "the Jewish problem" before the war: Stepan Baran, "Nasha zhydivska probliema," *Dilo*, no. 16 January 23, 1936, 1-2.
425 Kozak wrote to Kurdydyk: "Please send us several good anti-Jewish articles. We have been tasked with conducting an anti-Jewish campaign, but we lack

A SCHOOL OF HATE 119

Kuzyk,[426] Olena Kysilevska,[427] Luka Lutsiv,[428] Oleksander Mokh[429]) and four were non-Western Ukrainians (Levko Lukasevych,[430] Yurii Lypa,[431] Evhen Malaniuk,[432] Oleksander Mytsiuk[433]). It is unclear whether Baran, Lukasevych, and Malaniuk even responded to Kozak's solicitations.[434] Lypa wrote back with "a lengthy letter," which is missing from the editorial archive.[435] The other six, five

---

enough material. We want serious in-depth articles, which would illuminate the disintegrative [rozkladovu] role of Jewry both on us and on the world." See: Letter from Mariian Kozak to Anatol Kurdydyk May 22, 1943. PAA, Michael Chomiak fonds, File PR1985.0191/40.

426 Kuzyk was asked to write about "Jewish exploitation and demoralization of Boiko region." See: Letter from Mariian Kozak to Kost Kuzyk May 15, 1943. PAA, Michael Chomiak fonds, File PR1985.0191/40.

427 Kysilevska was asked to write about "Jewish exploitation and demoralization of Hutsul region." See: Letter from Mariian Kozak to Olena Kysilevska May 15, 1943. PAA, Michael Chomiak fonds, File PR1985.0191/40.

428 It seems that Kuzyk suggested Lutsiv to Kozak as a potential contributor to the campaign. See: Letter from Mariian Kozak to Kost Kuzyk May 29, 1943. PAA, Michael Chomiak fonds, File PR1985.0191/40.

429 Mokh was asked to write about "the harmful and disintegrative [rozkladovu] role of the Jewish element in literature, press, art and philosophy." See: Letter from Mariian Kozak to Oleksander Mokh May 15, 1943. PAA, Michael Chomiak fonds, File PR1985.0191/40.

430 Lukasevych was asked to write articles on the following topics: "1) 'Jewish role in 1917-1921'; 2) 'Jewish cooperation with the Bolsheviks'; 3) 'Causes of the pogroms'; 4) 'Jews and the assassination of Petliura.'" See: Letter from Mariian Kozak to Levko Lukasevych May 15, 1943. PAA, Michael Chomiak fonds, File PR1985.0191/40. Incidentally, Lukasevych was hiding a Jew in his apartment at the time: Lukasevych, *Rozdumy na skhylku zhyttia*, 243.

431 Lypa was asked to write on Jewish topics from the perspective of "Ukrainian racial questions or Ukrainian national interest" and to address "the role of Jews in the [Ukrainian] liberation struggles of 1917–1921 ... and the assassination of Otaman Petliura." See: Letter from Mariian Kozak to Yurii Lypa May 15, 1943. PAA, Michael Chomiak fonds, File PR1985.0191/40.

432 Malaniuk was asked to write articles "revealing the harmful effects of Jewish influence on cultural and civic life." See: Letter from Mariian Kozak to Evhen Malaniuk May 26, 1943. PAA, Michael Chomiak fonds, File PR1985.0191/40.

433 Mytsiuk was asked to write on the topic: "The negative role of Jews in Ukraine, particularly in economic life." See: Letter from Mariian Kozak to Oleksander Mytsiuk May 12, 1943. PAA, Michael Chomiak fonds, File PR1985.0191/40.

434 Himka believes that they refused to participate in the campaign: Himka, "*Krakivski visti* and the Jews," 89.

435 Lypa's letter is mentioned here: Letter from Mariian Kozak to Yurii Lypa May 26, 1943. PAA, Michael Chomiak fonds, File PR1985.0191/40. Himka speculates that the editors of *Krakivski Visti* destroyed the letter to protect Lypa: Himka, "*Krakivski visti* and the Jews," 83.

Galicians and one non-Western Ukrainian, sent their contributions. One of them, "An Old Enemy" by Kurdydyk, was eventually rejected.[436] The rest appeared in the newspaper without using the authors' full names.

Oleksander Mokh (1900-1975) was a journalist, literary critic and publisher with religious interests. His lifelong cause was the popularization of Catholicism among Ukrainians.[437] Mokh's piece was the first and the least original contribution to the anti-Semitic campaign in *Krakivski Visti*. It appeared as a series of nine articles (each with a different title) under the initials M. L.[438] The majority of the text was compilation of quotations from American, British, French, Italian, German, and Polish authors (Joseph Eberle, Henry Ford, Otto Forst de Battaglia, Jules Du Mesnil-Marigny, Giovanni Papini, Robert Schneider, Werner Sombart, Arnold White, Marian Zdziechowski, etc.), which Mokh used to characterize Jews as an anti-European and anti-Christian force seeking global domination through the economy (financial capitalism), ideology (liberalism and Bolshevism) and media control.

---

436 Kozak wrote to Kurdydyk: "[your] article about Jews could not be published because you touched on too many issues. Moreover, it is untenable to take the stance that Jews are to blame for everything." See: Letter from Mariian Kozak to Anatol Kurdydyk June 18, 1943. PAA, Michael Chomiak fonds, File PR1985.0191/40. The title of Kurdydyk's article is mentioned in: Letter from Mariian Kozak to Anatol Kurdydyk July 22, 1943. PAA, Michael Chomiak fonds, File PR1985.0191/41.
437 About Mokh see: Tetiana Shprinher, "Oleksandr [sic] Mokh yak literaturnyi krytyk, zhurnalist i vydavets," *Visnyk Lvivskoho universytetu. Seriia zhurnalistyka*. Vyp. 36 (2012): 168-178. The article makes no mention of Mokh's anti-Semitism or his contributions to *Krakivski Visti*.
438 M. L. [Oleksander Mokh] "U dzherel vsesvitnoi zmovy," *Krakivski Visti*, no. 109 (847) May 25, 1943, 2; M. L. [Oleksander Mokh] "Taina vplyviv i uspikhiv," *Krakivski Visti*, no. 114 (852) May 30, 1943, 2; M. L. [Oleksander Mokh] "Za dushu inteligenta," *Krakivski Visti*, no. 117 (855) June 3, 1943, 2; M. L. [Oleksander Mokh] "Natsia desperadiv," *Krakivski Visti*, no. 118 (856) June 4, 1943, 2; M. L. [Oleksander Mokh] "Zhydy depravaiut Evropu," *Krakivski Visti*, no. 119 (857) June 5, 1943, 2; M. L. [Oleksander Mokh] "Ideyaly i nosii rozkladu," *Krakivski Visti*, no. 121 (859) June 8, 1943, 3-4; M. L. [Oleksander Mokh] "Yak spomahaly bolshevykiv," *Krakivski Visti*, no. 122 (860) June 9, 1943, 2; M. L. [Oleksander Mokh] "Spravedlyvi u Sodomi," *Krakivski Visti*, no. 123 (861) June 10, 1943, 3; M. L. [Oleksander Mokh] "Pered naizdom Dzhingiskhana," *Krakivski Visti*, no. 124 (862) June 11, 1943, 3.

He did not mention Nazi authors though it is safe to assume, judging from his interest in anti-Semitism, that he was aware of their writings on the subject. Mokh's anti-Semitism had primarily religious, not racial, reasoning. For him, Jews were spiritual rebels against the Christian order (how did they dare to reject Christ?) in the same sense as Satan rebelled against God. He credited Jewry with the creation of two archenemies of contemporary Christianity — Masonry and Bolshevism. For Mokh, Jews were a primordial chaotic force in the world, an element antithetical to any order and structure, and if allowed within would inevitably work toward their disruption. This Jewish irritability, wrote Mokh, was well spotted by Ukrainians in the past, which is proved by the old Ukrainian saying describing someone with idiosyncratic behavior — "vertytsia yak zhyd u tserkvi" (twists like a Jew in a church).[439] The most interesting passage in the series was Mokh's discussion of the anti-Semitic classic *The Protocols of the Elders of Zion*. He was not afraid to admit that the text could be a forgery — but even in that case *The Protocols* were still a prophetic description of the Jewish peril. Therefore, he wrote, it warned about Jews accurately in either case.[440]

The little-known Sambir-based journalist Kost Kuzyk (a regular contributor to the newspaper) submitted two pieces for the campaign. The first one was published under initials K. K. and looked at writings of Ivan Franko (1856-1916), the most famous Western Ukrainian writer, about Jews.[441] Kuzyk challenged the mainstream interpretation of Franko as a "zhydofil" (Judeophile), which according to him was constructed by the Ukrainian socialists (Franko was a socialist) on the basis of his literary works such as the poem "Moses" and the novel "Boryslav is Laughing." This reputation of

---

439 M.L. [Oleksander Mokh] "Natsiia desperadiv," *Krakivski Visti*, no. 118 (856) June 4, 1943, 2.
440 M.L. [Oleksander Mokh], "U dzherel vsesvitnoi zmovy," *Krakivski Visti*, no. 109 (847) May 25, 1943, 2.
441 K. K. [Kost Kuzyk], "Ivan Franko i zhydivske pytannia," *Krakivski Visti*, no. 112 (850) May 28, 1943, 3-4. The Ukrainian historian Yaroslav Hrytsak, in his biography of Ivan Franko, erroneously attributes the authorship of this article to Anatol Kurdydyk: Yaroslav Hrytsak, *Prorok u svoii vitchyzni: Franko ta ioho spilnota, 1856-1886* (Kyiv: Krytyka, 2006), 526.

Judeophilia, according to Kuzyk, was further cemented both by Ukrainian liberal circles and by the Bolsheviks. The latter used Franko for their own ideological agenda as became evident during the 25th anniversary of Franko's death in Soviet Galicia in 1941. Kuzyk regarded this reputation as one-sided and brought attention to Franko's journalistic work in which he viewed Jews "realistically," specifically in three articles (two in German, one in Polish) that Franko published in the 1880s. They appeared in Ukrainian for the first time in 1914 in Franko's collection of texts that he wrote for Polish- and German-language periodicals.[442] The fact that Franko himself selected those three pieces and republished them in 1914 proved to Kuzyk that he had not changed his views about the "Jewish issue."

Kuzyk went on to summarize the three articles providing occasional quotations. The first of Franko's pieces, according to him, exposed a conspiracy of Viennese Jews to acquire large landholdings in Galicia through the façade of a Jewish educational society. Such conspiratorial methods, Kuzyk quotes Franko, exemplify "Jewish tactics within our society which under cover of emancipation wants to achieve factual hegemony."[443] Franko drew a parallel between this land-grabbing tactic in Galicia with the story of the Jewish conquest of Canaan from the Book of Judges (Old Testament) and came to the conclusion that soon the majority of Galician land would become Jewish property, turning the crownland into the "homeland of Judas."[444] In reply to Franko's claims, the Lviv Jewish newspaper *Der Israelit* published an article calling his piece a "disgusting crime." Franko responded with an article (the second piece summarized by Kuzyk) citing land statistics to prove his claim about Jewish land-grabbing in Galicia, adding that Jews were not only trying to take over land but had already taken over the Galician economy and commerce through dishonest competition, forcing the Ukrainian peasantry into economic dependency on

---

442 Ivan Franko, *V naimakh u susidiv: zbirnyk prats pysanykh polskoiu ta nimetskoiu movamy v perekladi z poiasnenniamy ta dodatkamy avtora* (Lviv, 1914).
443 K.K. [Kost Kuzyk], "Ivan Franko i zhydivske pytannia," *Krakivski Visti*, no. 112 (850) May 28, 1943, 3
444 Ibidem, 4.

Jewish businesses.[445] Kuzyk used Franko's third article, "Semitism and anti-Semitism in Galicia," to prove that its author looked at the "Jewish question" not only as a socioeconomic issue but as a moral one as well. In this text Franko praised the apostle Paul for breaking away with Jewish tradition through "liberating the Christian ethic from Jewish formulas and Jewish formalism."[446] Kuzyk ended his piece by quoting Franko's warning from the third article that if Jews should ignore the growing dissatisfaction with them of the Galician non-Jewish population, then both the region (Galicia) and its Jews might face "untold threats" in the future. "Life showed that Franko's predictions were correct," ended Kuzyk, which may be interpreted as a hint at the ghettoization and extermination of Galician Jews by the summer 1943.[447] It is worth noting that the subject of Franko's anti-Semitism remains an issue of intellectual and public controversy.[448]

Kuzyk's second contribution to the campaign was published under the pseudonym "Boiko." In this text, "Tin Ahasfera nad Boikivshchynoiu" (Ahasver's shadow over the Boiko region), he tried to answer the old question of Ukrainian poverty: how come Ukrainians are so poor despite living in a land so rich with natural resources?[449] Kuzyk's answer was quite straightforward — Jews were one of the main reasons for Ukrainian poverty. The title of the article was somewhat misleading since Kuzyk looked beyond the Boiko region in his argument. He started with a brief historical outline of how Jews came to live in Ukraine pointing out that their rise to economic dominance was rooted in the medieval Polish kingdom, when both Polish royals and lords passed the collection of taxes and entrusted the management of their landed estates to Jews.

---

445   Ibidem.
446   Ibidem.
447   Ibidem.
448   See a collection of articles: Alois Woldan and Olaf Terpitz, eds. *Ivan Franko und die jüdische Frage in Galizien: Interkulturelle Begegnungen und Dynamiken im Schaffen des ukrainischen Schriftstellers* (Wien: Vienna University Press; Göttingen: V&R unipress, 2016). The Ukrainian edition was published in the same year.
449   Boiko [Kost Kuzyk], "Tin Ahasfera nad Boikivshchynoiu," *Krakivski Visti*, no. 113 (851) May 29, 1943, 2-3.

From there he immediately jumped to the late 19th-early 20th century and described the relations of Jews to the Ukrainian population as economic exploitation (*vyzysk*). The most successful tool of this exploitation in Ukrainian villages was the Jewish tavern. It was from these taverns that Boikos primarily got alcohol, which kept them demoralized and impoverished. After Jewish taverns spread throughout Ukrainian villages—Kuzyk likened this expansion to the spreading of an infectious disease—Jews took over the best lands in the region, forests, commerce and crafts.[450]

But the largest profits off Ukrainians, in Kuzyk's opinion, were made by Jews during the oil boom in Eastern Galicia before World War I. Here Ukrainians served as white slaves to Jewish masters in the same manner as Europeans exploited colonial populations overseas. To support this claim Kuzyk quoted from the fiction of two Ukrainian writers, Ivan Franko and Stefan Kovaliv. Both wrote short stories about the oil industry in Boryslav (the center of the Galician oil boom) and the social conditions surrounding it. But, continued Kuzyk, Jews were not satisfied with their traditional dominance in commerce and crafts. They also expanded into the so-called free professions, especially law and medicine, leading to a Jewish monopoly among lawyers and doctors. According to him, the number of Jews registered as lawyers in Eastern Galicia rose from 40.1% in 1890 to 60.8% in 1910 and doctors from 24.8% to 34.8% in the same period.[451]

That so many Jews pursued law and medicine, wrote Kuzyk, was not a problem per se. The problem was that they lacked any moral principles and entered those fields purely for profit. This resulted in further exploitation of Ukrainian peasants as Jewish lawyers encouraged them to pursue even the most hopeless cases, giving them false hope and, in the process, milking them of their savings. Jewish lawyers rightfully had the reputation of being the most corrupt lawyers in Galicia since they were not shy to suggest that their clients bribe the judge. Jewish doctors were no better in Kuzyk's opinion: they pushed out non-Jewish competition by

---

450 Ibidem, 2.
451 Ibidem.

A SCHOOL OF HATE   125

charging less per visit, and most people naturally went to the cheapest doctors, the only doctors that they could afford. But Jewish doctors made more money because they persuaded their clients to come much more often and, in addition, always charged for various useless injections during these visits. The Jewish work ethic, surmised Kuzyk, is profit-oriented and built around the exploitation of goys (non-Jews).[452]

But when it came to specifically Jewish-Ukrainian relations the harmful effect of Jewish influence was not limited to economic exploitation alone. According to Kuzyk Jews were always hostile to "our people and our culture." During World War I many Galician Ukrainian peasants and members of the intelligentsia ended up in the Thalerhof internment camp because of Jewish denunciations, claimed Kuzyk. During the interwar period, Jews, on the one hand, served Polish interests and were carriers of Polish culture in Eastern Galicia. On the other hand, Jews were also responsible for spreading communist ideas, thus contributing to a lack of national unity among Ukrainians. But it was during the Soviet occupation of 1939-1941 that the Jewish presence in Galician Ukrainian society reached new heights. Jews eagerly took positions in Soviet institutions, including the NKVD. It is thanks to these local Galician Jews and their knowledge of the Ukrainian community that the Bolshevik terror in the Boiko region was so devastating. Kuzyk ended his article on an optimistic note: "today [May 1943] our national organism has shaken off Jewry."[453] As a result, the Ukrainian economy, culture and public life will continue to grow because the "Boiko region will never be Jewish again."[454] Both of Kuzyk's articles were the most sophisticated and best-written contributions to the anti-Semitic campaign in *Krakivski Visti*.

The third contributor was Luka Lutsiv (1895-1984), a well-educated (Ph.D. in literature from Charles University in Prague) Ukrainian journalist and literary critic.[455] He wrote two articles for

---

452 Ibidem, 3.
453 Ibidem.
454 Ibidem.
455 The most detailed study of Luka Lutsiv is a Ph.D. dissertation by Solomiia Kovaliv: Solomiia-Mariia Kovaliv, "Literaturoznavchi kontseptsii Luky Lutsiva.

the campaign published under his usual pseudonym "L. Hranychka." Both dealt with literary themes. The first was on the role of laughter and humor in literature.[456] Lutsiv reminded readers that Ukrainian national literature started as a humorous experiment, meaning Ivan Kotliarevskyi's *Eneida*. But contemporary Ukrainian literature, according to him, contained more lamentation than laughter. In the wrong hands, laughter can do more harm than good, as we can see, wrote Lutsiv, from Jewish control over the press, cinemas and theatres, which were used by Jews to promote a new "progressive" human being, liberated from any moral "chains." Jews made fun of religion (Lutsiv meant Christianity), national traditions, the noble character of some nations (which ones Lutsiv did not specify), and most importantly of marital fidelity. Instead, Jews praised religious indifference, cosmopolitanism, liberal permissiveness, and sexual depravity. Jews never had access to "our [Ukrainian]" press to preach this message directly, but there were always Ukrainian journalists and writers willing to spread their "demoralizing" influence under the guise of "Western" ideas. Lutsiv ended his article with the call: "Let's make fun of our sins and praise our virtues! Not the other way around!"[457]

Lutsiv's second article, "Deshcho pro roliu zhydivskykh pysmennykiv" (Something about the role of Jewish writers), was perhaps the most primitive text in the whole campaign.[458] He claimed that any national literature accepting Jewish authors would eventually suffer from their demoralizing influence. To prove his point, Lutsiv went on to list a number of writers who published as Germans, Russians, and Italians, but in reality, all were Jewish and should be regarded as such. "This national incognito

---

Dysertatsiia na zdobuttia naukovoho stupenia kandydata filolohichnykh nauk" (Lvivskyi Natsionalnyi Universytet imeni Ivana Franka, 2018). The dissertation makes no mention of Lutsiv's anti-Semitic articles in *Krakivski Visti*.

456 L. Hranychka [Luka Lutsiv], "Pro smikh, zhydiv, radnyka Shchypku i Makolondru Miska (Nashym humorystam pid uvahu)," *Krakivski Visti*, no. 115 (853) June 1, 1943, 3-4.
457 Ibidem, 4.
458 L. Hranychka [Luka Lutsiv], "Deshcho pro roliu zhydivskykh pysmennykiv," *Krakivski Visti*, no. 136 (874) June 27, 1943, 4.

was used to lull the national sensitivity of some peoples."[459] The writings of these authors, often praised, "only demoralized our people." For example, Erich Maria Remarque, whose most famous novel Lutsiv mistitled as "Na zakhodi bez zmin" (No changes in the West), deserved none of the praise lavished on him as the novel celebrated "defeatism" and made a mockery out of "real heroism and true [...] patriotism." The reason why Jewish writers did not penetrate Ukrainian literature as much as German or Russian literature was because Jews "pushed" into literatures with large readerships where they could make "good money" from sales. "Ukrainian books before the world war [that is, before 1914] had very low print runs so no Jew wanted to be our writer."[460] Jewish authors — those "Shchupaks, Pervomaiskyis, Holovanivskyis and Stebuns" — started to write in Ukrainian only when the Soviets started to mass publish Ukrainian-language books for "propaganda purposes." Lutsiv believed that "these 'Ukrainian' writers made a good profit from [writing] Ukrainian books and at the same time served Muscovite imperialism."[461]

The fourth contributor was Olena Kysilevska (1869-1956), one of the most frequent authors of *Krakivski Visti* who specialized in "women's" topics and general hygiene. For the campaign she submitted one article — "Khto ruinuvav Hutsulshchynu?" (Who ruined the Hutsul region?) — which was published under the initial "Kh."[462] The article had quite telling subheadings — *Yak zhydy znyshchyly bahatstvo hutsuliv* (How Jews destroyed Hutsul wealth); *Yak zhydy vykydaly hutsula z khaty* (How Jews threw out the Hutsul from his home); *Yak zhydy nyshchyly kylymarstvo* (How Jews destroyed carpet-making); *Yak zhydy obmotuvaly hutsula* (How Jews wrapped up the Hutsul); *Zhydy i poshyriuvannia bolshevyzmu* (Jews and the spreading of Bolshevism). According to Kysilevska, out of all Ukrainians, the Hutsuls (a Ukrainian ethnic group that still lives in the Carpathian Mountains) suffered the most from Jewish

---

459 Ibidem.
460 Ibidem.
461 Ibidem.
462 Kh. [Olena Kysilevska], "Khto ruinuvav Hutsulshchynu?" *Krakivski Visti*, no. 126 (864) June 16, 1943, 2; no. 127 (865) June 17, 1943, 2.

economic exploitation because they were totally uneducated and had no intelligentsia of their own. This allowed Jews—those "cunning, flattering, greedy, unscrupulous in methods, insolent and inquisitive" people—quickly to become "false" friends of Hutsuls after settling among them.[463]

Just as the British colonizers drove Australian aboriginals to ruin through alcohol, Jews did the same to Hutsuls, who were a well-to-do people before the Jewish arrival in the region, wrote Kysilevska. In Jewish taverns, Hutsuls lost their memory, reason, houses and lands. Jewish alcohol drove this primitive but innocent Ukrainian tribe even to visible physical deterioration—cretins, retards or physically deformed children became common among Hutsuls.[464] According to her, the efforts of Ukrainian priests, including Metropolitan Andrei (Sheptytskyi), to stop this plague of alcoholism bore little result. Through control of moneylending and trade in the region, Jews made slaves of the Hutsuls in all but name. They took over each of the economic activities in which Hutsuls engaged—sheep breeding, carpet-making, fruit growing—and pushed out any non-Jewish competitors, especially Ukrainian cooperatives and stores. Jews actively encouraged Hutsuls to buy on credit and drive themselves into debt. In addition, during the interwar period, Jews contributed further to the worsening of Hutsul life by spreading Bolshevik propaganda. Like Kuzyk in his article about Boikos, Kysilevska ended her article on the optimistic note that the "Jews are gone [now] from the [Carpathian] mountains" which meant that the "old owners [Hutsuls]" finally had a chance at economic and societal revival.[465]

John-Paul Himka discovered that after the war Kysilevska—now an émigré—wrote another article on the Jews. Originally titled "Do spravy zhydivsko-ukrainskykh vidnosyn" (On the issue of Jewish-Ukrainian Relations) and then renamed as "Za dobre imia ukrainskoho narodu" (For the Good Name of the Ukrainian

---

463 Kh. [Olena Kysilevska], "Khto ruinuvav Hutsulshchynu?" *Krakivski Visti*, no. 126 (864) June 16, 1943, 2.
464 Ibidem.
465 Kh. [Olena Kysilevska], "Khto ruinuvav Hutsulshchynu?" *Krakivski Visti*, no. 127 (865) June 17, 1943, 2.

People), the article claimed that "the Jews were the enemies of the Ukrainians in Galicia—they exploited them and got them drunk, and they actively collaborated with their oppressors; nonetheless, Ukrainian peasants helped and fed Jews during the war."[466]

The fifth and last contributor to the campaign was Oleksander Mytsiuk (1883-1943), the only non-Western Ukrainian and the most outstanding figure out of all five contributors. He was a prominent Ukrainian Socialist-Revolutionary before and during the Ukrainian Revolution of 1917-1920 and served briefly (for almost two months) as the Minister of Internal Affairs in the government of the Ukrainian Directory in 1918-1919. After 1920 Mytsiuk, like the majority of his party colleagues, became an émigré, settling in Czechoslovakia, where he made a fine career at the Ukrainian Free University in Prague, eventually becoming its rector in 1938-1941. Unlike the other contributors, Mytsiuk had a record of writing about Jews before the war and under his real name: in 1931-1933 he wrote a series of articles on the "agrarianization of Jewry" for the official journal of the OUN *Rozbudova Natsii* (Nation Building).[467] For the campaign in *Krakivski Visti* Mytsiuk wrote a series of six articles under one title—"Zhydy v Ukraini" (Jews in Ukraine), which appeared under his initials O. M.[468]

The first article dealt with Jewish traits in general. According to Mytsiuk, the Jewish psyche had lost any notion of fatherland or homeland. Jews have the mentality of nomads rather than settlers—they stay in one place only as long as it suits their needs and leave promptly once it does not. They are the quintessential stateless people, for they feel no need for state or state borders. Their ideal

---

466 Himka, "*Krakivski visti* and the Jews," 87-88.
467 The articles were republished in a small book: Oleksander Mytsiuk, *Ahrary-zatsiia zhydivstva na tli zahalnoi ekonomiky* (Prague, 1933). Taras Kurylo and John-Paul Himka consider it "one of the most serious anti-Jewish publications that ever came out of Ukrainian intellectual tradition." See: Taras Kurylo and Ivan Khymka [John-Paul Himka], "Yak OUN stavylasia do ievreiv? Rozdumy nad knyzhkoiu Volodymyra Viatrovycha," *Ukraina Moderna* no. 13 (2008): 256.
468 O. M. [Oleksander Mytsiuk], "Zhydy v Ukraini," *Krakivski Visti*, no. 125 (863) June 12/15, 1943, 7-8; no. 137 (875) June 29, 1943, 2; no. 144 (882) July 7, 1943, 2; no. 175 (913) August 12, 1943, 2; no. 176 (914) August 13, 1943, 4; no. 201 (939) September 11, 1943, 4.

environment is an open world without any borders and nation-states. This is the reason why international socialism and communism attracted so many Jews, wrote Mytsiuk: the leading role of Jews in Bolshevism is not the result of some conspiracy, but a natural outcome of their predisposition. The Jewish drive to global dominance comes from their self-perception as "the chosen people" accompanied by arrogant attitudes toward goys, whom Jews treat very differently from their fellow tribesmen. When it comes to the economy, the Jewish ideal is to have as little state regulation as possible, but in the communist Soviet Union Jewry pursued an opposite course—regulation of everything (Mytsiuk did not bother to explain this logical contradiction).[469]

The rest of the series dealt with Ukrainian Jews specifically. Mytsiuk described them as unwelcome migrants who were never invited by Ukrainians to come to their lands but came on the invitation of Polish landlords to help exploit the Ukrainian people. Since then, the Jewish presence among Ukrainians has been a source of economic hardship. Mytsiuk provided the traditional list of grievances against the Jewish role in the economy of Ukrainian lands: control over trade, merciless exploitation of Ukrainian peasants for the benefit of Poles, impoverishment of the Ukrainian population through Jewish taverns, etc. After surveying the economic role of the Jews, Mytsiuk arrived at a powerful conclusion: the reason why Ukrainians never fully developed, never acquired their own burgher class, was because of Jewish competition. Jews, he added, would win in economic competition with anyone, for they are an utterly dishonest and corrupt people. They even managed to turn two peasant emancipations—Habsburg of 1848 and Romanov of 1861—in their favor, further exploiting Ukrainian peasants in both empires through usury.[470]

As for the demographic distribution of Jews in the Ukrainian ethnic lands, Mytsiuk found their highest percentage in

---

469 O. M. [Oleksander Mytsiuk], "Zhydy v Ukraini," no. 125 (863) June 12/15, 1943, 7-8.
470 O.M. [Oleksander Mytsiuk], "Zhydy v Ukraini," *Krakivski Visti*, no. 137 (875) June 29, 1943, 2; no. 144 (882) July 7, 1943, 2; no. 175 (913) August 12, 1943, 2; no. 176 (914) August 13, 1943, 4.

Transcarpathia (up to 14%). This fact, in his view, was not a coincidence: Jews gravitate to live near settlements that are least resistant to their demographic penetration. Mytsiuk measured this resistance in poverty: the poorer a village was, the easier it was for Jews to gain a foothold in it. This explains, wrote Mytsiuk, why most Transcarpathian Jews live in the poorest Ukrainian villages of the region since it is harder for them to take advantage of wealthier and better-educated peasants.[471]

Though Mytsiuk saw no need for conspiracy theories to explain either Jewish competitiveness or their affinity to Bolshevism, he did come up with his own conspiracy theory about research on Jews. According to him, any study of Ukraine's history, economy, statistics, folklore and demography would reveal a negative image of the Jew. Such studies showing "real" Jews were done in the Russian Empire in the 19th century by Mykhailo Drahomanov, Fedir Vovk and Pavlo Chubynskyi. But in the early 20th century such works stopped appearing. The first generation of Ukrainian socialists, argued Mytsiuk, people like Drahomanov, Podolynskyi, Pavlyk, and Navrotskyi openly professed anti-Jewish feelings since, as true socialists, they were against any exploitation, including Jewish exploitation of Ukrainians. However, subsequent generations of socialists did not tolerate critical views about Jews; such people were condemned as anti-Semites and expelled from the socialist parties. Fiction went through a similar pattern. Nineteenth-century authors—Pushkin, Gogol, Shevchenko, Saltykov-Shchedrin, and Dostoevsky—portrayed Jews as they really were. But in the early 1900s, such negative depictions of Jews became a taboo. Why? Mytsiuk explained this shift by the successful infiltration of Russian and Ukrainian scholarship and literature by Jews in the early 20th century, who then directed their development away from Jewish issues.[472]

---

471 O.M. [Oleksander Mytsiuk], "Zhydy v Ukraini," *Krakivski Visti*, no. 125 (863) June 12/15, 1943, 7-8.
472 O.M. [Oleksander Mytsiuk], "Zhydy v Ukraini," *Krakivski Visti*, no. 201 (939) September 11, 1943, 4.

Mytsiuk ended his series with the strong claim that the emancipation of Jews should never have happened because when the same rules apply to Jews and to the local population, the former will always outcompete the latter. This thesis, according to him, was best demonstrated in Transcarpathia whose local Ukrainian population ended up "in death throes" under the "Jewish yoke," which was well described in the famous Egán report.[473] Egán died in Transcarpathia in 1901 under mysterious circumstances (most likely killed by local bandits). But Mytsiuk had no doubts—local Jews murdered him for telling the truth about their exploitation.[474]

The editorial correspondence contains no hints whether the occupation authorities were (dis)satisfied with how the editors accomplished the task to conduct an anti-Semitic campaign in *Krakivski Visti*. As for the Ukrainian public's reaction, there is very little evidence—just two letters by Mykhailo Khomiak from 1943. In the first one, from July 10, Khomiak defended the publication of articles about Jews, though in his own words their reception was negative:

> I have to confess that we have written enough on the Jewish subject, and we [also] have heard enough disapproval from many people that we are conducting or, rather, justifying the action against the Jews, also for our dishonesty and provincialism, and our escape from reality and responsibility, but that is a minor matter. To us it seems that we are approaching every matter in the most objective way and that we strive to cover those problems that life itself pushes onto us or throws at us. We strive to do this 'sine ire et studio' [without anger and zeal]. As for how good we are at that, let history issue its harsh judgment someday.[475]

More than one month later, in a letter from August 20, Khomiak described the reaction to the "Jewish" articles as mixed: "Many

---

473 Ede Egán (1851-1901) was a Hungarian official and economist, who wrote a lengthy report on the social and economic conditions of Transcarpathia in the 1890s. On Egán and his report see: Paul Robert Magocsi, *The Shaping of a National Identity: Subcarpathian Rus', 1848-1948* (Cambridge, MA: Harvard University Press, 1978), 71, 384.
474 O.M. [Oleksander Mytsiuk], "Zhydy v Ukraini," *Krakivski Visti*, no. 201 (939) September 11, 1943, 4.
475 Letter from Mykhailo Khomiak to Volodymyr Levynskyi, July 10, 1943. PAA, Michael Chomiak fonds, File PR1985.0191/41. John-Paul Himka translates this fragment in a slightly different way. See: Himka, "*Krakivski visti* and the Jews," 89.

people are upset that we are touching upon this sensitive theme in such conditions in which we are now forced to live. It is also true that very many people express their approval of the good manner in which the authors approach this painful problem."[476]

After the war, Khomiak returned to the subject of the Jewish-Ukrainian relationship at least once more. In 1958 he wrote to Vasyl Kosarenko-Kosarevych (1891-1964), a Galician Ukrainian nationalist and émigré who at the time lived in New York. In the letter, Khomiak praised Kosarenko-Kosarevych's book published a year earlier—"Moskovskyi sfinks: mit i syla v obrazi Skhodu Evropy" (The Moscow sphinx: myth and power in the image of Eastern Europe).[477] The book was an anti-Russian/Soviet treatise, but it was its penultimate chapter—"Zhydy i Skhid Evropy" (Jews and Eastern Europe)—that drew Khomiak's attention. The chapter provided a historical review of Jewish-Ukrainian relations from Kyivan Rus to World War II, and like many other Ukrainian nationalist writings on the subject, it tried to accomplish two seemingly unrelated tasks. On the one hand, the chapter blamed Jews for various hardships that Ukrainians suffered throughout history, and on the other hand, it attempted to exonerate Ukrainians from accusations of anti-Semitism. It is curious how Kosarenko-Kosarevych applied victim blaming in the case of Jewish suffering but did the opposite for Ukrainian suffering. Besides that, he repeated a number of the usual anti-Semitic tropes: the Soviet Union was a Jewish state, Jews were a nation of exploiters, Jews exploit other nations because they consider themselves "chosen people," Jews control the media, Jews dream of global domination, etc.[478] Khomiak praised the author for his "bravery" in writing the chapter that showed the "decisive influence of Jewry" (Khomiak did not specify influence on what) and recommended its expansion into a separate book.[479]

---

476 Letter from Mykhailo Khomiak to Oleksander Mytsiuk, August 20, 1943. PAA, Michael Chomiak fonds, File PR1985.0191/41. Translation by John-Paul Himka.
477 Vasyl Kosarenko-Kosarevych, *Moskovskyi sfinks: mit i syla v obrazi Skhodu Evropy* (New York, 1957).
478 Kosarenko-Kosarevych, *Moskovskyi sfinks*, 409-429.
479 Letter from Mykhailo Khomiak to Vasyl Kosarenko-Kosarevych March 31, 1958. PAA, Michael Chomiak fonds, File PR1985.0191/170.

The third and final group of anti-Semitic content in *Krakivski Visti*, after texts from the Axis press and the commissioned pieces in 1943, were articles submitted by willing Ukrainian authors. Not all of them dealt exclusively with Jews and some mentioned them only in passing, but the general message was clear enough—Jews should be regarded as a hostile group that at most supports Ukrainian enemies or at least benefits and profits from Ukrainian suffering. Before June 1941 Jews were linked with the Polish oppression of Ukrainians. It was not uncommon for these articles to associate Jews with dirtiness, bad smells, infectious diseases and visual repugnance.

The article by V. Nemyrych, which I discussed earlier in this chapter in the framework of anti-Polish content, was the first text in *Krakivski Visti* that contained a negative comment, though in passing, on Jews. Expressing his contempt for interwar Poland as an "artificial" country, Nemyrych also injected a note of disgust at Poland by adding that it was densely populated by the "Jewish infection [*zaraza*]."[480] The article "Miska spozhyvcha kooperatsiia" (City grocery cooperatives) argued that Poles, by their nature, are incompetent in matters of economy, which allowed "Jewish exploiters" to easily run the Polish economy until the Germans arrived in 1939.[481] These comments about Jews were often accompanied by calls to seize new opportunities. Yu. Radiievych in his article called for a revival of Ukrainian handicraft, trade and small industry since Jewish "leeches," which had prevented their development for centuries, are now gone from Ukrainian towns and villages.[482] "Za sylnu organizatsiiu ukrainskoho kupetstva" (For a strong organization of Ukrainian merchants) pointed out that German dejewification (*vidzhydivlennia*) of trade in the General Government is an opportunity which Ukrainian merchants should take full advantage of.[483] Bohdan Halit noted that now is the time, thanks to the

---

480 V. Nemyrych, "Pevnym krokom vperid!" *Krakivski Visti*, no. 2 January 11, 1940, 2.
481 "Miska spozhyvcha kooperatsiia," *Krakivski Visti*, no. 4 January 17, 1940, 4.
482 Yu. Radiievych, "Za nashu hospodarsku samovystarchalnist," *Krakivski Visti*, no. 5 January 21, 1940, 4.
483 "Za sylnu organizatsiiu ukrainskoho kupetstva," *Krakivski Visti*, no. 5 January 21, 1940, 4.

dejewification of cities, for Ukrainians to move in and urbanize themselves.[484] The Ukrainian takeover of the former Jewish properties was regarded as a positive development that needed to be encouraged. Slava Holovinska praised how quickly Ukrainians were recovering under the German order from the previous Polish rule and gave an example of such recovery: the best shops in the former Jewish market in the city of Belz were now in Ukrainian hands.[485]

There were also calls for intensifying German anti-Jewish policies. For example, Yurii Tarkovych complained that the German dejewification of the economy was not going fast enough: yes, the Jewish "leeches" have lost their monopoly and can no longer impoverish Ukrainians, but there are still too many Jewish shops around. The German order to mark them with the star of David made their presence even more visible and thus, in Tarkovych's eyes, even more irritating since Ukrainians had suffered the Jewish presence long enough during the two interwar decades of the "Polish-Jewish rule" so that even in purely Ukrainian villages by the end of the 1930s, "we could only see a Jew, a Pole, a Jew and once more a Jew."[486] In another article, Tarkovych explained more fully what he meant by "Polish-Jewish rule": according to him, in interwar Poland, Poles and Jews worked hand in hand to keep Ukrainians backward. Poles hindered the national and cultural development of Ukrainians and Jews did the same for their economic advancement.[487]

Besides texts that linked Jews with either Polish or Soviet/Russian rule over Ukrainians, *Krakivski Visti* also published a number of *purely* anti-Semitic pieces: in other words, articles that regarded Jews in their relationship to Ukrainians as a hostile element on their own, without Poles or Soviets/Russians. One such author of a purely anti-Semitic mindset was the Carpatho-

---

484 Halit, "Za torhovelnu osvitu," *Krakivski Visti*, no. 13 February 21, 1940, 3.
485 Slava Holovinska, "Ne vmirae dusha nasha," *Krakivski Visti*, no. 35 May 9, 1940, 7.
486 Yu. Tarkovych, "Za rozbudovu kredytovykh kooperatyv na Lemkivshchyni," *Krakivski Visti*, no. 6 January 25, 1940, 5.
487 Yurii Tarkovych, "Yak pratsiuie 'Lemkivskyi Soiuz Kooperatyv' u Sianotsi?" *Krakivski Visti*, no. 12 February 18, 1940, 3.

Ukrainian writer and journalist Vasyl Grendzha-Donskyi (1897-1974).[488] In terms of national consciousness, Grendzha-Donskyi went through a rapid transformation from a Margaryized Rusyn in the 1910s to a Carpatho-Ukrainian nationalist in the 1930s. In 1919 he served in the Red Hungarian Army. In the interwar period, he made his living as a bank clerk in Uzhhorod, but his ambition lay in journalism and writing fiction (some of which he self-published). In the all-Ukrainian cultural context, he was a second-rate, maybe even third-rate, writer, but within the confines of his home region, Transcarpathia (or Carpatho-Ukraine as his generation preferred to call it), he grew into a titan of local Ukrainian journalism and literature. The highlight of his life occurred in 1938-1939 when Carpatho-Ukraine received autonomy within Czechoslovakia, and he worked as an editor for its autonomous government.

Grendzha-Donskyi's conversion to anti-Semitism did not occur overnight. His writings from the 1920s show no trace of it. It started to develop in him in the 1930s in a rather disturbing way—not from reading anti-Semitic literature, but from observing Jews in their relations with the local population in Transcarpathian villages and towns as he traveled through almost all of them, collecting material for his journalist articles. A prejudice formed through real-life interactions is much stronger and deeper than one formed by reading a brochure or watching a movie. By the end of the 1930s, his anti-Semitism was not yet public, but his diary showed clear signs that it had taken root. By that time Grendzha-Donskyi's Ukrainian nationalism radicalized as well. He also developed a strong nativist attitude, according to which all of Transcarpathia was the property of Rusyns and whatever wealth was made by other ethnic groups—Czechs, Hungarians and Jews living in the region—was actually owed to Rusyns. In other words, their gains were the Rusyns' losses. In his mind he established a causal link between the destitution of Rusyn villages and the Jewish presence within them.

---

488 Grendzha-Donskyi's daughter Zirka has written a biography of him: Zirka Hrendzha-Donska, *"My ie lyshen korotki epizody": zhyttia i tvorchist Vasylia Hrendzhi-Donskoho* (Uzhhorod: Sribna zemlia, 1993). It makes no mention of her father's anti-Semitism.

In his diary, he noted his impressions of two Transcarpathian villages in the 1930s. The one with Jews was "forsaken by God and people, poor, enslaved and unhappy."[489] In the other village, local peasants refused to deal with Jewish traders, and now "they are making profits themselves." The peasants in this village also favored temperance, so local Jewish taverns had to close down. Unable to trade and sell alcohol, "all Jews fled [the village], they have nothing to do here, there is nobody here whom they can cheat out of money."[490] Thus the absence of Jews meant better economic opportunities for Ukrainians. But the very demographic presence of Jews also felt alienating to Grendzha-Donskyi. In his diary, he noted that he had never liked Mukachevo, or "Palestine" as he called it: a dirty town with a Jewish majority, which made it look like an "oriental" locality. For him, the Jewish presence made a place non-European.[491] But all those thoughts remained confined to his diary. The war let them out.

In summer 1941 Grendzha-Donskyi published three pieces in *Krakivski Visti* in which he publicly voiced his anti-Semitism. The first two made anti-Semitic comments in passing: "Judeobolshevism has to disappear from the face of the earth so no trace will be left of it"[492] and "Instead of Judeo-Bolshevik Marxism, we must give full rights to our national culture."[493] The third article, "Na vlasnykh sylakh" (Using our own strength), was published at the time (August 1941) when German troops were rapidly advancing into Soviet Ukraine. Grendzha-Donskyi, still uncertain about German plans for the "liberated" territories, advocated a nativist approach to their reconstruction — Ukrainians must rebuild Ukraine themselves. He warned against involving Jews in the economic revival of the territories, even temporarily: "under no circumstances should Jews be allowed into any sector of the economy. A Jew may

---

489 Vasyl Grendzha-Donskyi, *Shchastia i hore Karpatskoi Ukrainy: Shchodennyk. Moi spohady* (Uzhhorod: Zakarapattia, 2002), 99.
490 Grendzha-Donskyi, *Shchastia i hore*, 135.
491 Grendzha-Donskyi, *Shchastia i hore*, 56.
492 V. Grendzha-Donskyi, "Slovatska ta khorvatska presa pro bolshevytski zvirstva nad ukraintsiamy," *Krakivski Visti*, no. 164 (319) July 29, 1941, 4.
493 V. Grendzha-Donskyi, "Vidpovidalnist pered istoriieiu," *Krakivski Visti*, no. 165 (320) July 30, 1941, 1.

not engage in trade, openly or not, because he is an element difficult to safeguard against—he will get in anywhere, will elbow in to exploit."[494]

***

One of the goals of the German authorities in the General Government was to put its multiethnic population through a "school of hate": propaganda of ethnic hatred aimed at dividing the population along ethnic lines and forming attitudes based on group identity. Historically speaking, such a policy was not original. Already ancient rulers understood that it is easier to rule over a divided population. However, in the General Government, this German task was made easier by pre-existing ethnic tensions that Polish policies of assimilation and denationalization produced by 1939. Anti-Semitism constituted the core of German propaganda in the General Government throughout the war which is unsurprising considering that its territory was the central killing ground of the Holocaust, so it was important to keep the local population hostile or at least unsympathetic toward Jews. *Krakivski Visti* was an obedient cog in this propaganda machine: following German orders and/or encouragement, it also attacked Jews, Poles and Russians/Soviets, often featuring texts (translated or paraphrased) from the Axis press. However, is it enough to describe it as a "Nazi" newspaper? It is precisely how many commentators referred to *Krakivski Visti* in spring 2017 when Mykhailo Khomiak/Michael Chomiak—grandfather of Canadian politician Chrystia Freeland—became a hot subject in the Canadian media.[495]

---

494 Vasyl Grendzha-Donskyi, "Na vlasnykh sylakh," *Krakivski Visti*, no. 189 (344) August 28, 1941, 4.
495 Two examples: Robert Fife, "Freeland knew her grandfather was editor of Nazi newspaper," *The Globe and Mail*, March 7, 2017, https://www.theglobea ndmail.com/news/politics/freeland-knew-her-grandfather-was-editor-of-naz i-newspaper/article34236881/; Paula Simons, "'School of hate': Was Foreign Affairs Minister Chrystia Freeland's grandfather a Nazi collaborator?" *Edmonton Journal*, March 8, 2017, https://edmontonjournal.com/news/politics/pa ula-simons-school-of-hate-was-foreign-affairs-minister-chrystia-freelands-gra ndfather-a-nazi-collaborator

In my opinion, a more accurate description of the newspaper would be "collaborationist" rather than "Nazi." We need to distinguish between the proper Nazi press (such as *Völkische Beobachter* or *Der Stürmer*) that was published in the Third Reich and the collaborationist press in the German-occupied territories. Blanketing all of them as "Nazi" distorts rather than clarifies. There were nontrivial differences between the two groups—Nazi and collaborationist newspapers—in the circumstances in which they were published, content policy, the motivation of editors and authors, etc. Nuance matters. As I stated before, the Ukrainian authors of *Krakivski Visti* engaged in campaigns against Jews, Poles and Russians/Soviets for reasons that had little or nothing to do with National Socialism. The original Ukrainian anti-Semitic discourse of the newspaper was dominated by historical and socio-economic, not racial, arguments often framed in anti-colonial rhetoric (Ukrainian natives vs Jewish interlopers).[496] The Nazi fear of Jewish blood polluting the Aryan race was alien to Ukrainians since interethnic marriages between them and Jews were almost non-existent (marriages between Poles and Ukrainians were a different matter, see next chapter).[497] Finally, the power imbalance between the two anti-Semitisms was immense: Nazi anti-Semitism was served by a powerful security apparatus that, by the end of the war, exterminated up to six million Jews; Ukrainian anti-Semitism had no state behind it whatsoever.

However, describing *Krakivski Visti* as "Nazi," even though I disagree with the label, points to an important issue of accountability. Should we hold the editors of the legal press accountable for the entire content that appeared in them, including Nazi propaganda that they had to include (or lose their jobs or worse), or only for the portion that they had editorial control over? Most Canadian commentators wrote their pieces on Khomiak/Chomiak in 2017 as if they answered the question's first part in the affirmative. But it

---

496 Unfortunately, a comprehensive study of anti-colonial discourse in Ukrainian nationalism of the 1930s-40s does not exist yet. My suspicion is that Ukrainian nationalists (including Ounites) borrowed much of it from the Comintern publications of the 1920s about anti-colonial movements in Africa and Asia.
497 Mick, *Lemberg, Lwów, L'viv*, 212.

would also be interesting to consider the editors' perspective. Ostap Tarnavskyi wrote in his memoirs that as an editor of *Lvivski Visti*, he essentially had nothing to be ashamed of: "At the time, I thought that we had fulfilled our [editorial] task honestly. We informed our community about events, and by daily information on Ukrainian life we helped to ensure that our social and cultural life did not stagnate under the circumstances [of the occupation] and [even] developed. It is true that the [Ukrainian] underground press ... sometimes called us 'nightingales' from *Lvivski Visti*, but these nightingales could also sing native [Ukrainian] songs. None of us came out with any odes in honor of great Germany, or with praises in honor of the German leader or even a German soldier. If there was news about the army or the front, it was a translation of official reports from the German command."[498] As we can see, Tarnavskyi limited the occupation content of the newspaper to war reports and omitted that it included official anti-Semitic propaganda (which it published with regularity).

Unfortunately, Mykhailo Khomiak did not leave memoirs, but his wartime and postwar correspondence show no feelings of remorse or regret over the publication of Nazi propaganda in the newspaper that he edited. Both *Krakivski Visti* and *Lvivski Visti* featured the occupation regime's propaganda of seasonal work in the Third Reich aimed at young Ukrainians in the General Government.[499] In September-October 1943 Khomiak toured Ukrainian labor camps in the Reich and was shocked by their poor conditions. Upon his return, he wrote to a fellow editor: "On Tuesday the fifth of this month, I returned from a ten-day trip through the camps of Ukrainian workers in Germany. The situation [in the camps] is tragic. [What I saw was enough] material for an indictment."[500] Yet

---

498 Tarnavskyi, *Literaturnyi Lviv*, 129.
499 *Krakivski Visti* called on Ukrainians to sign up for work in Germany as early as July 1940, see: "Sprava robitnychykh transportiv do Nimechchyny," *Krakivski Visti* no. 62 July 10, 1940, 7; "Na pratsiu do Nimechchyny," *Krakivski Visti* no. 65 July 17, 1940, 2.
500 Letter from Mykhailo Khomiak to Ivan Nimchuk October 9, 1943. PAA, Michael Chomiak fonds, File PR1985.0191/41. Khomiak also wrote a formal report (twelve pages, untitled and undated) about his tour of the labor camps, see:

the thought that he, as the chief editor of *Krakivski Visti*, might be somewhat responsible for the "tragic" situation never surfaces in his correspondence. John-Paul Himka wrote about Ukrainian war criminality during World War II as "a blank spot in the collective memory of the Ukrainian diaspora," noting almost two decades ago that "there persists a deafening silence about, as well as reluctance to confront, even well-documented war crimes, such as the mass murder of Poles in Volhynia by the Ukrainian Insurgent Army (UPA) and the cooperation of the Ukrainian auxiliary police in the execution of the Jews."[501] The postwar memoirs of Ostap Tarnavskyi and correspondence of Mykhailo Khomiak show that this selective historical amnesia affected not only the war criminality, but also Ukrainian participation in spreading the propaganda of the German occupiers.

PAA, Michael Chomiak fonds, File PR1985.0191/62. Photographs taken during the tour are here: PAA, Michael Chomiak fonds, File PR1985.0191/75.

501 John-Paul Himka, "War Criminality: A Blank Spot in the Collective Memory of the Ukrainian Diaspora," *Spaces of Identity* 5 Special Issue: War Crimes (2005), 10. Available at https://soi.journals.yorku.ca/index.php/soi/article/view/7999 (accessed August 13, 2024)

III "A nation aware of its glorious past and national strength will never disappear": Ukrainian History, Historical Memory and Nation in *Krakivski Visti*

Two main ideological trends dominated *Krakivski Visti*'s original materials throughout its existence. The first, which I termed a "school of hate" (see chapter 2), taught readers of the newspaper who were Ukraine's historical enemies: Poles, Jews and Russians/Soviets. Images of enemies, the Others, can be quite useful for any project of nationality construction: they frame that which should be excluded or eliminated. But the success of any national project is determined through assertion, not negation. If the "school of hate" was the negative construction (what our nation is not) then the second ideological trend was the positive construction (what our nation is or should be), reflected in articles about Ukrainian history, historical memory and national issues. In this regard *Krakivski Visti* was an important part of the larger program pursued by the UCC and Kubijovyč personally to elevate Ukrainians as a nation, to raise their educational and cultural level in the direction of broadening and deepening national consciousness. This is also quite evident through the publication catalog of the UPH, which included primers, textbooks, popular fiction and nonfiction, though the latter appeared in lesser numbers than Kubijovyč wanted due to German censorship restrictions (see chapter 1).[502]

Krakivski Visti's official mission statement, contained in a short editorial ("Vid redaktsii") in the very first issue, was rather vague.[503] It declared that the majority of its subscribers (in reality, it had none at the time) were peasants. Therefore, the newspaper would focus on publishing practical texts for their agricultural needs. The editorial also promised to write about "general" and

---

[502] See: L. V. Holovata, "*Ukrainske vydavnytstvo" u Krakovi-L'vovi, 1939-1945: Bibliohrafichnyi dovidnyk* (Kyiv: Krytyka, 2010).
[503] "Vid redaktsii," *Krakivski Visti*, no. 1 January 7, 1940, 2.

"legal-professional" (*pravno-fakhovi*) subjects. Ukrainian scholars and writers were to be involved in the "literary-scholarly" weekly supplement to *Krakivski Visti*.[504] The editorial was a stark contrast to the UCC's internal memorandum for the newspaper's editors. The latter document is unsigned and undated, but most likely it was prepared in fall 1940, since it refers to *Krakivski Visti* as a "daily" which it became in November 1940.[505] Unlike the editorial, the memorandum was a well-formulated, precise outline of the newspaper's "ideological and political direction," which was "to stand on the platform of Ukrainian nationalism" (this should not be equated to the ideology of either OUN) according to its vision by the UCC's leadership.[506] History, or rather certain use of history (stressing the importance of having your own state), was an important part of that vision.

Articles on Ukrainian history appeared in *Krakivski Visti* frequently, constituting one of the largest blocks of content in the newspaper after texts about the war and politics. Among the contributors were both professional and amateur historians. In terms of literary style and the presentation of historical material, the articles were quite uneven. An absolute majority of them were of inferior intellectual and literary quality, but one must take into account that these texts (and much of the newspaper) were not aimed for a highly sophisticated public: their purpose was not to stimulate nuanced thinking or enrich understanding. The primary goal of these articles was to tell Ukrainians in simple language who they had been in the past, so they knew what directions to follow in the future. Due to the large numbers of these materials, I will limit myself to discussion of three historians and a selection of texts which I found typical of this general ideological line.

---

504 Ibidem. The Literary and Scholarship supplement (Literaturno-naukovyi dodatok) appeared only in four issues of the newspaper—no. 3, 7, 11, and 15 (1940).
505 "Pravylnyk dlia Redaktsiï shchodennyka 'Krakivski Visti.'" PAA, Michael Chomiak fonds, File PR1985.0191/28.
506 Ibidem.

History and commemoration

The first two professional historians to collaborate with the newspaper were Mykola Andrusiak (1902-1985) and Myron Korduba (1876-1947).[507] Both were Galician Ukrainians and reputable historians by 1940. To a degree, Andrusiak was Korduba's protégé, at least during the late 1920s – early 1930s. Under the German occupation both found themselves in financial need, especially Andrusiak who even before the war struggled to secure an income. When in 1934 Korduba tried to help young Andrusiak with employment, a Polish official told him that Poland had enough unemployed historians to fill teaching positions in the whole of Europe and even after that there would still be a significant leftover.[508] Unsurprisingly, both turned to *Krakivski Visti* to improve their income situation in 1940. Before the war Andrusiak wrote for *Dilo*: according to Maryna Cheban's estimate he wrote thirty articles and book reviews for the newspaper in 1929-1937. In 1937 Andrusiak stopped writing for *Dilo* due to a conflict with its chief editor, Ivan Nimchuk.[509]

For *Krakivski Visti* Andrusiak wrote a series of twelve articles vaguely titled "Istorychni narysy" (Historical Sketches).[510] It surveyed Ukrainian history from the settlement of Slavs until the Union of Lublin (1569). Andrusiak started the series by briefly discussing the relationship of Slavic and Germanic peoples to the Aryan race. Both groups of peoples and their languages, according to him,

---

507 On Andrusiak see: Maryna Cheban, *Mykola Andrusiak: istoriia istoryka* (Lviv: Instytut ukrainoznavstva im. I. Krypiakevycha, 2015). On Korduba: Oleh Pikh, *Myron Korduba (1876-1947)* (Lviv: Instytut ukrainoznavstva im. I. Krypiakevycha, 2012).
508 Oleh Pikh and Maryna Cheban, "Myron Korduba and Mykola Andrusiak: do istorii vzaiemyn," *Ukraina-Polshcha: istorychna spadshchyna ta suspilna svidomist* no. 5 (2012): 164.
509 See: Cheban, *Mykola Andrusiak*, 76.
510 N. A. [Mykola Andrusiak], "Istorychni narysy," *Krakivski Visti*, no. 23 March 27, 1940, 7; no. 25 April 4, 1940, 7; no. 29 April 17, 1940, 7; no. 30 April 21, 1940, 7; no. 36 May 11, 1940, 7; no. 39 May 17, 1940, 7; no. 40 May 19, 1940, 10; no. 41 May 22, 1940, 7; no. 42 May 24, 1940, 4, 7; no. 43 May 27, 1940, 11; no. 44 May 29, 1940, 7; no. 45 May 31, 1940, 7.

originated from the same "Aryan root."⁵¹¹ The implication of this claim was quite significant: in other words, Germans and Slavs were both equally Aryan and thus racially on the same level. Curiously enough, the German occupation authorities of the General Government never took a clear, official stance on whether Ukrainians and Poles constituted Aryans or not.⁵¹² They allowed Ukrainians to identify as Aryans (meaning non-Jews), which many of them, especially educated ones, did.⁵¹³

Andrusiak placed the historical fatherland of Aryans somewhere between the Ukrainian steppe and ancient German forests. Over time Aryans divided into peoples who migrated out of the ancestral land. But Germans and Slavs forever remained neighbors. At the time of their earliest history, even their languages were much closer to each other than they are now. From this introduction Andrusiak moved to the Kyivan Rus (*kyivsko-ruska*) state. He followed the usual narrative of its history: the rise of the state in the 9-10th centuries, the adoption of Christianity by Volodymyr the Great, fragmentation after the 11th century and separation of one Rus into several Ruses, subsequent Mongolian invasions, and finally, the decline and disappearance of Rus principalities. As we can see, Andrusiak made no changes to the established grand narrative.

---

511 N. A. [Mykola Andrusiak], "Istorychni narysy," *Krakivski Visti*, no. 23 March 27, 1940, 7.

512 For example, Himmler considered "racially valuable Poles" suitable for "Germanization." See: Doris L. Bergen, "The Nazi Concept of 'Volksdeutsche' and the Exacerbation of Anti-Semitism in Eastern Europe, 1939-45," *Journal of Contemporary History* 29, no. 4 (1994): 574. Hitler said that his racial ideas were "somewhat shaken" after visiting Poltava on June 1, 1942. According to his so-called table talks, there he had seen "so many blue-eyed, blond [Ukrainian] women that—thinking of the photographs of Norwegian or even Dutch women submitted to me with applications for permission to marry—I would speak of the need to 'Southify' [*Aufsüden*] rather than 'Nordicize' [*Aufnorden*] our northern European states." Quoted from: Majer, *"Non-Germans" under the Third Reich*, 608. The authenticity of the table talks has been recently questioned by a well-researched book: Mikael Nilsson, *Hitler Redux: The Incredible History of Hitler's So-Called Table Talks* (London; New York: Routledge, 2021).

513 See CVs of contributors submitted to *Krakivski Visti*: PAA, Michael Chomiak fonds, File PR1985.0191/31. Many of them added "Aryan" to describe their ethnic background. For example, Bohdan Osadchuk wrote in his CV that he was a "Ukrainer, arischer Abstammung" (Ukrainian, Aryan descent): "Lebenslauf" July 9, 1941. PAA, Michael Chomiak fonds, File PR1985.0191/31.

However, he did make several important claims on specific issues. The fact that the earliest Rus chronicles made no mention of Slavic tribes on the territory of contemporary Western Ukraine did not mean for him that it was not a part of Kyivan Rus. The chronicles made no mention of the tribes because at the time when they were written (mid-11th century), "tribal names in Western Ukraine had completely perished."[514] Andrusiak strongly objected to the popular claim of Polish historiography that before 981 (Volodymyr's conquest of the so-called Cherven towns) the Galicia and Chełm regions had belonged to the Polish state of Mieszko I. The claim is based on the confusion of the name *liakhy* with Poles, he wrote. Andrusiak agreed with another authoritative Ukrainian historian, Stepan Tomashivskyi (1875-1930), that *liakhy* was originally the name of the Eastern Slavic tribe neighboring the Dulibs. Association of *liakhy* with Poles exclusively, according to Andrusiak, was a later development.

Moreover, Andrusiak claimed that the Polish region of Mazowsze (Mazovia) and its people were also originally Eastern Slavic. Thus, in his opinion, not only was Galicia, without a doubt, a historical Ukrainian region from the outset of Slavic history, but the historical border between Ukraine and Poland lay through the river Vistula. In terms of racial divisions within Slavdom, Andrusiak claimed that Ukrainians were closest not to Russians and Belarusians but to Bulgarians, Serbians and Croatians.[515] The name Ukraine, stressed Andrusiak, has nothing to do with *okraina* (borderland): the Ukrainian folk songs clearly show the usage of *ukraina* in the meaning of "land" and "country." In the same way, it was used by Rus chronicles beginning from the 12th century. Use of *ukraina* in the meaning of "borderland" Andrusiak blamed on the Polish and Lithuanian officials from the 15-16th centuries.[516]

---

514 N. A. [Mykola Andrusiak], "Istorychni narysy," *Krakivski Visti*, no. 23 March 27, 1940, 7.
515 N. A. [Mykola Andrusiak], "Istorychni narysy. Slavianski plemena v skhidnii Evropi," *Krakivski Visti*, no. 25 April 4, 1940, 7.
516 N. Andrusiak [Mykola Andrusiak], "Istorychni narysy. Nazva narodu," *Krakivski Visti*, no. 36 May 11, 1940, 7.

According to Andrusiak, Christianity first entered Ukraine from the west: it started to spread in Western Ukraine from Great Moravia soon after the latter received the mission of Ss. Cyril and Methodius. Prior to the adoption of Christianity, there was very little linguistic and ethnic difference between Slavic tribes, who were separated primarily by their pagan gods. Prince Volodymyr chose Christianity mainly because he saw in it a unifying ideology for the various tribes in his state.[517] Though Volodymyr adopted Christianity from Byzantium, his vision was to follow the European kingdoms of the time.[518] "Already in the Kyiv state, there was a contest of influences between Byzantine and Western European cultures."[519] Volodymyr's European orientation was followed by his most famous son, Yaroslav the Wise, who paid special attention to the western border of the Kyiv state. As soon as circumstances allowed, he reconquered lands lost to the Polish kingdom in 1018.[520] But it was in the successor state, Halych-Volyn, where the Europeanizing trend of Ukrainian medieval history manifested itself most clearly, claimed Andrusiak. When Galician boyars demanded privileges from their princes, they only followed the examples of the Hungarian magnates who made similar demands on their kings. The Halych-Volyn state also became entangled in European politics: already at the end of the 12th century, the kingdoms of Poland and Hungary and the Holy Roman Empire were involved in its internal affairs.[521] The arrival of the Mongols in the 1240s further strengthened the European connection, as both the Halych-Volyn and European states now had a powerful common enemy.[522] By the

---

517 N. A. [Mykola Andrusiak], "Istorychni narysy. Khrystiianstvo na Ukraini," *Krakivski Visti*, no. 29 April 17, 1940, 7.
518 M. Andrusiak, "Istorychni narysy. Nazva narodu," *Krakivski Visti*, no. 39 May 17, 1940, 7.
519 N. A. [Mykola Andrusiak], "Istorychni narysy," *Krakivski Visti*, no. 44 May 29, 1940, 7.
520 [Mykola Andrusiak], "Istorychni narysy. Rozvytok i rozpad kyivskoi derzhavy," *Krakivski Visti*, no. 40 May 19, 1940, 10.
521 [Mykola Andrusiak], "Istorychni narysy. Halytsko-Volynska derzhava," *Krakivski Visti*, no. 41 May 22, 1940, 7.
522 N. A. [Mykola Andrusiak], "Istorychni narysy. Halytsko-volynska derzhava," *Krakivski Visti*, no. 42 May 24, 1940, 7.

end of the 13th century this connection was solidified by dynastic ties with the Hungarian, Polish, Czech, and Austrian dynasties.[523]

On the significance of the Halych-Volyn state in Ukrainian history, Andrusiak not only agreed with Stepan Tomashivskyi that it was the first truly Ukrainian state but went further. His claim was that without the Halych-Volyn state, there would be no "contemporary national-political and cultural, and partially linguistic, independence of Ukraine among the Slavs."[524] First, the historical experience and legacy of the state were so profound that, even though it died with its last ruler in 1340, it secured the Ukrainian character of its lands (Western Ukraine) for the next seven centuries. Second, its resistance to the Polish "onslaught" for two centuries shielded Ukrainian territories east of it, allowing them to develop and expand for the "benefit of the Ukrainian nation."[525] Facing the problem of how to continue Ukrainian history after the end of the Halych-Volyn state in 1340, Andrusiak, like many Ukrainian historians before and after him, changed his focus from states and rulers to culture and language. The solution to state discontinuity was to emphasize "Ukrainization" of the foreign dynasties and states that came into possession of the Ukrainian lands in the 14-15th centuries by adopting "Ukrainian" culture and language in a similar way to how ancient Rome was influenced by Greek culture after the conquest of Greece.

Traditionally, Ukrainian historians concentrated on the Lithuanian dynasty of the Gediminids to showcase this process of Ukrainian transfer from state to culture. But Andrusiak mentions it only in passing. Instead, he based the claim about the gravitational attraction of Ukrainian culture on a different case—Moldavia. In Andrusiak's view, the Ukrainian population was culturally superior to Wallachians, so it was no surprise that the latter, he claimed, started to adopt the culture of the former. Besides Ukrainian culture, Wallachians also experienced Bulgarian cultural influence.

---

523 N. A. [Mykola Andrusiak], "Istorychni narysy. Halytsko-volynska derzhava," *Krakivski Visti*, no. 43 May 27, 1940, 11.
524 N. A. [Mykola Andrusiak], "Istorychni narysy," *Krakivski Visti*, no. 44 May 29, 1940, 7.
525 Ibidem.

Together, according to Andrusiak, those two cultures Slavicized Wallachians and their rulers, who adopted Ukrainian as the official language of "the new Moldavian state."[526] This Ukrainization manifested itself, wrote Andrusiak, among other things by the very title of Moldavian rulers—*hospodar* (a Ukrainian word which usually means "owner")—and by the name which they favored—Bogdan.[527]

The Lithuanian princes who came to rule Ukrainian lands also soon Ukrainianized and from representatives of a foreign dynasty in these lands, they evolved into representatives of local nobility vis-à-vis Poland and Lithuania. Eventually, they rebelled against both Polish kings and Lithuanian grand dukes, but none of the revolts were successful. As a result, the Ukrainianized princes and their principalities were liquidated. They were replaced by land magnates, who were Polonized "at first politically, and then nationally" after the Union of Lublin (1569). With their Polonization "they stopped being carriers of the Ukrainian statehood idea, but [at the same time] it appeared among Cossackdom."[528] It is not clear whether Andrusiak intended to end his series with the Union of Lublin. He developed a strong personal conflict with the newspaper's chief editor Mykhailo Khomiak (see chapter 1) and stopped his collaboration with *Krakivski Visti*. In any case, the UPH republished the series as a small book in 1940.[529]

Unlike Andrusiak's general *Istorychni narysy* Myron Korduba's contributions to the newspaper dealt with narrow and specific themes. Korduba was one of Mykhailo Hrushevskyi's students at Lviv University in the 1890s and in Ukrainian historiography he is regarded as a historian belonging to the Hrushevskyi school. He was one of the very few Ukrainian historians in interwar Poland who managed to make a career at Polish universities. He taught at Warsaw University from 1929 until its closure by the German

---

526 Ibidem.
527 Ibidem.
528 N. A. [Mykola Andrusiak], "Istorychni narysy. Chuzhi dynastii na Ukraini," *Krakivski Visti*, no. 45 May 31, 1940, 7.
529 Mykola Andrusiak, *Istorychni narysy (kniazha doba)* (Krakiv: Ukrainske Vydavnytstvo, 1940).

occupation authorities in 1939. Korduba specialized in the medieval history of Western Ukraine and wrote to the newspaper on related subjects. Unlike Andrusiak, Korduba developed a good working relationship with Khomiak, though he was occasionally displeased with changes made to his articles.[530]

Korduba began to write for *Krakivski Visti* shortly after Andrusiak severed ties with the newspaper. His first submission was a series of articles titled "Boleslav-Yurii II. Ostannii samostinyi volodar Halytsko-Volynskoi derzhavy. Z nahody 600-littia ioho smerty" (Bolesław-Yurii II. The last independent ruler of the Halych-Volyn state. On the occasion of 600 years since his death). The title was somewhat misleading as the series was not so much a biography of the last ruler of the Halych-Volyn state but a study of the state during his rule (1323-1340).[531] Compared to Andrusiak's *Istorychni narysy*, which was quite popular in style, the series was closer to an academic text, with quotations in original Latin and their translation into Ukrainian.

This series is important for two reasons. First, it fit the newspaper's general trend before June 1941 to focus on Ukrainian lands within the General Government. Second, it looked at the crucial moment in Ukrainian history — the loss of their medieval state. The series explained how Ukrainians lost their state in 1340 in the same way as Kedryn's series "Prychyny upadku Polshchi," published simultaneously in the newspaper, explained how Poles lost theirs in 1939. Both series pointed at leadership as the main reason: both peoples lost their states because of choices made by their leaders. Incidentally, the hero of Korduba's series was a Pole. Before

---

530 Letter from Myron Korduba to Mykhailo Khomiak June 17, 1940; Letter from Myron Korduba to Mykhailo Khomiak June 22, 1940. PAA, Michael Chomiak fonds, File PR1985.0191/33; Letter from Myron Korduba to Mykhailo Khomiak August 30, 1943. PAA, Michael Chomiak fonds, File PR1985.0191/41. In the letter from August 30, 1943 Korduba complained to Khomiak that "правоправности" in his original text was changed to "православности" in the published version, resulting in a totally different sentence: "в Росії почуття православности було дуже слабко розвинене."

531 Myron Korduba, "Boleslav-Yurii II. Ostannii samostinyi volodar Halytsko-Volynskoi derzhavy. Z nahody 600-littia ioho smerty," *Krakivski Visti*, no. 52 June 17, 1940, 6-7; no. 53 June 19, 1940, 4-5; no. 54 June 21, 1940, 4-5; no. 55 June 24, 1940, 4-5.

becoming Yurii II, the last ruler of the Halych-Volyn state was named Bolesław, a Roman Catholic princeling from the neighboring principality of Mazovia, who took a new name after converting to Orthodoxy and ascending the throne. We do not know whether the prince was elected by the local nobility or chosen by foreign powers. Korduba's own theory was that Bolesław won the competition for the crown (the two other contenders were Polish and Lithuanian princes) because he was favored by local boyars, burghers and the Golden Horde, to whom the rulers of the Halych-Volyn state had been bound by oath since 1245.[532]

The main attraction of Bolesław to these three parties, speculated Korduba, was his political weakness. He was tied neither to the Grand Duchy of Lithuania nor to the kingdoms of Poland and Hungary — mighty powers and neighbors of the Halych-Volyn state at the time. Instead, he was a petty prince from a small principality and thus politically unthreatening. But why had no Rus princes competed for the vacant seat in 1323? Korduba's answer was that the Halych-Volyn state became a victim of its own success: it was ruled by the local dynasty of Romanovychi for so long (nearly 150 years) that other Riurikids no longer considered it a part of their common dynastical house. This dynastical separation was also facilitated by the fact that the Romanovychi, over the course of their rule, increasingly intermarried not only with neighboring Polish and Hungarian royals, but also with distant Austrian and Lithuanian ones. The last time a Romanovych had married another Riurikid, pointed out Korduba, was in 1259.[533] Later on, *Krakivski Visti* published alarmist articles on how interethnic marriages threatened Ukrainian national survival (discussed further in this chapter).

In discussing Bolesław-Yurii's foreign policy, Korduba emphasized that he always sought out positive or at least neutral relations with the Teutonic Order, or the German Order as Korduba

---

532 Myron Korduba, "Boleslav-Yurii II. Ostannii samostinyi volodar Halytsko-Volynskoi derzhavy. Z nahody 600-littia ioho smerty," *Krakivski Visti*, no. 52 June 17, 1940, 7.
533 Ibidem.

preferred to call it. In this regard, Bolesław-Yurii faithfully continued the foreign policy of previous rulers of the Halych-Volyn state.[534] On the other hand, his relationship with Poland, even though Bolesław-Yurii was an ethnic Pole, eventually turned from neutral to hostile, resulting in an open conflict. In 1337 Bolesław-Yurii went to war with the Polish king Casimir III the Great, who was his relative (both belonged to the Piast dynasty). The two rulers warred over Lublin and neighboring lands—taking them was an "old temptation" for the Halych-Volyn rulers, according to Korduba. The war was unsuccessful for Bolesław-Yurii: after besieging the city for twelve days, Rus troops had to withdraw because their Tatar allies, whose commander was killed on the twelfth day, abandoned the siege.[535] Korduba devoted a lot of attention to how Casimir III the Great managed to secure an alliance with Hungarian king Charles Robert (Károly Róbert) against Bolesław-Yurii in 1339. The latter failed to counter this diplomatic combination with one of his own.

He also failed to foresee a domestic threat that eventually cost him his life: a year later, he was poisoned by the "enemy party." Korduba wrote that this "work of Cain" against the "great ruler" was completed with the help of a "neighboring state" (a hint at Poland).[536] It is puzzling why Korduba was reluctant to clearly name the "enemy party" and that neighboring state. But what is even more interesting is how carefully Korduba minimized throughout the series the importance of the sovereigns of the Halych-Volyn state—the Golden Horde—in the history of this Rus principality, mentioning it only in passing. He did not explain how and why after 1340 this sovereign allowed Hungary and Poland to partition the Halych-Volyn state, which was an important staging ground for

---

534 Myron Korduba, "Boleslav-Yurii II. Ostannii samostinyi volodar Halytsko-Volynskoi derzhavy. Z nahody 600-littia ioho smerty," *Krakivski Visti*, no. 53 June 19, 1940, 4-5; no. 54 June 21, 1940, 4-5.
535 Myron Korduba, "Boleslav-Yurii II. Ostannii samostinyi volodar Halytsko-Volynskoi derzhavy. Z nahody 600-littia ioho smerty," *Krakivski Visti*, no. 54 June 21, 1940, 4.
536 Myron Korduba, "Boleslav-Yurii II. Ostannii samostinyi volodar Halytsko-Volynskoi derzhavy. Z nahody 600-littia ioho smerty," *Krakivski Visti*, no. 55 June 24, 1940, 5.

Tatar raids into the two kingdoms. In the end, Korduba's narrative implied that the Halych-Volyn state disappeared not because of a simple dynastical crisis, but because its last ruler stood alone against enemies foreign and domestic. The historical lesson here was clear: the Ukrainian nation had strong enemies against which she required strong allies. The series mentioned only one such ally—the German Order. Korduba returned to the subject of the Halych-Volyn state in a popular history of the Chełm and Podlasie regions published by the UPH, arguing that they were historical Ukrainian lands.[537] It was praised in *Krakivski Visti* for demonstrating that the medieval "Ukrainian state ... was equal in might and value [sic] to other states of that time."[538]

The third major historian to collaborate with *Krakivski Visti* was Dmytro Doroshenko (1882-1951), perhaps the most eminent Ukrainian historian to write for the newspaper.[539] His most notable contribution was a series of eight articles on Viacheslav Lypynskyi (1882-1931).[540] Both Doroshenko and Lypynskyi were original Ukrainian historians and conservative thinkers. At one point, the latter was a subordinate of the former: in 1918, when Doroshenko served as the minister of foreign affairs in the Skoropadskyi regime, Lypynskyi served as its ambassador to Austria-Hungary. As politicians both failed: the Ukrainian governments for which they had worked lost Ukrainian independence by 1920. Both were important figures in the Hetmanite movement in the interwar period. Lypynskyi was the main ideologue of the movement until falling out with

---

537 Myron Korduba, *Istoria Kholmshchyny ï Pidliashshia* (Krakiv: Ukrainske Vydavnytsvo, 1941).
538 I. Iruk, "Perehliad knyzhok," *Krakivski Visti*, no. 39 (195) February 24, 1941, 6.
539 On Doroshenko see: Thomas M. Prymak, "Dmytro Doroshenko: A Ukrainian Émigré Historian of the Interwar Period," *Harvard Ukrainian Studies* 25, no. 1/2 (Spring 2001): 31-56.
540 D. Doroshenko, "Pamiati Viacheslava Lypynskoho (Storinka z moikh spomyniv)," *Krakivski Visti*, no. 136 (874) June 27, 1943, 3; no. 139 (877) July 1, 1943, 3; no. 140 (878) July 2, 1943, 4-5; no. 141 (879) July 3, 1943, 4; no. 142 (880) July 4, 1943, 4; no. 143 (881) July 6, 1943, 3-4; no. 186 (924) August 25, 1943, 3-4; no. 187 (925) August 26, 1943, 3-4. On Lypynskyi see: Jaroslaw Pelenski, ed., *Harvard Ukrainian Studies* vol. 9 no. 3/4 (December 1985): The Political and Social Ideas of Vjačeslav Lypyns'kyj; I. H. Perederiï, *Viacheslav Lypynskyi: etnichnyj poliak, politychnyj ukrainets* (Poltava: PoltNTU, 2012).

Pavlo Skoropadskyi in 1930. The movement failed as well: it never came close to its primary goal, which was the restoration of the Ukrainian state as a monarchy with Skoropadskyi's dynasty. But as historians both succeeded tremendously: their works are still widely read by Ukrainian historians, and their interpretations, especially on the role of the Cossack elite, have entered mainstream Ukrainian historiography.

Doroshenko's series on Lypynskyi was primarily a memoir about the life of his political ally and former diplomatic colleague, but it also contained tidbits of historiographical and political analysis. But foremost it was a sympathetic portrayal of the man who, according to the author, was one of the "greatest Ukrainian intellects of recent decades."[541] According to Doroshenko the most defining feature of Lypynskyi as a character and as a thinker was his "Western Europeanness," which the author attributed to his Polish upbringing and connections.[542] This was a rare instance when Polishness was described as something positive in *Krakivski Visti*.

Doroshenko and Lypynskyi met for the first time in 1909 and that is when the series begins. By then Lypynskyi was already known in Ukrainian national circles due to his efforts to turn Polish and Polonized nobility in Ukraine toward the Ukrainian national cause.[543] How successful was Lypynskyi in his Ukrainophile campaign? Doroshenko praised his efforts — lectures and publications — but had to recognize that it failed, or in his own words, "it was not met with great sympathy."[544] Most of the Polish and Polonized circles to which Lypynskyi directed his pro-Ukrainian message looked at him as some sort of Trojan horse, designed to undermine from within Polish superiority over Ukrainians. *Przegląd Krajowy*, a biweekly that Lypynskyi published for "Ukrainians of Polish culture" to publicize his program, failed to attract financing

---

541 D. Doroshenko, "Pamiati Viacheslava Lypynskoho (Storinka z moikh spomyniv)," *Krakivski Visti*, no. 136 (874) June 27, 1943, 3.
542 Ibidem.
543 D. Doroshenko, "Pamiati Viacheslava Lypynskoho (Storinka z moikh spomyniv)," *Krakivski Visti*, no. 139 (877) July 1, 1943, 3.
544 D. Doroshenko, "Pamiati Viacheslava Lypynskoho (Storinka z moikh spomyniv)," *Krakivski Visti*, no. 140 (878) July 2, 1943, 4.

and subscribers, so only fourteen issues appeared.[545] This "disappointment" prompted Lypynskyi to move from politics and public affairs to historical research. Through the latter he wanted to prove to the Polonized nobility in Ukraine that their ancestors in the 17th century were "carriers of the Ukrainian state idea" and thus to make them receptive to the call of "blood and soil" (a rather curious choice of words by Doroshenko which directly echoed the Nazi slogan of *Blut und Boden*). Only by heeding this call would they manage to stop feeling like "colonists" in their native land and become its "citizens."[546]

In Doroshenko's eyes, Lypynskyi represented the third generation of the Polonized nobility in Ukraine that heeded the call. The first was the Polish romantics at the beginning of the 19th century. They "idealized historical Poland, but also loved Ukraine," leading to the creation of the so-called "Ukrainian school" in Polish literature. The second was the *khlopomany* of the mid-19th century, who were drawn to the Ukrainian national cause by populism (*narodoliubstvo*), the idea that the educated class must help and serve the lower masses (*narodni masy*). Neither generation, pointed out Doroshenko, created a "political program" or some "wider movement." Politicization was achieved in the third generation, which Lypynskyi personified for him. But Lypynskyi and his few followers were not just another step in "the tradition of the return of Polonized nobility to the Ukrainian nation." They represented a "certain finale," bringing with them a firm conviction toward "regaining ... [Ukrainian] statehood."[547]

When Lypynskyi and his followers entered the Ukrainian national scene the idea of Ukrainian independence was not popular, wrote Doroshenko. At the time, most Ukrainian activists were socialists who "subjugated political and national aspirations to social issues." Their ideal was an autonomous Ukraine within a socialist Russian republic. The idea of independent Ukraine, wrote

---

545 Ibidem, 5.
546 D. Doroshenko, "Pamiati Viacheslava Lypynskoho (Storinka z moikh spomyniv)," *Krakivski Visti*, no. 141 (879) July 3, 1943, 4.
547 Ibidem.

Doroshenko using the famous phrase of Ivan Franko, in their eyes was "beyond the bounds of the possible" (*poza mezhamy mozhlyvoho*).[548] Doroshenko blamed the generation of *khlopomany* for Ukrainians' lack of appreciation for independent statehood. It was they who injected into the Ukrainian national idea the naïve belief that national existence can (and should) be achieved "without serfs or lords" (*bez khlopa i pana*), which meant pursuit of social justice at the expense of all other goals, including national independence. Doroshenko also accused the *khlopomany* and Ukrainian "democratic historians" of falsifying the history of Cossack Ukraine and idealizing its (alleged) democratic character. Doroshenko claimed that Mykhailo Drahomanov was right, when he wrote that democracy in Cossack Ukraine existed only at the very bottom level of society, but at the top level of hetman and *starshyna* (the upper echelon of Cossacks) it was a monarchy.[549]

Doroshenko credited Lypynskyi for revealing a completely different picture of the Cossack *starshyna*—not as exploiters of the peasantry (as in the view of the *khlopomany*), but as Ukrainian state-builders. By 1912 Lypynskyi's research into Ukrainian history resulted in the publication of *Z dziejów Ukrainy*, a collection of articles and primary sources that he edited. It proved that most of Bohdan Khmelnytskyi's colonels, including those that were believed to come from the lower classes, belonged to the Polish and Rus *szlachta*. "Together with the great hetman Bohdan they were co-creators of the Ukrainian Cossack State," wrote Doroshenko. They directed the revolutionary tide into a constructive, state-building direction. Unfortunately, in the end the tide proved to be too strong for them: the steppe nature of Cossackdom, with its "unlimited drive to freedom," and the unfortunate geographical location of the Cossack state—between Poland and Muscovy—led to the territorial division of Ukraine between Warsaw (Right-Bank) and Moscow (Left-Bank). The Cossack *starshyna* of the two halves, seeking to be

---

548 Ibidem.
549 Ibidem.

co-opted into the ruling elites, respectively Polonized and Russified itself over time.[550]

This "historical experience," digressed Doroshenko from discussing *Z dziejów Ukrainy*, should warn Polonized Ukrainians that there is no future for them among Ukrainians if they persist in identifying as Poles. They can find "salvation" only by returning to their people. Otherwise, the next "great social or political cataclysm will sweep them [Poles] away."[551] These were prophetic words, considering that they were written before the Volhynian massacre and published on July 4, just a week before UPA attacked en masse Polish villages in Volhynia on July 11, 1943.[552] The importance of *Z dziejów Ukrainy* and its reassessment of the Cossack elite in the Khmelnytskyi uprising was recognized right away by leading Ukrainian historians, for example by Ivan Krypiakevych and Mykhailo Hrushevskyi, though the latter in his political and social views was the antithesis of Lypynskyi. But *Z dziejów Ukrainy* received the coolest reception from its intended audience: the Polonized Ukrainian nobility for whom Lypynskyi produced this volume simply ignored it.[553]

After 1912 Doroshenko lost track of Lypynskyi. They met again, randomly, on a street in Kyiv in January 1918. The city had just been occupied by the Bolsheviks and Lypynskyi was visibly depressed. Their conversation was brief: Doroshenko recalled that they said farewell to each other as people who did not expect to see each other "for a century." But thanks to rapidly changing circumstances—Ukraine's peace with the Central Powers, the arrival of their troops to drive the Bolsheviks out, a coup d'état with German assistance which removed the socialist Ukrainian government and replaced it with conservatives and liberals (many of whom were Russified Ukrainians)—they met in Kyiv in May 1918. Doroshenko

---

550 D. Doroshenko, "Pamiati Viacheslava Lypynskoho (Storinka z moikh spomyniv)," *Krakivski Visti*, no. 142 (880) July 4, 1943, 4.
551 Ibidem.
552 Grzegorz Motyka, *Od rzezi wołyńskiej do Akcji "Wisła": konflikt polsko-ukraiński 1943-1947* (Kraków: Wydawnictwo Literackie, 2011), 137-138.
553 D. Doroshenko, "Pamiati Viacheslava Lypynskoho (Storinka z moikh spomyniv)," *Krakivski Visti*, no. 143 (881) July 6, 1943, 3.

was offered the position of deputy foreign minister in the new government. Upon learning that the ministerial position was to be given to the former Russian ambassador to Vienna in 1913-14, Nikolai Shebeko (1863-1953), Doroshenko categorically refused. The problem, in his eyes, was that Shebeko was an ethnic Pole and thus incapable of representing Ukrainian interests: "how could such a [Polish] minister defend the interests of Western Ukrainian lands?"[554]

According to Doroshenko, when Hetman Pavlo Skoropadskyi learned about the reasons behind Doroshenko's refusal he changed his mind and instead offered the ministerial position to Doroshenko. When the latter accepted it, one of his first tasks was to appoint a new Ukrainian ambassador to Vienna. Doroshenko offered the position to Lypynskyi, who agreed on the condition that he would select all diplomatic staff for the embassy. Doroshenko eagerly accepted the condition, but when Lypynskyi presented him with the list of candidates—"I confess, I was in doubt."[555] All of the candidates were Roman Catholics and hence "Poles" in the eyes of the Ukrainian public, whom Doroshenko did not want to antagonize. After a heated discussion with Lypynskyi, he understood what motivated the selection. Lypynskyi chose those people because he wanted to prove in political practice what he had argued before the war with his journalism and historical research: Polonized *szlachta* could be turned toward the Ukrainian cause (*ukrainstvo*). "It must be acknowledged that Lypynskyi's candidates proved themselves good Ukrainians and skilled diplomats."[556]

At this point—issue 143 (July 6) of *Krakivski Visti*—the publication of Doroshenko's series was interrupted by German

---

554 Ibidem. Even if Shebeko's ethnic background were indeed Polish, he was deeply Russified and his national sympathies were on the Russian, not on the Polish, side. During the Russian Civil War, he supported the Whites and served in Denikin's regime. After 1920 Shebeko, together with thousands of Russian Whites, settled in France where he was a member of an organization of Russian monarchists. See: S. V. Volkov, *Ofitsery rossiiskoi gvardii: Opyt martirologa* (Moskva: Russkii put, 2002), 531-532.
555 D. Doroshenko, "Pamiati Viacheslava Lypynskoho (Storinka z moikh spomyniv)," *Krakivski Visti*, no. 143 (881) July 6, 1943, 4.
556 Ibidem.

censorship. From the correspondence between Khomiak and Doroshenko in July 1943 it is not clear what the issue was exactly.[557] One thing is certain: the chief editor was not a completely powerless figure. Khomiak liked the series and wanted to finish its publication, so after a couple of attempts he received permission to continue. The publication of the series was resumed in issue no. 186 (August 25).

For Lypynskyi's service as a diplomat, Doroshenko had nothing but praise. He represented Ukraine with aplomb: in Vienna "Lypynskyi was known and respected."[558] As a politician and diplomat, he had the ability to see a bigger picture. When negotiating with Habsburg officials regarding the division of the Austrian crownland of Galicia into Ukrainian and Polish halves, Lypynskyi advised his superiors in Kyiv to agree with the Austrian proposal, which left the Chełm region in the Polish half. Doroshenko quoted a letter from Lypynskyi: "It is better for us, in case it is necessary [that we] give something up, to give up Kholmshchyna rather than to give up the division of [the crownland] Galicia." Lypynskyi's reasoning was that the state borders of Ukraine must be determined not only by ethnic but also by geographical considerations. Losing the Chełm region for the sake of Galicia would also provide it with the natural border of the Carpathian Mountains. But most importantly, this matter must be solved now "so we can turn all our strength toward the [future] fight (which will be very difficult) with the East [Russia]." It was not Lypynskyi's fault, suggested Doroshenko, that these negotiations resulted in nothing.[559]

After the conservative regime of Skoropadskyi was overthrown by the socialist Directory in December 1918, Lypynskyi offered his resignation but was convinced to stay in the position. Instead of the Ukrainian Hetmanate he now represented the Ukrainian People's Republic in Vienna. In April 1919 he was ordered to visit Ukraine, to meet with the head of Directory, Chief Otaman

---

557 See: PAA, Michael Chomiak fonds, File PR1985.0191/41.
558 D. Doroshenko, "Pamiati Viacheslava Lypynskoho (Storinka z moikh spomyniv)," *Krakivski Visti*, no. 186 (924) August 25, 1943, 3.
559 Ibidem.

Petliura. The meeting, in Lypynskyi's eyes, was a complete disaster. Lypynskyi, who assumed that he was called to discuss some important political matter, in fact was only treated to a social chat (20-25 minutes) with Petliura and then told to return to Vienna. Doroshenko believed that Petliura simply wanted to take a personal look at Lypynskyi, who was considered an exotic figure in Ukrainian circles. But Lypynskyi was furious with Petliura for this trip, pointless, in his eyes: he had traveled with great personal risk through "Bolshevized Hungary, Galicia and Volhynia" to meet with him. During the return trip, he ran into Doroshenko. In a conversation, both shared their pessimism regarding the statesmanship skills of Petliura and his Directory, agreeing that they would bury "the cause of Ukrainian statehood."[560] In the end, Lypynskyi resigned after a Ukrainian commander, whom he valued, Otaman Bolbochan, was executed on Petliura's order in June 1919. He settled in the Austrian countryside to treat his "old lung illness" (tuberculosis), in Reichenau an der Rax, a small town in Lower Austria.

Doroshenko arrived in this sleepy Austrian town as well, attracted by its cheap rental rates. He had almost "daily" conversations with Lypynskyi, discussing at length Ukrainian history and politics. Lypynskyi argued strongly against democracy as a form of political order, regarding it as "ineffective," especially for emerging states. (Most likely this was an allusion to the failings of the young Ukrainian democracies in 1917-20.) In his view, the next most important task of Ukrainian politics was the regeneration of the "leading class" (*providna verstva*) from the Right- and Left-bank Ukrainian nobility. Without them Ukrainian statehood would not be restored, said Lypynskyi. And without their own state, "Ukrainians will never become a real nation."[561] The values of having your own state and political elite were highlighted in the last two major works of Lypynskyi, which he completed in Reichenau—the historical monograph *Ukraina na perelomi 1657-1659* (Ukraine at the turning

---

560 Ibidem, 4.
561 D. Doroshenko, "Pamiati Viacheslava Lypynskoho (Storinka z moikh spomyniv)," *Krakivski Visti*, no. 187 (925) August 26, 1943, 3.

point 1657-1659, 1920) and the political treatise *Lysty do brativ-khliborobiv* (Letters to fellow farmers, 1926). The latter was to serve as a political Bible of the Hetmanite movement, which Lypynskyi joined in 1920, becoming its main ideologue. "He poured into this movement all his strength and, one can say, [because of that] burned out like a candle, shining with the fire of love and devotion to the Ukrainian cause."[562] In 1926 Lypynskyi left Reichenau for Berlin, to be closer to the court of Pavlo Skoropadskyi. This relocation complicated his health issues: a year later he left again for Austria, this time for Badegg (a small village not far from Graz). Doroshenko saw him for the last time in fall 1930. Lypynskyi was bedridden and depressed: he was tormented by doubts about whether the path he had chosen in life was for nothing. He died the next year.[563] Doroshenko's series on Lypynskyi, especially when compared to their correspondence and his other writing about the man, was hagiographical to a degree.[564] Certain key topics — the question of Lypynskyi's mental illness, explosive conflicts with fellow Hetmanites (Osyp Nazaruk) and Ukrainian conservatives (Stepan Tomashivskyi), falling out with Skoropadskyi in 1930 — Doroshenko, despite having the first-hand knowledge, avoided completely.

The three historians (Andrusiak, Korduba, Doroshenko) and their articles showcase the use of history for the general political line of the newspaper, which stressed the primary importance of the state and strong leadership for national survival. In addition, it reminded readers about historical friends and enemies of Ukrainians. The editorial archive of *Krakivski Visti* reveals that publications on Ukrainian history were not some sentimental pursuit. At least one of the editors, Mykhailo Khomiak, thought in historical terms. For example, in a letter to Volodymyr Levynskyi (1880-1953) Khomiak explained that the newspaper would not wage a campaign, as some Ukrainian nationalists demanded, against Mykhailo

---

562 Ibidem, 3-4.
563 Ibidem, 4.
564 See: M. Zabarevskyi [Dmytro Doroshenko], *Viacheslav Lypynskyi i ioho dumky pro ukrainsku natsiiu i derzhavu* (Vienna: Vyd. zakhodamy O. Zherebka, 1925); Ivan Korovytskyi, ed., *Lysty Dmytra Doroshenka do Viacheslava Lypynskoho* (Philadelphia: W. K. Lypynsky East European Research Institute, 1973).

Drahomanov's reputation in Ukrainian history: though Drahomanov did not support the idea of Ukrainian independence, his activity and writings were nonetheless a significant contribution to the development of the Ukrainian nation.[565] In another letter to Vsevolod Petriv (1883-1948) Khomiak asked him to write an article against the Ukrainian nationalist "partisans," who had started to operate in the General Government, that is, against the Ukrainian Insurgent Army (UPA), though Khomiak did not use the term. Again, his argument was historical: during the Ukrainian liberation war of 1918-1920 (in which Petriv fought), reliance on Ukrainian guerillas had proven to be disastrous.[566]

History was evoked in the newspaper for political, social, national, agricultural and other causes. For example, an excerpt from the Halych-Volyn chronicle was published to prove that the Chełm region was originally a Ukrainian land.[567] An anonymous series on Bohdan Khmelnytskyi's uprising wanted to prove that the Ukrainian state may again rise like a phoenix and strike down its enemies, i.e. the Poles.[568] Readers were reminded that Ukrainian merchants were the economic backbone of Kyivan Rus and the Halych-Volyn state; therefore, it was a matter of national importance to develop a Ukrainian merchant class in the General Government.[569] There was no lack of publications stressing the importance of knowing Ukraine's "glorious" history just for the sake of patriotism or national dignity. As one anonymous author put it in his article about

---

565 Letter from Mykhailo Khomiak to Volodymyr Levynskyi July 10, 1943. PAA, Michael Chomiak fonds, File PR1985.0191/41. Khomiak argued that Drahomanov played a positive role in Ukrainian history in this letter as well: Letter from Mykhailo Khomiak to Oleksander Mokh June 10, 1943. PAA, Michael Chomiak fonds, File PR1985.0191/40.
566 Letter from Mykhailo Khomiak to Vsevolod Petriv August 25, 1943. PAA, Michael Chomiak fonds, File PR1985.0191/41.
567 "Zasnuvannia Kholmu," *Krakivski Visti*, no. 3 January 14, 1940, 6.
568 "Pryhadaimo sobi nashe mynule," *Krakivski Visti*, no. 13 February 21, 1940, 4; no. 14 February 25, 1940, 2; no. 15 February 28, 1940, 4; no. 16 March 3, 1940, 4; no. 17 March 7, 1940, 3; no. 19 March 13, 1940, 4; no. 20 March 17, 1940, 4; no. 21 March 20, 1940, 4; no. 22 March 24, 1940, 4; no. 23 March 27, 1940, 4; no. 24 March 31, 1940, 4; no. 26 April 7, 1940, 4.
569 Mykola Derevianko, "Mozhemo buty hordi z nashykh starokupetskykh tradytsii," *Krakivski Visti*, no. 46 June 3, 1940, 4-5; no. 47 June 6, 1940, 4.

the education of Ukrainian youth: "a nation [*narod*] aware of its glorious past and national strength will never disappear."570

Calls for commemorating Ukrainian history routinely appeared in the newspaper before Pentecost (*Zeleni Sviata*). For example, an article with the same title praised Ukrainians because they had developed "piety" toward the "creators of our statehood, fighters for freedom." Ukrainian "glory" is undying, argued its author, despite the fact that so many Ukrainian historical monuments and sites had been destroyed beginning with the Mongolian invasion in the 13th century and ending with the destruction of princely tombs in the Chełm cathedral by "barbarous ruin" (implying: by Poles).571 Another article reminded readers about "the dear graves of [Ukrainian] heroes, which densely cover our land" and how their presence infuses "stronger faith in the great mission of Ukrainian life." The graves guaranteed Ukrainian "national eternity ... sanctified by the blood of our heroes." The article's author—Bohdan Hoshovskyi (1907-1986)—welcomed their sacrifices: in 1917-1918 they gave birth to the "Myth of the Great Warrior," who will lead Ukrainians on the Great March (to Ukraine's independence, presumably).572 Yulian Tarnovych, in his article "Kult poliahlykh" (Cult of the fallen), used similar symbolic language. "All cultured people," he claimed, honor their fallen, because there is no greater national "treasure" than to die for your fatherland. So many Ukrainian heroes sacrificed themselves for the sake of their homeland that their cumulative sacrifices make Ukrainians a nation "wealthy with glory." Tarnovych overdramatized an obscure event from recent Ukrainian history—the battle at Łupków Pass in 1918 where "less than a hundred" paramilitary Ukrainians fought unsuccessfully against "at least" 800 Polish troops—and declared "this was our Thermopylae!"573

The theme of national glory and sacrifice dominated articles and short notices about honoring Ukrainian military graves, which

---

570 "Za vykhovannia molodi," *Krakivski Visti*, no. 46 June 3, 1940, 9.
571 L., "Zeleni sviata," *Krakivski Visti*, no. 52 June 17, 1940, 1.
572 [Bohdan Hoshovskyi], "Mohyla—Zapovit," *Krakivski Visti*, no. 52 June 17, 1940, 2.
573 Yu. Tarnovych, "Kult poliahlykh," *Krakivski Visti*, no. 52 June 17, 1940, 4-5.

started to appear in the newspaper after June 1940. One of the first was "Sviato heroiv u Krakovi" (Holiday of heroes in Cracow) which was remarkable because it specifically mentioned the Ukrainian Galician Army, whose fighters were honored at the event, rather than the usual nonspecific category of "fallen," and the presence of Vasyl Kuchabskyi (1895-1971), an original Ukrainian political thinker, who spoke at the event. The article stressed that for the first time in twenty-one years, such an event was held by Ukrainians without the surveillance of the Polish police.[574]

In July 1940 *Krakivski Visti* introduced a regular rubric, "Sviato poliahlykh" (Holiday of the Fallen), to report on this kind of event, which became common in the General Government.[575] Quite often this ritual of grave honoring was enacted even in places where no Ukrainian military graves existed at the time; instead of real graves, symbolic ones were prepared for "fighters for freedom" or the "Unknown Sharpshooter" (*Nevidomyi Strilets*)."[576] According to *Krakivski Visti*, commemorations of fallen heroes were also held by Ukrainians at German military graves (from World War I).[577]

However, it seems that these practices did not evolve into genuine care for graves. Evhen Malaniuk in his essay "Na nevchasnu temu" (On an untimely topic) published in the journal *Nashi Dni* in 1943 praised Ukrainians for their love of burials: "no other nation in Europe reached such perfection as ours ... in the art of burying." But after burials are done, Ukrainians usually forget their graves. It was most evident, according to Malaniuk, in the cemeteries where both Roman and Greek Catholics were buried. When you enter such cemeteries, he wrote, even if you knew nothing about the Polish-Ukrainian divide, you would notice a stark visual difference. The "Roman" part would be ordered and well-cared for, but the

---

574 "Sviato heroiv u Krakovi," *Krakivski Visti*, no. 53 June 19, 1940, 7.
575 "Sviato poliahlykh," *Krakivski Visti*, no. 58 July 1, 1940, 10; no. 59 July 3, 1940, 6; no. 60 July 5, 1940, 6.
576 See for example: "Sviato heroiv u Dubrivtsi," *Krakivski Visti*, no. 64 July 15, 1940, 9; "Sviato mohyl u Chulchytsi," *Krakivski Visti*, no. 65 July 17, 1940, 6; "Sviato mohyl u Bohorodytsi," *Krakivski Visti*, no. 66 July 19, 1940, 6; "Sviato mohyl u Vanivtsi," *Krakivski Visti*, no. 68 July 24, 1940, 7.
577 "Z kniazhoho horoda Yaroslava," *Krakivski Visti*, no. 68 July 24, 1940, 7.

"Greek" would be usually covered with wild grass and flowers conquering the surface.[578]

Commemorations of specific events and persons were also reported, for example of General Myron Tarnavskyi (1869-1938) and of the Chortkiv Offensive (1919), which was the last major operation of the Ukrainian Galician Army in the Polish-Ukrainian war of 1918-1919.[579] Initially, the newspaper reported on commemorations of Symon Petliura (1879-1926) and Yevhen Konovalets (1891-1938) without mentioning their names. Instead, *Krakivski Visti* alluded to them as "Parisian" and "Rotterdam" tragedies—the cities where Petliura and Konovalets were assassinated respectively.[580] Curiously, the newspaper also reported on the commemoration of Petro Bolbochan (1883-1919), the Ukrainian military commander executed on Petliura's orders.[581]

Two and a half men of the Ukrainian literary cult

Despite this militaristic and heroic pathos in *Krakivski Visti*, the Ukrainian historical figures featured the most in it were not generals or hetmans, but three writers: Taras Shevchenko (1814-1861), Ivan Franko (1856-1916) and Markiian Shashkevych (1811-1843). Such focus on literary figures was not accidental: Ukrainian literature was not just an important, but a crucial factor in developing and propagating Ukrainianness, especially in the 19th century. Any comprehensive history of the Ukrainian national movement, besides political programs, parties, personalities and ideologies, must also deal with Ukrainian literature because the two were often intertwined. In this regard, Taras Shevchenko arguably deserves the

---

578 E. M. [Evhen Malaniuk], "Na nevchasnu temu," *Nashi Dni* no. 10 October 1, 1943, 7.
579 "U druhi rokovyny," *Krakivski Visti*, no. 58 July 1, 1940, 5; "Pomynky po gen. Tarnavskim," *Krakivski Visti*, no. 59 July 3, 1940, 2.
580 "Dvi akademii v Kholmi," *Krakivski Visti*, no. 51 June 15, 1940, 6; "V rokovyny paryskoi trahedii," *Krakivski Visti*, no. 63 July 12, 1940, 6; "Spivpratsia dvokh sil," *Krakivski Visti*, no. 63 July 12, 1940, 6.
581 For example: "V nediliu," *Krakivski Visti*, no. 64 July 15, 1940, 11. On Bolbochan and his death see: V. Sidak, T. Ostashko, T. Vronska, *Polkovnyk Petro Bolbochan: trahedia ukrainskoho derzhavnyka* 2nd ed. (Kyiv: Tempora, 2009).

most important place in the history of the Ukrainian national "awakening": it is not an exaggeration to say that without his poetry, it most likely would not have happened.

The cult of Shevchenko started to form in Austrian Galicia in the 1860s (almost at the same time as it was formed in Russian Ukraine) and since then played an important role in the symbolic culture of the Ukrainian national movement in this region.[582] Articles about Shevchenko in *Krakivski Visti* always appeared in March (the month in which he was born and died), typically with one issue fully devoted to the poet. In 1940 there was an additional reason to commemorate Shevchenko—it was the centenary of the publication of *Kobzar* (1840), his first poetic collection and the whole issue of *Krakivski Visti*—no. 18 (March 10) 1940—celebrated *Kobzar*. The tone of most articles in the newspaper about this truly great Ukrainian poet ranged between eulogical and over-eulogical. An anonymous author claimed that for Ukrainians, the celebration of Shevchenko's birthday should be equal to the celebration of Christ's birth by Christians.[583] Shevchenko was described as a national genius,[584] awakener,[585] and prophet.[586] The newspaper published numerous reports on the commemoration of Shevchenko's life and work by Ukrainians in the General Government and beyond,[587] for some time even running a specific rubric "Krai u

---

582 Ostap Sereda, "'As a Father among Little Children': The Emerging Cult of Taras Shevchenko as a Factor of the Ukrainian Nation-building in Austrian Eastern Galicia in the 1860s," *Kyiv-Mohyla Humanities Journal* no. 1 (2014): 159–188.
583 "Poklin Tarasovi Shevchenkovi," *Krakivski Visti*, no. 18 March 10, 1940, 2.
584 Volodymyr Horbovyi, "Nevmirushchist Geniia Ukrainy," *Krakivski Visti*, no. 33 May 4, 1940, 2; "Selo Terepcha—heniievi Ukrainy," *Krakivski Visti*, no. 34 May 6, 1940, 10.
585 Svii, "Probudytelevi Ukrainy," *Krakivski Visti*, no. 35 May 9, 1940, 2; Prysutnyi, "Probudytelevi Ukrainy," *Krakivski Visti*, no. 35 May 9, 1940, 6.
586 "Prorokovi Ukrainy," *Krakivski Visti*, no. 37 May 13, 1940, 7.
587 See: "Shevchenkivska akademiia v Krakovi," *Krakivski Visti*, no. 22 March 24, 1940, 1; "Pidliashshia vshanovuie pamiat T. Shevchenka," *Krakivski Visti*, no. 34 May 6, 1940, 2; Poinformovanyi, "Horlychchyna Kobzarevi," *Krakivski Visti*, no. 35 May 9, 1940, 2; "Volia Myhova Tarasovi," *Krakivski Visti*, no. 37 May 13, 1940, 11; "Pratsia v seli Krasnii," *Krakivski Visti*, no. 39 May 17, 1940, 2; "Shevchenkivske sviato u Vidni," *Krakivski Visti*, no. 40 May 19, 1940, 11; Yaroslav Naddnistrianskyi, "Velychavyi kontsert v chest Tarasa Shevchenka v ukrainskii Krynytsi," *Krakivski Visti*, no. 42 May 24, 1940, 4; "Zhidlyva pratsia u seli," *Krakivski Visti*, no. 42 May 24, 1940, 6; "My vyderzhaly polsku nevoliu,"

pokloni Shevchenkovi" (The land bowing to Shevchenko) for this kind of report.[588]

Sophisticated articles about Shevchenko were rare. The real Shevchenko was a complicated figure and so were his writings. He was claimed as "our own" by Ukrainophiles as well as "Little Russians" in the 19th century, by atheists and religious activists, and by Ukrainian nationalists and Soviet patriots in the 20th century.[589] For *Krakivski Visti*'s authors it was important to reclaim Shevchenko only for the Ukrainian national cause. Thus, the prominent Ukrainian socialist Antin Chernetskyi (1887-1963), in the article "Prysud bolshevykiv na Shevchenka" (The Bolshevik judgement of Shevchenko), argued that the Soviets had been using Shevchenko for their ideological campaigns in Ukraine not because of sympathy toward his views, but because of the popularity of his name among the Ukrainian masses.[590] The Bolsheviks had proven to be the "masters of demagogy," claimed the author, by converting popular historical Ukrainian figures such as Khmelnytskyi, Shevchenko and Franko into "heralds" of their policies.

According to him, the steps that the Bolsheviks had taken to commemorate Shevchenko—the opening of his museum, publication of doctored editions of his writings, numerous monuments and "bombastic" celebrations at his grave in summer 1939—served their political needs only. Moscow's main goal was to deceive and manipulate Ukrainians, especially those naïve and simpleminded "malorosy" (Little Russians) among them. This deceptive Soviet use of Shevchenko was directed both outward and inward. To foreigners, the Soviets wanted to show how much they valued this

---

Krakivski Visti, no. 42 May 24, 1940, 6; H., "Z zhyttia ukrainskoi hromady u Brni," *Krakivski Visti*, no. 46 June 3, 1940, 4; "Pratsia v seli Dubrivka," *Krakivski Visti*, no. 62 July 10, 1940, 6.

588 "Krai u pokloni Shevchenkovi," *Krakivski Visti*, no. 24 March 31, 1940, 2; no. 25 April 4, 1940, 2; no. 26 April 7, 1940, 2; no. 27 April 11, 1940, 2; no. 29 Apr 17, 1940, 2; no. 30 Apr 21, 1940, 2.

589 A biography of Shevchenko by Ivan Dziuba offers an excellent analysis of these and other (mis)uses of the poet, see: I. M. Dziuba, *Taras Shevchenko. Zhyttia i tvorchist* (Kyiv: Kyievo-Mohylianska Akademia, 2008).

590 A. Ch. [Antin Chernetskyi], "Prysud bolshevykiv na Shevchenka," *Krakivski Visti*, no. 113 (851) May 29, 1943, 4.

"genius of the Ukrainian people" so that reports about their anti-Ukrainians policies would not be taken as credible. For Soviet Ukrainians, this glorification served to "dull" their enmity toward the Bolshevik regime, which used the history of Shevchenko's contacts with the Russian revolutionary democrats to frame Russification as something beneficial for "Ukrainian culture."[591]

The real Shevchenko, claimed the article, would be an inconvenient figure to Bolsheviks since his poetry can be easily interpreted in an anti-Bolshevik way. But Shevchenko's fame among Ukrainians was too great for the Bolsheviks to ignore or turn against him. Thus, their laudation of Shevchenko as a "great Ukrainian poet" and "fighter for the exploited peasant masses" was just pure agitation. To prove his point, Chernetskyi quoted the 1934 theses on Shevchenko by the Department of Culture and Propaganda of Leninism at the Central Committee of the Communist Party(b) of Ukraine.[592] The theses (one can only wonder how he got hold of this Soviet publication) revealed what the Bolsheviks really thought about Shevchenko. They described him as a representative of "bourgeois democratic" and "nationalist" positions and as someone who never rid himself of his "petty bourgeois illusions."[593] In the contemporary Soviet Union, such labels would constitute a death sentence according to Chernetskyi. He had no doubt that if Shevchenko were still alive under the Bolsheviks, the fate of Khvyliovyi and Zerov would await him.[594] Only naïve "khakhly" (Russian ethnic slur for Ukrainians), concluded Chernetskyi, can believe that Bolsheviks "truly honor" Shevchenko.[595]

---

591 Ibidem.
592 T. H. *Shevchenko 1814-1934: Tezy viddilu kultury i propahandy leninizmu TsK KP(b)U do 120-richchia vid dnia narodzhennia T.H. Shevchenka* (Kharkiv, 1934).
593 A. Ch. [Antin Chernetskyi], "Prysud bolshevykiv na Shevchenka," *Krakivski Visti*, no. 113 (851) May 29, 1943, 4.
594 Mykola Khvyliovyi (1893-1933) was a Soviet Ukrainian writer and essayist who committed suicide in protest against Stalinist policies in Ukraine. Mykola Zerov (1890-1937) was a Soviet Ukrainian literary critic and translator who was arrested in 1935 and executed two years later by the Soviets.
595 A. Ch. [Antin Chernetskyi], "Prysud bolshevykiv na Shevchenka," *Krakivski Visti*, no. 113 (851) May 29, 1943, 4.

It is puzzling that *Krakivski Visti*, a newspaper run by Galician Ukrainians, paid much less attention to arguably the most important Galician Ukrainian writer, Ivan Franko, than to Shevchenko. For example, in the first half of 1940 the newspaper published 19 texts on the latter, but only 3 on the former. Though Franko had certainly lost to Shevchenko in the number of articles written about him in the newspaper, he was somewhat ahead in terms of their quality. The first large article on Franko in *Krakivski Visti*, "Velykyi syn halytskoi zemli" (The Great son of Galician land), appeared on May 29, 1940 to commemorate 24 years since his death on May 28, 1916.[596] It was better written than half of the laudatory articles on Shevchenko. The author recognized that as a national poet, Shevchenko was greater than Franko (whom he called the "Great Teacher of the Ukrainian nation"). The article drew parallels between Franko and the biblical prophet Moses, about whom Franko wrote one of his most famous poems (the article's author regarded it as his best poem). Both—Moses and Franko—loved their people (the article's author carefully avoided specifying who Moses' people were), but at the same time, they were not blind to their people's shortcomings. Franko saw that centuries of *nevoli*,[597] meaning not having a state of their own, influenced Ukrainians negatively, turning them into "voluntary slaves, serving without resistance to anyone" who owned their chains (this could also allude to Ukrainian behavior under the German occupation).

According to the article, to remove this "slavery of mind and body," Franko became, through his writings, a blacksmith of Ukrainian consciousness, forging it as "a Ukrainian Moses" and showing to the Ukrainian people their ultimate goal—"Ukrainian statehood."[598] The latter would be attained through hard work and struggle, in which Ukrainians, as Franko wrote in one of his poems, would have to achieve "either victory or death!"[599] It is worth mentioning that the author slightly manipulated quotations from

---

596 V. K., "Velykyi syn halytskoi zemli," *Krakivski Visti*, no. 44 May 29, 1940, 1-2.
597 The word is usually translated as slavery, but it literally means non-freedom.
598 Most likely this was also an allusion to Franko's father, who was a village blacksmith.
599 V.K., Velykyi syn halytskoi zemli," *Krakivski Visti*, no. 44 May 29, 1940, 1.

Franko. For example, the following passage was quoted as a single verse:

Або смерть, або побіда!	Either death or victory!
Це наш оклик боєвий,	That is our battle cry,
Хто ненавидить кайдани,	Those who hate chains,
Тому війни нестрашні.[600]	Are not afraid of wars.

But the lines come from two different poems of Franko: the first and second from "Konkistadory" (1904), the third and fourth from "Velyki rokovyny" (1898).[601]

That Franko was more than just a literary figure was the subject of a speech by one of *Krakivski Visti*'s editors, Lev Lepkyi, at the concert commemorating the writer in Cracow. In Lepkyi's opinion, Franko was not merely a Ukrainian poet but a "great citizen and statesman," which is a strange claim since Franko's involvement in politics was hardly prominent (he thrice, unsuccessfully, ran in elections). Lepkyi also called for the protection of Franko's legacy from those (unspecified) who try to "debronze" (*vidbronzovuiut*), that is, to deglorify or demythologize, his image.[602] In the history of Ukraine and Ukrainian literature Franko is rightfully regarded as one of the most mythologized figures, contending for first place in that category only with Taras Shevchenko.

One of the myths, which Franko himself created and propagated, was of his peasant origin (his mother belonged to the

---

600 Ibidem.
601 For an interesting comparison between the two poems and their appeals to heroism see: Yevhen Nakhlik, "Frankovi 'Konkistadory': poetyzatsiia zdobuvnytskoho heroizmu," May 28, 2018 https://zbruc.eu/node/80144 (accessed August 15, 2024).
602 "Kontsert u chest Ivana Franka u Krakovi," *Krakivski Visti*, no. 57 June 28, 1940, 7. "Bronze" in this context was a reference to *Zabronzovuimo nashe mynule!* (Let us cast our past in bronze!) by the Ounite intellectual Volodymyr Martynets. Originally it was published as a series of newspaper articles and then as a brochure: Volodymyr Martynets, *Zabronzovuimo nashe mynule!* (Paris: Vydannia "Ukrainskoho Slova," 1937). According to Martynets, Ukrainian national activists focused too much on past misfortunes, defeats and gloomy pages of Ukrainian history ("dark myth"). He proposed to counterbalance this negativity by glorifying ("bronze") the Ukrainian past.

szlachta).⁶⁰³ Another myth, or rather self-image, was that of a working-class man, a rock miner (*kameniar*).⁶⁰⁴ Both myths were regularly featured in the newspaper. For example, Bohdan Hoshovskyi in his article "Pisnia i pratsia" (Song and work), inspired by the eponymous poem by Ivan Franko from 1883, described him as a "son of Ukrainian peasant depths," born of peasant parents, and as the "Rock miner" whose "testament" to the next generations of Ukrainians was the "law of unceasing labor-struggle," because, in the words of Franko, "nations gain nothing for free."⁶⁰⁵ Hoshovskyi also described Franko as a "Giant of Ukraine," "the Moses of the Ukrainian people" and assigned him equal significance in the "great cult of the [Ukrainian] past" with Taras Shevchenko, whom he called the "immortal sovereign of Ukraine." Hoshovskyi presented Ukrainians as a people strongly inclined toward myths; commemoration of historical events and figures gained among them "specific, often deep and unique forms." For Ukrainians, the "cult of the past" with such figures as Franko and Shevchenko was not just an expression of "love" toward the fatherland but also "proof of their vitality" as a nation.⁶⁰⁶

The Galician Ukrainian writer Markiian Shashkevych (1811-1843) had neither Shevchenko's talent nor Franko's industriousness (but to be fair, Shashkevych died prematurely from tuberculosis). His most famous accomplishment was the literary almanac *Rusalka Dnistrovaia* (The Dniester Nymph, 1837), which he compiled with Yakiv Holovatskyi (1814-1888) and Ivan Vahylevych (1811-1866). All three were Greek Catholic priests and were known collectively as the Ruthenian Triad. Only Shashkevych is commemorated by Ukrainians: Holovatskyi later chose Russian national identity, converted to Orthodoxy and moved to the Russian Empire;⁶⁰⁷

---

603 See: Yaroslav Hrytsak, "Ivan Franko—selianskyi syn?" *Ukraina: kulturna spadshchyna, natsionalna svidomist, derzhavnist* no. 15 (2006-2007): 531-542.
604 See: Tamara Hundorova, *Franko ne kameniar. Franko i kameniar* (Kyiv: Krytyka, 2006).
605 B. Danylovych [Bohdan Hoshovskyi], "Pisnia i pratsia," *Krakivski Visti*, no. 44 May 29, 1940, 2.
606 Ibidem.
607 On Holovatskyi see: Zynovii Matysiakevych, *Ukrainskyi istoryk Yakiv Holovatskyi* (Lviv: Litopys, 2002); F. I. Steblii, *Spodvyzhnyk Markiiana Shashkevycha: Yakiv*

Vahylevych converted to Lutheranism and worked closely with Polish national and cultural organizations, for which he was ostracized by contemporary Ukrainian circles as a Polonophile.[608] *Rusalka Dnistrovaia* did not produce the same cultural and emotional impact as Shevchenko's *Kobzar* in Ukrainian history. Already by the 1860s Shashkevych was semi-forgotten in Galicia. But since the almanac was published in vernacular Ukrainian in phonetic script and Shashkevych never joined either the Polish or Russian orientation in Galicia (maybe thanks to his early death), in the 1890s he was rediscovered in the Galician Ukrainian national movement and coopted as a founder figure. The first large demonstration of the movement in 1893 was the commemoration of fifty years since Shashkevych's death.[609] Shashkevych and his almanac served as proof that the Ukrainian national movement in Austrian Galicia developed sui generis. This was an important counterargument to claims, which evoked feelings of cultural inferiority among Galician Ukrainian activists, that the Ukrainian national idea was imported into Galicia from "Greater Ukraine" (*Velyka Ukraina*).

Since the choice of Shashkevych for the national pantheon was based on a formal criterion (the vernacular language of *Rusalka Dnistrovaia*) rather than on the actual content of his output, his cult lacked substance. Commemorations of Shevchenko and Franko could be easily fitted into the Ukrainian national framework just through quotations from their writings—on Ukraine, heroism, work, sacrifice, etc. Commemoration of Shashkevych offered no such opportunity. This is quite evident from the articles that *Krakivski Visti* published to commemorate 100 years since his death. Ivan Pankevych (1887-1958) in his article "Markiian Shashkevych

---

Holovatskyi—diiach ukrainskoho natsionalnoho vidrodzhennia (Lviv: In-t ukrainoznavstva im. I. Krypiakevycha, 2004).

608 On Vahylevych see: Peter Brock, "Vahylevych and the Ukrainian National Identity," *Nationbuilding and the Politics of Nationalism: Essays on Austrian Galicia*, ed. Andrei Markovits and Frank Sysyn (Cambridge: Harvard Ukrainian Research Institute, 1982), 111–148.

609 Lidia Lazurko, "Sviatkuvannia ukrainskykh natsionalnykh iuvileiv u Halychyni (kinets XIX—pochatok XX st.)," *Z istoriii zakhidnoukraiinskykh zemel* no. 10-11 (2015): 191; Ihor Chornovol, "Markiian Shashkevych: mekhanizmy kultu," *Krytyka* no. 1-2 (2005): 1-2.

na tli zakhidno-evropeiskykh idei" (Markiian Shashkevych against the background of Western European ideas) said little about Shashkevych per se: most of the text dealt with Herder, Schlegel brothers, Goethe and Šafárik and how Shashkevych *may* had been inspired by their works when he was compiling the almanac. In fact, the way in which Pankevych wrote the article can be easily interpreted as a depiction of Shashkevych as some sort of second-rate imitator.[610]

Luka Lutsiv contributed the article "Talant, shcho zhas peredchasno" (The talent which was extinguished prematurely) to the commemoration.[611] Unlike Pankevych who was a linguist, Lutsiv was a literary critic. In this sense, he was better prepared to write about Shashkevych and his place in the history of Ukrainian literature, but similarly to Pankevych, he did not deal with Shashkevych per se. Instead, Lutsiv focused on his reception. The last two commemorations related to the poet — the centenary of the publication of *Rusalka Dnistrovaia* in 1937 and the centenary of his death in 1943 — Lutsiv described as underwhelming, or in his own words as "too humble" (*zaskromno*). In his view, the commemoration that preceded them — the centenary of Shashkevych's birth in 1911 — was much more "celebratory."

Lutsiv's explanation for this difference in commemorative intensity was not political: he did not point out that the political regimes under which the commemorations were held in 1911, 1937 and 1943 were quite different from each other. Instead, as a literary critic, he offered an explanation rooted in literary criticism. Nineteen-Eleven was the year when another literary critic, Mykola Yevshan, published his famous article against the commemoration

---

610 Ivan Pankevych, "Markiian Shashkevych na tli zakhidno-evropeiskykh idei," *Krakivski Visti*, no. 170 (908) August 6, 1943, 3; no. 171 (909) August 7, 1943, 3; no. 172 (910) August 8, 1943, 3-5. Pankevych was a talented Ukrainian linguist who specialized in Carpathian Ukrainian dialects. About him see: P. M. Fedaka, ed., *Materialy naukovoi konferentsii, prysviachenoi pamiati Ivana Pankevycha (23-24 zhovtnia 1992 roku)* (Uzhhorod: Uzhhorodska typohrafiia, 1992); Mykola Mushynka, ed., *Ivan Pankevych ta pytannia literaturnoi movy. Statti ta materialy* = Mikuláš Mušinka, ed., *Ivan Paňkevyč a otázky spisovného jazyka. Štúdie a materiály* (Priashiv, 2002).

611 L. Hranychka [Luka Lutsiv], "Talant, shcho zhas peredchasno," *Krakivski Visti*, no. 174 (912) August 11, 1943, 3-5; no. 175 (913) August 12, 1943, 3.

of Shashkevych, strongly questioning his significance.[612] In Yevshan's view, he was not worthy of being called a poet, and as a literary figure, he lacked originality. There was nothing to commemorate, argued Yevshan, so the centenary of Shashkevych's birth should be just another day in the calendar.[613] In response to such a devastating critique from the influential critic, Lutsiv listed opinions on Shashkevych by other authors who described him as an important figure—Yakiv Holovatskyi, Ivan Franko, Serhii Yefremov, Bohdan Lepkyi and Mykola Hnatyshak. The latter described Shashkevych in 1937, who, according to Yevshan, was a poet of "lamentations," as an embodiment of "spiritual strength ... and pathos of struggle." For Yevshan, Shashkevych was not an example of national awakening but of Galician literary parochialism (*zahuminkovosty*). Lutsiv argued (with no evidence but with much emotion) the opposite: Shashkevych was "our first [Ukrainian] poet in Galicia," who nationally "awakened" Galician Ukrainians through the publication of *Rusalka Dnistrovaia* just as Shevchenko did with *Kobzar* for Ukrainians in the Russian Empire.[614] This claim is difficult to tie with the facts: the almanac played little to zero role in turning the Galician Ruthenian intelligentsia toward the Ukrainian idea in the 1860s-80s. It was other texts that accomplished this turn.[615]

---

612 On Yevshan see the introduction to a volume of his collected writings: Natalia Shumylo, "Mykola Yevshan (1889-1919)," in Mykola Yevshan, *Krytyka. Literaturoznavstvo. Estetyka* ed. Natalia Shumylo (Kyiv: Osnovy, 1998), 3-11.
613 L. Hranychka [Luka Lutsiv], "Talant, shcho zhas peredchasno," *Krakivski Visti*, no. 174 (912) August 11, 1943, 3.
614 L. Hranychka [Luka Lutsiv], "Talant, shcho zhas peredchasno," *Krakivski Visti*, no. 175 (913) August 12, 1943, 3. This part of the article appeared under the title "Ivan Pankevych. Markiian Shashkevych na tli zakhidno-evropeiskykh idei." The newspaper issued a correction in the next issue, see: "Spravlennia pomylky," *Krakivski Visti*, no. 176 (914) August 13, 1943, 5.
615 See: Ostap Sereda, "Shaping of a National Identity: Early Ukrainophiles in Austrian Eastern Galicia, 1860-1873" (PhD diss., Central European University, 2003), 63-70.

The national body and its borders

History was evoked in the newspaper not only for defining the geographical borders of Ukraine (Vistula etc.), but also the borders of the national body. Who is Ukrainian? Where does Ukrainianness begin and where does it end? In this regard *Krakivski Visti* published one of the most interesting articles in its history—on the so-called *latynnyky* and mixed marriages. The three largest ethnic groups of Galicia—Ukrainians, Poles and Jews—had a very high degree of correlation between religion and nationality. By knowing the former, you could usually tell the latter and vice versa: Greek Catholics were typically Ukrainians, Roman Catholics—Poles, and followers of Judaism—Jews.[616]

However, as often happens when diverse groups coexist, hybrids begin to appear. By the end of the 19th century, two groups had become numerous enough in Galicia to attract public, political and academic attention—Greek Catholics who used Polish in everyday life and Roman Catholics who used Ukrainian in the same way. The latter group became commonly known as *latynnyky* since they were people of the Latin (Roman Catholic) rite. Their population size and exact origins remain a contentious subject in historiography. One of the highest estimates put them at over 500,000 in 1914.[617] Some consider them Poles who acculturated to the Ukrainian environment; others consider them Ukrainians who converted or were converted to Roman Catholicism. Both theories have concrete historical evidence behind them.[618] But, most importantly, they are not mutually exclusive.

Though *latynnyky* spoke Ukrainian in daily life, very few of them had Ukrainian national consciousness. In the battle of Polish

---

616 There was also a social aspect to this triangle—most of the nobility were Poles, most of the tradesmen were Jews and most of the peasants were Ukrainians. See: John-Paul Himka, "The Galician Triangle: Poles, Ukrainians and Jews under Austrian Rule," *Cross Currents: A Yearbook of Central European Culture* no. 12 (1993): 125-146.
617 Oleh Pavlyshyn, "Dylema identychnosty, abo istoria pro te, yak 'latynnyky' (ne) staly ukraintsiamy/poliakamy (Halychyna, seredyna XIX—persha polovyna XX st.)," *Ukraina Moderna* no. 21 (2014): 191.
618 Ibidem, 179-186.

and Ukrainian national projects in Galicia, this group was caught in the crossfire: their language pulled them toward Ukrainian identity, but their religion, since churches were becoming increasingly nationalized, toward Polish identity. Both Polish and Ukrainian nationalists looked at *latynnyky* with a mixture of hope and suspicion because they were an important demographic gain for either national project, but from their perspective, they also stood with one leg (language or religion) in the enemy camp. The group also raised complex questions of national identity for Polish and Ukrainian nationalists, who preferred simple answers to those questions.

The issue of *latynnyky* was also important to Kubijovyč personally. Though he was not one of them, but similarly to many *latynnyky* he was an offspring of a mixed Polish-Ukrainian marriage and his first marriage was with a Polish woman. The UCC under his leadership made certain efforts to turn *latynnyky* to the Ukrainian side. For example, it was for them that the UPH published a special edition of Shevchenko's *Kobzar*. The book was in the Ukrainian language but in Latin script so that *latynnyky*, most of whom by 1939 had experienced only Polish schooling and thus had little exposure to the Cyrillic script, could read the text.[619] The group was a recurring theme in *Krakivski Visti*. Interestingly, the very first article about them avoided the term *latynnyky*. Instead, it referred to the group as "Ukrainian Roman Catholics" (*ukraintsi rymo-katolyky*), though it was clear from the text that it meant *latynnyky*.[620] The author claimed that Roman Catholic Ukrainian peasants in Podlasie want to be regarded as Ukrainians: his proof was that they come "almost daily" to register themselves with local branches of the UCC. These registrations most likely had more to do with material assistance provided by the UCC to "Ukrainians" only (Poles would be turned away and directed toward their national committees), but the article made no mention of that.

---

619 The Latinized *Kobzar* was advertised in: *Krakivski Visti*, no. 64 July 15, 1940, 3. According to Kubijovyč its print run was six thousand copies: Kubijovyč, *Ukraintsi v Heneralnii Hubernii*, 269.
620 -Ya-, "Ukraintsi rym.-kat. na Pidliashshi tverdo zaiavliaiut svoie ukrainstvo," *Krakivski Visti*, no. 11 February 14, 1940, 3.

According to the author, more Roman Catholic Ukrainian peasants would register as Ukrainians if not for two obstacles. First, many of them feared retaliation from their Polish neighbors and Polish officials in the occupied administration. This fear was "nonsense," because "Poland will not rule over Ukrainian lands ever again!!!"[621] Second, Poland achieved great success in spreading within its borders the conviction that "every Roman Catholic is a Pole." The author argued that who is Ukrainian and who is not should be determined through "only belonging by blood, only lineage and internal feelings" (*lyshe krovna prynalezhnist, lyshe pokhodzhennia i vnutrishnie vidchuttia*) — notice the order of the criteria and absence of either language or religion in them. For a thousand years, Podlasie had suffered demographic losses to "Polishness," but now, thanks to "contemporary favorable conditions" (i.e., the German occupation), the presence of the Ukrainian population in this region could be "strengthened."[622] The implication of this suggestion was clear: the shortest path to increase Ukrainian demographic presence in Podlasie was through attracting these Roman Catholic peasants into the Ukrainian nation.

The article that made the strongest case that identifying as a Roman Catholic did not exclude identifying as a Ukrainian was written by a priest with the initials D. N. The author openly recognized that it would be difficult to integrate *latynnyky* into the Ukrainian nation and not only because of the Polish propaganda that "you are Poles because you are Roman Catholics."[623] Ukrainians are guilty of this assumption as well: "how many times, perhaps unconsciously, our intelligentsia — teachers, officials, cooperators — pushed away a *latynnyk*-Ukrainian with the words: 'You are a Pole! [So] go to the Poles!'" As a result, "we have done nothing to [nationally] save those Roman Catholics, former Ukrainians." And so *latynnyky* found themselves with both sides saying the same: on the one hand, Polish priests and bureaucrats kept telling them that

---

621 Ibidem.
622 Ibidem.
623 D. N., "Nashi zavdannia na zakhid vid Kholmshchyny," *Krakivski Visti*, no. 56 June 26, 1940, 5.

they are Poles because they are Roman Catholics, and on the other hand "we [Ukrainians] are doing" the same. "So how will this unfortunate *latynnyk* become a Ukrainian?" The author warned that if this Ukrainian attitude continued, *latynnyky* would inevitably become Poles. But where was the root of this attitude, he asked?[624]

The author blamed it on the Russian state: to think that faith defined national identity was an "old Muscovite habit." *Latynnyky* in the Chełm region, claimed the author, were a product of the Russian persecution of Uniates. Those among the latter who refused to convert to Orthodoxy were regarded by Russian officialdom as Poles, and thus, "hundreds of thousands" of them were pushed into Roman Catholicism. "We must not tread this old path." Depolonization should not mean losing one's faith, in this case Roman Catholicism, argued the author. He used the example of Lithuanians who also were once Polonized through the Roman Catholic Church, but eventually, they reversed this process of denationalization by removing Polishness (*polshchyna*) from "parishes, churches, sermons, and … schools." The author also appealed to Ukrainian and German historical experiences. Zaporozhian Cossacks, according to him, accepted anyone who believed in the Christian God and in contemporary Germany faith played no role in determining whether someone was a German.[625] So if religion could (and should) no longer be a valid tool for deciding one's national identity, then what was?

In his answer, D. N. went much further than the previous author, who still took into account lineage and blood relations. According to D. N., the only thing that mattered, the foundation on which we build "life and progress of a nation," was not faith or even language, but a "conscious feeling of national belonging," that is national consciousness. Such an approach to national identity that did not prioritize ethnicity, language, and faith was rare in Ukrainian circles at the time. The author's definition of national identity followed a practical goal. Besides *latynnyky* he was also interested in so-called Zaveprianska Ukraine, that is, the region by the river

---

624 Ibidem.
625 Ibidem.

Wierpz (one of the Vistula's tributaries). According to Ukrainian historians, whom he trusted, this region was once a part of the Halych-Volyn state but was lost to the Polish kingdom in 1302. The local population of this region, the author claimed, was ethnically Ukrainian, but it had been Polonized and Latinized already by the beginning of the 19th century. They no longer remembered the Ukrainian language and most Ukrainian traditions; only a vague sense of distinct identity separated them from neighboring Masurians. Yet through "our theater, our song, our press, and ... our cultural, ideological work," they and their "orphaned" land could be returned to Ukraine, thus restoring the Polish-Ukrainian border along the Vistula, which was a "just and natural boundary" between the two nations.[626]

The anonymous author of "Pidliashshia nashe" (Podlasie is ours) wrote about the same group—Roman Catholic Ukrainian peasants—in a much more pessimistic tone despite the assertive title. Since the Roman Catholic church in the region was dominated by the Polish clergy, a religious conversion from the Orthodox or Greek Catholic to the Roman Catholic faith usually resulted in a national conversion from Ukrainian to Pole. The Polish *księdzy* would teach the converts "that becoming a Catholic is becoming a Pole, which means becoming an enemy of everything non-Catholic and non-Polish." Thus, our "blood brothers" would turn against the Ukrainian national cause. The article implied that as long as *latynnyky* remained Roman Catholics, they would remain easy prey for Polonization. The author warned that if these "confused" (*zbalamucheni*) converts will not return "to their own people," they will disappear "in the Polish sea."[627] It is worth mentioning that most of the time, *Krakivski Visti* described the Polish Roman Catholic church as a stronghold of anti-Ukrainian sentiment in interwar Poland: a Polish monastery was a "nest of [anti-Ukrainian] hate,"[628] the Polish Felician Sisters were more Polish chauvinists than nuns, etc.[629]

---

626 Ibidem.
627 "Pidliashshia nashe," *Krakivski Visti*, no. 64 July 15, 1940, 9.
628 "Polskyi manastyr hnizdom nenavysty ta brudu," *Krakivski Visti*, no. 10 February 11, 1940, 3.
629 "Oraty i siiaty musymo perelih," *Krakivski Visti*, no. 40 May 19, 1940, 6.

While most authors who wrote about *latynnyky* used the term in the established sense—Roman Catholic peasants who used Ukrainian in everyday life—at least one author, Ivan Nimchuk (1891-1956), for some reason tried to expand it to the urban population as well. In a series of four articles under the misleading title "Shche pro lvivskykh rymo-katolykiv" (Once more about Lviv Roman Catholics) he wrote about Greek Catholics, presumably all Ukrainians, who converted to Roman Catholicism in Lviv in 1919-1939.[630] In his opinion, they were *latynnyky* as well, which was a rather strange claim since these converts lived in the city and Nimchuk had no proof that they kept their everyday communication in Ukrainian.[631] Most of the text is a close reading of statistics from three Lviv Greek Catholic parishes during the abovementioned period, showing how many Greek Catholic faithful officially changed to the Latin rite per year. The point of this arithmetic exercise was revealed in the last article of the series, in which Nimchuk tried to extrapolate his findings (10,139 converts) onto seven other Greek Catholic parishes of Lviv, for which he had no data. He estimated that at least 15,000 Lviv Greek Catholics converted to Roman Catholicism during the interwar period. He guessed that for the period of 1880-1919 the number would be at least 10,000, so for the two periods combined the total would be at least 25,000. Taking into account possible demographic growth from these converts, which he also based on a guess, he doubled it to at least 50,000. "Now let's remember," wrote Nimchuk, that contemporary Lviv had around 80,000 Ukrainians and 150,000 Poles. If Ukrainians could regain those "lost" 50,000, the numbers would be respectively at 130,000 and 100,000, meaning that Lviv would have a Ukrainian demographic majority and thus the city would be under its control.[632]

---

630 I. N. [Ivan Nimchuk], "Shche pro lvivskykh rymo-katolykiv," *Krakivski Visti*, no. 73 (811) April 7, 1943, 2; no. 78 (816) April 14, 1943, 2; no. 80 (818) April 16, 1943, 2; no. 82 (820) April 18, 1943, 2-3.
631 I. N. [Ivan Nimchuk], "Shche pro lvivskykh rymo-katolykiv," *Krakivski Visti*, no. 73 (811) April 7, 1943, 2.
632 I. N. [Ivan Nimchuk], "Shche pro lvivskykh rymo-katolykiv," *Krakivski Visti*, no. 82 (820) April 18, 1943, 2

Could Ukrainians regain those "lost" converts? Nimchuk was not optimistic: the fight for the national identity of these people was "essentially a competition between two cultures," Polish and Ukrainian, and he implied that the latter was a much weaker contender. This was evident from a broad list of changes he thought it needed to go through just to reach an equal footing in the competition, which involved book publishing, theatre, sports, philanthropy, etc. But most importantly, Ukrainians, in his opinion, had to get rid of their "primitive, parochial approach" to matters of great importance and lose their strong feelings of "inferiority."[633] The Ukrainian Greek Catholic Church also must get involved in this reclamation process because its negligence was one of the reasons why so many Ukrainians had converted to Roman Catholicism in the first place.[634]

Mixed marriages

The issue of *latynnyky* was closely tied to discussions of mixed marriages between Ukrainians and Poles in Galicia. Historically, such intermarriages were a significant phenomenon (going back to the medieval period), steadily increasing through the Habsburg period with the growth of the urban population. A Ukrainian author in the early 1900s estimated that one-third of Roman Catholics in Galicia came from mixed marriages between Poles and Ukrainians.[635] This reality was reflected by a slightly exaggerated contemporary statement that the Polish-Ukrainian border in Galicia lay not through geographical space, but through the marriage bed.[636] In Lviv alone, on the eve of World War I, marriages between Greek Catholics and Roman Catholics constituted almost 17% of all marriages in the city. As Polish-Ukrainian relations in Galicia took a turn for the worse after 1918 due to the war between Poland and the Western Ukrainian People's Republic, so did the rate of marriages between the two

---

633 Ibidem.
634 Ibidem, 3.
635 Pavlyshyn, "Dylema identychnosty," 186.
636 Ivan L. Rudnytsky, *Essays in Modern Ukrainian History* ed. Peter L. Rudnytsky (Edmonton: Canadian Institute of Ukrainian Studies, 1987), 326.

UKRAINIAN HISTORY, HISTORICAL MEMORY AND NATION 183

ethnic groups, dropping to 5% in Lviv in 1922. But the mutual gravitation between the two groups must have been too strong to break because even in the unfavorable conditions of interwar Poland, which treated Ukrainians (and other minorities) as second-class citizens, the rate of mixed marriages between Ukrainians and Poles kept rebounding, eventually reaching 12% in Lviv on the eve of World War II.[637]

A discussion about mixed marriages developed on the pages of *Krakivski Visti* in 1943, that is, in the same year when Polish-Ukrainian enmity exploded into mutual ethnic cleansings and assassinations. In this paroxysm of violence mixed families were often singled out.[638] Based on the editorial archive, it does not seem that these submissions were instigated or orchestrated by the editors: they were written out of genuine concern for the issue of mixed marriages. In terms of tone, the articles ranged from calm and measured to alarmist, but all of them described mixed marriages as a negative phenomenon in Ukrainian national life.[639] Four authors — Antin Chernetskyi, Myron Konovalets, Ivan Mirchuk and Ivan Nimchuk — took part in the discussion.

The discussion was started off by Antin Chernetskyi's article "Denatsionaliztsiia i urbanizatsiia" (Denationalization and urbanization), which touched on mixed marriages in the urban environment.[640] According to him, ethnically mixed families were a major

---

637 Mick, *Lemberg, Lwów, L'viv*, 212.
638 Witold Szabłowski in his book "Sprawiedliwi zdrajcy. Sąsiedzi z Wołynia" (2016) described cases when UPA soldiers in Volhynia in 1943, upon encountering mixed families, often ordered Ukrainians from these families to murder their Polish relatives. See: http://www.istpravda.com.ua/articles/57ec59cac001f/ (last accessed October 16, 2018).
639 In his memoirs Kubijovyč described his own mixed marriage (with a Polish woman) as a negative experience: "[Our] marriage was not smart and did not bring happiness to either partner. ... [we] soon came to conflicts: a wall rose between us since we belonged to two increasingly hostile nations. The mixed marriage was not good for the children either: the parents fought for national soul of their two daughters." See: Kubijovyč, *Meni 85*, 53.
640 A. Chernetskyi, "Denatsionaliztsiia i urbanizatsiia," *Krakivski Visti*, no. 11 (749) January 22, 1943, 1-2. This was not the only article that Chernetskyi wrote for *Krakivski Visti*. However, in his memoir written after the war he made no mention of his wartime articles or even of the newspaper. See: Antin Chernetskyi, *Spomyny z moho zhyttia* (Kyiv: Osnovni tsinnosti, 2001).

factor of Ukrainian denationalization in Galician towns and cities: usually, children from such families were not only "lost" to Ukrainianness (*ukrainstvo*) but would often become its "most ardent enemies."[641] Chernetskyi wrote that he could understand why Ukrainians of the "old age" (most likely, he meant the pre-1848 period) allowed themselves to marry non-Ukrainians, but he could not comprehend how such a "marvel" continued to happen in recent decades, "even among participants of the liberation struggle [of 1917-1920] and so-called nationalists." Here, Chernetskyi hinted at Ukrainian socialist leader Volodymyr Vynnychenko (1880-1951), who was married to a Jewish woman (Rozaliia Vynnychenko), and several prominent OUN members who were married to non-Ukrainians. Mixed families were a danger to a Ukrainian identity: they provided easier access to "alien language, press and books, alien culture, leading to ideas that were alien [and] hostile to us." Cities had always been "mostly an alien environment" for Ukrainians, stressed Chernetskyi, and "[Ukrainian] family and tradition" were the only means through which they could be "shielded" against urban denationalizing influence.[642]

Chernetskyi's article prompted a reaction from Ukrainian education activist Myron Konovalets (1894-1980), brother of Yevhen Konovalets.[643] In his article "Mishani podruzhzhia" (Mixed marriages) Konovalets agreed that mixed marriages between Poles and Ukrainians, with extremely rare exceptions, had always worked in

---

641 A. Chernetskyi, "Denatsionaliztsia i urbanizatsia," *Krakivski Visti*, no. 11 (749) January 22, 1943, 2. Interestingly, this observation echoed almost word for word one of the ten commandments of Ukrainian nationalist Mykola Mikhnovskyi that he wrote for the members of his leftist Ukrainian People's Party (Ukrainska narodna partiia) in 1903: "Do not take a wife from foreigners [chuzhyntsiv], for your children will be your enemies." See: Mykola Mikhnovskyi, *Suspilno-politychni tvory* (Kyiv: Smoloskyp, 2015), 212. The commandments are often regarded as a program document of modern Ukrainian nationalism.
642 Ibidem. He also wrote on the subject of how the Ukrainian national movement failed to spread in cities in his memoir, see: Chernetskyi, *Spomyny z moho zhyttia*, 157.
643 Myron K. [Myron Konovalets], "Mishani podruzhzhia," *Krakivski Visti*, no. 68 (806) April 1, 1943, 2; no. 69 (807) April 2, 1943, 2. In their internal documentation the newspaper's editors referred to Myron Konovalets as "Komisar Myron" (Commissar Myron). See: PAA, Michael Chomiak fonds, File PR1985.0191/32.

favor of the Polish nation and "contributed the most" toward Polonization of "our cities." In either case, whether the wife or husband was Roman Catholic, the result was usually the same—Polonization of the new family. The major difference was only in the length of the process: it usually happened faster in families with a Roman Catholic husband since normally the wife would convert to his faith even before the marriage. It is no surprise, wrote Konovalets, that Polish society historically has always been in favor of mixed marriages with Ukrainians: this was how the latter lost its "princes and boyars, *shliakhta* and petty bourgeoise" and became a nation of peasants.[644]

Konovalets, however, did not settle for yet another description of how the poor Ukrainians have been taken advantage of by their neighbor. He was interested in finding the root cause: why did mixed marriages in the urban environment always work in the Poles' favor? Konovalets suggested that the major, underlying reason was the Ukrainian feeling of "inferiority" in the Polish presence. This could be seen through language practice: when in a city a group of Ukrainians was joined by just one Pole, they would find it absolutely natural to switch the whole conversation "immediately to the Polish language." The social status of these Ukrainians was irrelevant—simple workers or members of the intelligentsia with university degrees—all would drop the Ukrainian language in the presence of Poles. The same applied to mixed marriages in cities. As a rule, all of them "almost exclusively" spoke Polish at home. Only in villages, "among the people," did Ukrainians continue to retain their language.[645]

Konovalets also blamed past leaders of the Ukrainian national movement and the Greek Catholic church for this dire situation with mixed marriages. "During Austrian times," the national activists and clergy were so focused on the "village" that they neglected Ukrainization of the "city." They did not oppose mixed marriages, which allowed for the slow Polonization of "our cities." Ukrainian

---

644 Myron K. [Myron Konovalets], "Mishani podruzhzhia," *Krakivski Visti*, no. 68 (806) April 1, 1943, 2.
645 Ibidem.

leaders awoke to this problem only after they lost the Polish-Ukrainian War of 1918-1919. What Konovalets meant here was that during the war most Galician cities and towns, due to their demographic composition, were on the Polish side or were easily swayed to it.[646] The interwar Polish regime rendered the situation with mixed marriages even worse for Ukrainians, wrote Konovalets. "Under Austria" one of the principal customs that regulated mixed marriages between Greek and Roman Catholics was that sons followed their father's faith, daughters—their mother's. Under the Polish regime this practice was broken: in most cases children of both genders from mixed marriages were baptized in the Roman Catholic church. But even those that were baptized as Greek Catholics would usually convert later: normally one of the parents would raise them "in the Polish spirit, in disdain for everything Ukrainian," but even without parental influence, the Polish-speaking "school, street, workplace and so on" would accomplish the same. The exceptions, which against all odds would somehow grow up into conscious Ukrainians, often had to deal with the Polish "chauvinism" of their close and distant relatives, leading to family tragedies.[647]

Besides Polish relatives, mixed families also suffered "misery" from their children, who were "embarrassed" by the fact that one of their parents was a Greek Catholic. Such children would emotionally "terrorize" their parent into conversion so that they did not have to live in "shame." Konovalets told a story about a funeral he witnessed in a Galician town not long before September 1939. The deceased, whom the whole town knew as a Pole, was buried by Greek Catholic priests to the surprise of the locals. It turned out that he was a closet Greek Catholic and only pretended to be a Roman Catholic under pressure from his wife and sons. The latter, officers of the Polish Army and other Polish relatives of the deceased in the funeral procession seemed to Konovalets more distressed (*prybyti*)

---

646 Ibidem.
647 Ibidem.

by the revelation of his true religious affiliation than by the fact of his death.[648]

The next question pondered by Konovalets was what made Ukrainians eager to marry Poles.[649] He did not consider the cultural proximity of the two ethnic groups (some cultures are closer than others), but instead offered the following three explanations. First, the naivete and emotional inexperience of young Ukrainian men who arrived from Ukrainian villages to study in cities. In most cases, such students would end up with Polish landladies, who often had daughters. Clever Polish mothers often used this renting situation to select a suitable husband for their daughters. This was how many Ukrainian men were "lost," wrote Konovalets, as if he were describing a battlefield.[650] Konovalets's first explanation repeated a very popular trope from Ukrainian accounts on the history of Polish-Ukrainian relations: cunning Poles taking advantage of naïve Ukrainians.

The second reason why Ukrainians sought marriages with Poles, according to Konovalets, was rooted in a desire for titles and stable income. "We are not a wealthy nation, even poor in comparison to some nations, but we have more ... directors, doctors, colonels and so on than the wealthiest state nations [*derzhavni narody*]." This obsession with titles (*tytulomaniia*) made young Ukrainian women in cities consider a Polish official or policeman a more desirable candidate than a Ukrainian artisan, even if the latter was doing well financially. But marrying him would be considered by Ukrainian women as a "great misfortune" (*velyke neshchastia*) because an artisan had neither title nor guaranteed state pension. During the interwar period Galicia was densely covered by Polish military garrisons, claimed Konovalets. As a result, many Ukrainian

---

648 Myron K. [Myron Konovalets], "Mishani podruzhzhia," *Krakivski Visti*, no. 69 (807) April 2, 1943, 2.
649 Incidentally, the occupation authorities also investigated the issue of Polish-Ukrainian marriages. In 1944 they issued a circular that declared them undesirable because they did not weaken the Polish presence in the General Government as their children "were normally brought up as Poles." See: Majer, *"Non-Germans" under the Third Reich*, 310.
650 Myron K. [Myron Konovalets], "Mishani podruzhzhia," *Krakivski Visti*, no. 69 (807) April 2, 1943, 2.

women chose to marry Polish NCOs rather than Ukrainian men. The former had a title and a stable income, while the latter suffered from a high rate of unemployment.[651]

The situation could have been rectified by marriages of these women with Greek Catholic priests, but at this time they were under orders of celibacy. Here, Konovalets referred to the decision of the Ukrainian Greek Catholic hierarchs on September 20, 1919, to make celibacy mandatory for priests in the church. The decision was not enforced in all eparchies.[652] But Konovalets claimed that it affected the whole priesthood of the Ukrainian Greek Catholic Church. Historically, he added, Greek Catholic priest families produced the best "Ukrainian intelligentsia."[653] The third reason why Ukrainians married Poles was a direct result of the Polish regime's policy of transfers. The regime intentionally took the best cadres of Ukrainians—teachers and officials—out of Western Ukraine and transferred them into ethnic Polish provinces where they naturally ended up marrying Polish locals. Konovalets advocated for a reversal of this policy of transfers so that these Ukrainians and their children could be "saved for the Ukrainian nation." Otherwise, they would disappear into the "Polish sea."[654]

The negative effects of mixed marriages on the Ukrainian nation, according to Konovalets, went beyond the usual claims of denationalization and Polonization. The marriages cost "us" material wealth—Ukrainian women marrying Poles often came with real estate and financial capital, accumulated by several generations of Ukrainian petty bourgeoisie. Thus, mixed marriages became a contributing factor toward the pauperization of Ukrainians, turning

---

651 Ibidem.
652 Oleh Yehreshii, *Yepyskop Hryhorii Khomyshyn: portret reliihno-tserkovnoho i hromadsko-politychnoho diiacha* (Ivano-Frankivsk: Nova Zoria, 2006), 54.
653 Myron K. [Myron Konovalets], "Mishani podruzhzhia," *Krakivski Visti*, no. 69 (807) April 2, 1943, 2. On the connection between Greek Catholic and Ukrainian identity in Galicia see: John-Paul Himka, *Religion and Nationality in Western Ukraine: The Greek Catholic Church and the Ruthenian National Movement in Galicia, 1867-1900* (Montreal; Kingston, Ontario; London; Ithaca: McGill-Queen's University Press, 1999).
654 Myron K. [Myron Konovalets], "Mishani podruzhzhia," *Krakivski Visti*, no. 69 (807) April 2, 1943, 2.

them into "grey proletarianized masses," more and more financially dependent on Poles and Jews. Konovalets concluded the article on a pessimistic note: Ukrainians still suffer from an "inferiority complex," and mixed marriages will continue to pose a "depopulating" threat "for a long time." To become an urban nation Ukrainians would have "to remove" previous "failures," among which Konovalets counted the phenomenon of "mixed marriages."[655]

The third contribution to the discussion of mixed marriages was "Nemalovazhne pytannia" (An important question) by the Ukrainian philosopher Ivan Mirchuk (1891-1961), written in direct response to Myron Konovalets's article discussed above.[656] The author agreed with Konovalets on all points, especially with his thesis of the "inferiority complex" as the primary reason why most mixed marriages turned out to be a national loss for Ukrainians. Since Konovalets had limited his discussion on the subject of marriages to "Western [Ukrainian] lands," Mirchuk sought to complement the thesis and demonstrate that Ukrainians suffered from an "inferiority complex" in relations not only with their "closest neighbor" (Poles) but "other nations" as well. He proposed to look at Ukrainian male students who studied at major centers of Ukrainian interwar emigration—Berlin, Vienna and Prague. "Thousands" of these students could not return back to their "native lands," so they stayed in Western Europe and married local women (*chuzhynky*). Mirchuk, who taught at Ukrainian émigré institutions in all three cities, claimed that he observed "hundreds" of these marriages, and they allowed him to postulate a "law," from which he saw "almost no exceptions."[657]

Mirchuk's "law" was simple: young Ukrainian men did not have the ability to make a good marital choice. The "foreign women" they chose were "neither pretty nor educated," and usually, they were not from families of higher "material or social" standing. According to Mirchuk, this was not a minor issue because

---

655 Ibidem.
656 I. M. [Ivan Mirchuk], "Nemalovazhne pytannia," *Krakivski Visti*, no. 122 (860) June 9, 1943, 1-2.
657 Ibidem, 1.

these poor marital choices had "long-term consequences for the future fate of the whole nation." It was an "absolute need" for the "stateless [Ukrainian] nation" to develop "connections" in political, art and academic circles of foreign countries. But the poor marital choices of young Ukrainian males ignored this "need."[658] Ukrainians often excused a poor marital choice by saying that marriage was an "individual thing." Mirchuk claimed that this "individualism" was born out of "Ukrainian spirituality," but in his opinion, individualism had no place "in the present time or under our [national] conditions." Both demanded subordination of individual desires to the collective need: "a human being does not live a separate life, it can develop only as part of collective, whose needs must be an internal imperative for an individual."[659]

Mirchuk clarified further that he did not propose for Ukrainian society to force marital choices on individuals, only that "education must go in the direction ... of individual desires attuning to the collective need."[660] Unfortunately, achieving such attunement, in his opinion, would be difficult because of the key component of the Ukrainian national character — "the superiority of the emotional element over pure rationality." It was normal to follow your heart in pursuit of marriage, wrote Mirchuk, but that should not mean ignoring your reason (*rozum*). Emotions often deceive and lead to delusions, while "intellect" offers a "sober and realistic" look at the world. Ignoring the "voice of reason" was "dangerous not only for an individual but for a [national] collective too," and on the issue of mixed marriages, Ukrainian youth, concluded Mirchuk, must learn to care for their individual desires without neglecting the needs of the national collective.[661]

---

658 Ibidem.
659 Ibidem, 2.
660 Ibidem.
661 Ibidem. Khomiak thanked Mirchuk for writing the article: "Heartfelt thanks for the very interesting article about mixed marriages. It will surely cause a lot of commotion among our various dignitaries. It was high time to address this extremely important issue and warn the youth against such foolishness. Let's hope that [our] youth will truly reflect on this critical matter." See: Letter from Mykhailo Khomiak to Ivan Mirchuk June 10, 1943. PAA, Michael Chomiak fonds, File PR1985.0191/40.

Mirchuk's article elicited the fourth and last contribution to the discussion—"Pora spynyty opust krovy!" (It is time to stop the loss of blood!) by the same Ivan Nimchuk.[662] The author agreed with Mirchuk's "law" that young Ukrainian males indeed make poor marital choices when it comes to foreign women and repeated his words about the women's lack of beauty, education, social status or wealth. Nimchuk lamented these marriages (the whole article is rather emotional) and blamed them for the alienation of "not hundreds or thousands, but dozens of thousands" of talented and educated Ukrainians from the "Ukrainian nation." Nimchuk's proof of this alienation was the contribution of these men to the "treasury of Ukrainian culture"—"none" in his words. You could not find these Ukrainians abroad, wrote Nimchuk, among financial donors for "Ukrainian national goals" or even among subscribers to Ukrainian periodicals. During the interwar period, the main Galician newspaper *Dilo* (Nimchuk was its last chief editor in 1935-39) had around 10 subscribers in Vienna and even fewer in Prague or Berlin. If such men could not bring themselves to support the "Ukrainian cause," what could we expect from "their children"? Nimchuk believed that they looked "with disdain" on the "Ukrainian nation," or at very best, they were "indifferent" toward it.[663]

From lamentation Nimchuk proceeded to explanation. Why did so many Ukrainian young men living or studying abroad end up marrying foreign women who, in all respects—from physical attractiveness to social status—stood "lower" than them? Nimchuk provided the same answer he did in his article about Lviv Roman Catholics[664] and other authors in the discussion about mixed marriages—"feelings of [Ukrainian] inferiority." Nimchuk claimed to know "many examples" of talented Ukrainian young men who were expected to become "leading individuals" of Ukrainian life abroad and who married the "first available" foreign woman— "waitress, florist or seamstress"—sometimes even with "not the

---

662 I. N. [Ivan Nimchuk], "Pora spynyty opust krovy!" *Krakivski Visti*, no. 129 (867) June 19, 1943, 1-2.
663 Ibidem, 1.
664 I. N. [Ivan Nimchuk], "Shche pro lvivskykh rymo-katolykiv," *Krakivski Visti*, no. 82 (820) April 18, 1943, 2.

best fame among informed youth" (most likely, this was a hint about their sexual reputation). All appeals to "reason" against such mésalliance usually would be turned away by the "stubborn Rusyn."[665] In other words, Nimchuk here repeated Mirchuk's argument about emotion subjugating reason as a primary feature of the Ukrainian psyche. After marrying these women, Ukrainian men would separate themselves from "our organized life" and "disappear" into the foreign nation.[666]

To illustrate this point, Nimchuk told a personal story of his acquaintance, a Ukrainian medical doctor who studied in Vienna before World War I and stayed in the city afterward. After the war, when Vienna and his native Galicia ended up in different states, he decided to organize other Ukrainian doctors in the city into a local chapter of the Lviv-based Ukrainian Physicians' Association (Ukrainske Likarske Tovarytsvo). All of the doctors, around twenty, were married to foreign women and none had any interest in belonging to or participating in a Ukrainian professional organization. "Their Ukrainianness extended only to their last names," wrote Nimchuk.[667] According to him, most of these doctors were sons of wealthy Galician Ukrainian priests and peasants: their parents had spent their life savings to give them an education in such an expensive city as Vienna.

For Nimchuk, this story of how hard-earned Ukrainian wealth and educated talent were so easily lost because of marriages to foreign women exemplified the whole tragedy of mixed marriages for the Ukrainian national cause.[668] Why had none of these doctors and other Ukrainians like them married Ukrainian women who were studying in Vienna (in smaller numbers) at the same time? What made them go after a "waitress or florist" rather than an educated Ukrainian woman? Nimchuk's answer was that "a Ukrainian [man] abroad avoided [such women]—he simply was afraid and ran away from an intelligent [Ukrainian] woman." He did not unpack

---

665 "Stubborn Rusyn" is a phrase from Ivan Franko's play "Uchytel" (1893).
666 I. N. [Ivan Nimchuk], "Pora spynyty opust krovy!" *Krakivski Visti*, no. 129 (867) June 19, 1943, 1.
667 Ibidem, 2.
668 Ibidem.

this answer, but it generally fitted with the diagnosis of an "inferiority complex."⁶⁶⁹

From explanation Nimchuk moved to solution. "This damned law [of mixed marriages] must be broken." Like other authors in the discussion, Nimchuk viewed mixed marriages as a dangerous enough threat to Ukrainian national development that they needed to be taken seriously. "Uneven" mixed marriages of Ukrainians abroad with lower women or mixed marriages abroad in general "should not be allowed to happen." Nimchuk proposed two policies. First, "both at home and school, we need to reeducate ... Ukrainian youth" in the sense that "any sense of inferiority, of being somehow lower, timidity, stupefaction [*zaturkanosty*] must be eliminated among them."⁶⁷⁰ Their education must be focused toward raising a "sense of national pride, we need to teach the younger generation not only to love, but to treasure the Ukrainian past and our cultural values."⁶⁷¹ His second policy recommendation was far less theoretical. Nimchuk proposed that two Ukrainian institutions that financed the education of many Ukrainians abroad — the Ukrainian Students' Aid Commission (KoDUS) and its parent organization, the UCC — should start monitoring "this matter [of mixed marriages] with the utmost attention" with regard to Ukrainian students receiving their stipends and should steer their marital choice in the correct direction, "just as Bulgarians and Japanese do with their own youth abroad."⁶⁷² Ultimately, this was a matter of Ukrainian national welfare both figuratively and literally. "We [as a nation] are too poor to allow ... this decades-long blood loss [of mixed marriages] to continue. It is time to stop it!"⁶⁷³

Krakivski Visti returned to the subject of mixed marriages with a long article once more in 1944. Marriages of young Ukrainians (male or female) were a matter of national importance, claimed Yurii Koshelnyk in his article "Mitsna simia — mitsna natsiia"

---

669 Ibidem.
670 Ibidem.
671 Ibidem.
672 Ibidem.
673 Ibidem.

(Strong family—strong nation).[674] A "national organism" was nothing more than a collective of families—"national cells." The stronger and healthier these "cells" were, the stronger and healthier was the nation made of them. This was the reason, wrote Koshelnyk, why marital choice could not be left "to follow a natural course [*na samoplyv*]," that is, allowing young people to marry whomever they want. The author turned to distant and recent history to prove his point. "Cultured people" understood the need "to regulate marriages" from "ancient times" and so did the Christian Church throughout its history. According to him, it was no accident that the Bolsheviks propagated unlimited "free love" and "freedom of marriage": the ruin of families meant the ruin of nations, which was the goal of "their internationalism." These Bolshevik policies resulted in the "reduction of the birthrate, an increase in the homeless population, prostitution and venereal disease" in the Soviet Union.

In addition, Soviet marriages became "internationalized": Ukrainians marrying "Russians, Poles, Jews" became a common thing. "[Soviet] Jews especially promoted love and marriages between individuals of different nations and races." Koshelnyk looked at "international" families as an aberration in a world where nations are supposed to be the norm: these families, according to him, almost never lived in harmony because they had conflicts within themselves about their national belonging. "Children from such families are very difficult to raise in a national spirit."[675] The author compared the Soviet practice of the "international" family with the Nazi practice of the "national" family. The latter received high praise from him: "the German people understood a long time ago the anti-national character of mixed marriages." Contemporary Germany, Koshelnyk wrote in reference to the Nuremberg laws of 1935, has a law regulating marriages, forbidding unions between Aryans and non-Aryans. The author advocated the same measure of top-down marriage regulation for the Ukrainian nation as well: "we ... would benefit from borrowing this foreign experience."

---

674 Yu. Koshelnyk, "Mitsna simia—mitsna natsiia," *Krakivski Visti*, no. 108 (1141) May 20, 1944, 1-2.
675 Ibidem, 1.

Unfortunately, he wrote, since Ukrainians did not have their own state at the time, they could not pass any state laws. "But this does not mean that such an important question as the marriages of our youth should be left to fate." The marital choices of Ukrainian youth needed to be controlled, concluded Koshelnyk, because some among them still did not understand the "anti-Ukrainian character of mixed marriages."[676]

A unique and fresh perspective on Polish-Ukrainian mixed marriages was offered by an article that appeared in January 1943, that is, before the discussion. Titled "Deshcho pro prychyny denatsionalizatsii" (A comment on the reasons of denationalization), it was written by Denys Savaryn (1902-?), who for some time worked as an editor at *Krakivski Visti*.[677] It was an autobiographical piece in which the author described his experience of growing up in a mixed family with a nationally conscious Ukrainian father and a Polonized German mother.[678] Following the rule of such marriages, he was baptized in his father's faith (Greek Catholicism), while his sisters — in his mother's (Roman Catholicism), which automatically made them "Poles in the understanding of the time."[679] *Krakivski Visti* usually described Polonization as a top-down process forced by "cunning" and "brutal" Polonizers (priests, officials, teachers, etc.) upon the Ukrainian masses. But this article is remarkable by its candid and calm view on Polonization from below. The author felt strong "Polonizing influences," both inside and outside his family while growing up, but none of those influences were, in his view, forced on him. It was "usual," he wrote, that in mixed Polish-Ukrainian families, one half eventually assimilated the other, but both his mother and sisters respected his choice of Ukrainian identity and none of them tried to "tug" him over to their

---

676 Ibidem.
677 According to the editorial chronicle he worked as an editor from February 15, 1943 until the newspaper's move to Vienna in October 1944: "Chleny Redaktsii 'Krakivskykh Vistei' i spivrobitnyky." PAA, Michael Chomiak fonds, File PR1985.0191/23.
678 D. S. [Denys Savaryn], "Deshcho pro prychyny denatsionalizatsii," *Krakivski Visti*, no. 3 (741) January 5, 1943, 2.
679 Ibidem.

national side. Similarly, nothing was forcing Polish identity on him in his social life.

The author's experience of those "Polonizing influences" came, as we would say today, from exposure to the soft power of Polonization: Polish culture (especially literature), which the author in no vague terms described as far superior to Ukrainian both in terms of literary quality and entertainment value. Since he was from a mixed family, both worlds—Polish and Ukrainian—were equally open to him. But the former was far more "attractive." His Ukrainian school friends were less "polished" and less "cultured" compared to his Polish friends. Polish books were even more superior: there was a wider selection of them (including translations), they were better written, more interesting and "passionately patriotic." Most Ukrainian literature, on the other hand, fell into the victimhood genre: look how "we have been abused" for all these centuries. It offered no "higher ideas." So how, in the end, despite having a Polish mother, sisters, friends, and books, did the author end up choosing a Ukrainian identity? Savaryn was honest: if not for the Ukrainian revolutionary events of 1918, he most likely would not have remained a "conscious Ukrainian."[680]

***

Were the articles on mixed marriages dealing with a genuine issue, or were they a Ukrainian echo of the pan-European paranoia about "blood mixing," which peaked in Nazi Germany, where it was elevated to an official policy? My answer is that they were both. Western Ukrainian society certainly did not escape general European trends before the war, including racial ideas. But there is also evidence to support Mirchuk's and Nimchuk's accusation that *some* Ukrainian men preferred non-Ukrainian women. Roman Volchuk wrote in his memoir that "wider intellectual interests were an exception rather than the norm among our [Western Ukrainian]

---

680 Ibidem.

young women."681 For some men, "intelligence is the ultimate aphrodisiac" (attributed to Timothy Leary). A contemporary of Volchuk, Ivan L. Rudnytsky, was harsher:

> Regarding Ukrainian girls from the intelligentsia in general. They say that the German woman is uninteresting. But from my student years, I recall German female classmates [*tovaryshky*] who were truly extremely interesting young women, real ladies, true world-class intellectuals, girls of immense energy and ability ("Tüchtigkeit"), again others possessed a genuine culture of the heart ("Innerlichkeit"). The type of the young Galician [Ukrainian] female is something dreadfully goosey and provincial, undeveloped both in brain and heart, uninteresting even as "spoiled."682

Six years later, Rudnytsky, already married to an American woman, returned to the subject in another letter, giving two reasons as to why he was attracted to foreign women. The first reason was social:

> The class, or rather "estate" [*stanovyi*] status, is very important to me. The point is not that my woman [*zhinka*] works in some intellectual profession or has a [university] diploma, but that she must organically belong to the same social formation as me by her mentality, background, etc. I hardly ever found such girls in the Ukrainian world, even among students and girls with [completed] school or university education. The Ukrainian intelligentsia as a stratum [*verstva*] is still very young, uncrystallized, and this lack of style and tradition is even more noticeable in the female half than in the male half.683

In other words, it was a systemic issue of two halves not being equally developed. The second reason was more personal:

> For many years now, I have been living in "two worlds," the Ukrainian and the foreign one. Ukrainian affairs mean a lot to me, but they often depress me with their tragedy and lack of hope; I may be oversensitive to Ukrainian faults, which often make me shudder, as if from some unpleasant dissonance in music. If "being at home" means feeling comfortable, relaxed, free, then I have always been "more at home" among foreigners than among my own. Ukrainianness is rather a responsibility, a duty, even an "obsession,"

---

681 Roman Volchuk, *Spomyny z povoennoi Avstrii ta Nimechchyny* (Kyiv: Krytyka, 2004), 83.
682 Letter from Ivan L. Rudnytsky to Nazar Yasinchuk February 26, 1947. UAA, Ivan L. Rudnytsky fonds, Accession no. 1984-155, File 745.
683 Letter from Ivan L. Rudnytsky to Bohdan Tsymbalistyi June 23, 1953. UAA, Ivan L. Rudnytsky fonds, Accession no. 1984-155, File 755.

> but it has little joy in it. I find balance and rest in the fact that it is the private, family sphere of my life that allows me to maintain a distance from Ukrainian affairs, to prevent myself from being absorbed by them.[684]

It is worth mentioning that Rudnytsky's first marriage fell apart in the early 1960s and ended in divorce in 1966. Two years later he married a Ukrainian émigré woman, who stayed with him until his death in 1984. In any case, his marriage with an American woman was an extremely rare phenomenon in his generation of Ukrainian émigrés.

---

684 Ibidem.

Conclusions

The German occupation of Poland in September 1939 resulted in the creation of the General Government (*Generalgouvernement*), a German colonial entity that, until the end of the war, was headed by a prominent Nazi figure, Hans Frank. The latter developed a set of policies in his domain that exploited and furthered pre-existing ethnic tensions among Jews, Poles and Ukrainians, favoring the latter. Each of the three ethnic groups came to be represented vis-à-vis the occupation authorities by umbrella organizations with headquarters in Cracow. In the case of the Ukrainians, it was the Ukrainian Central Committee (unofficially created in November 1939), led through the war by the prominent Ukrainian geographer Volodymyr Kubijovyč.

The Melnykite faction of the OUN played an important role both in the founding and functioning of the Committee (at least until June 1941). Though Kubijovyč was not a member of the OUN or any other Ukrainian political force, he was a Ukrainian nationalist who sought to elevate Ukrainians as a nation within the legal boundaries set by the occupation authorities. Kubijovyč and people like him were primarily situational, not ideological, collaborators: they worked with and for their German occupiers primarily because of a situation over which they had no control (war and invasion) and not because of some ideological sympathies toward National Socialism, though that also should not imply that they were free of racial or ethnic bias (Kubijovyč certainly was not). One of the important points of Kubijovyč's national program was to have a strong pro-Ukrainian newspaper that would replace the daily *Dilo*, which closed down in September 1939 due to the Soviet occupation of Western Ukraine. The first issue of this new newspaper, which received the name *Krakivski Visti* and was a semi-official organ of the UCC until the end of the war, was dated January 7, 1940. From November 1, 1940 it was issued as a daily and continued in this format until the last, 1406th issue on April 4, 1945 (the last five issues appeared under the name *Ukrainskyi Shliakh*). Except for the first month, the newspaper's chief editor was a former *Dilo* editor, a lawyer by education, Mykhailo Khomiak (he immigrated to Canada in 1948 as Michael Chomiak). However, the main intellectual force among the editors of *Krakivski Visti* was Mariian Kozak, who wrote most of the newspaper's editorials in 1940-1944. A weekly edition of the newspaper was also published from November 1940 until October 1944.

The three major blocks of content In *Krakivski Visti* were war, politics and culture. The newspaper was able to attract contributions from the most prominent Ukrainian intellectuals and cultural figures, especially in 1943-1944. The majority of authors wrote for *Krakivski Visti* for the sake of self-expression, income and status. Due to the advance of the Red Army the newspaper was transferred to Vienna in October 1944. This move proved to be detrimental for *Krakivski Visti*, as it lost the majority of its authors. Throughout the war, the newspaper's reception in the Ukrainian public was rather negative due to its lower intellectual and production quality compared with *Dilo*, but after the war it has been recognized as an important source for the history of Western Ukrainian lands under German occupation.

Ideologically, *Krakivski Visti* was a multi-layered product. On the surface, the newspaper was glazed with the official content of the German occupiers: anti-Semitism, anticommunism, glorification of Germany and other Axis powers (mainly Japan and Italy), praise of National Socialism and its leaders (mainly Hitler), and whatever short- or long-term ideological campaigns were pursued at a given time. Publication of these texts, often translated or summarized from the Axis press, was a price the newspaper paid for its existence under German occupation. In general, *Krakivski Visti* did not deviate from the official ideological direction set by the German authorities. However, underneath it contained its own original ideological layer—to be fair, it existed only because the Germans allowed it—of loyalist Ukrainian nationalism, which was realized primarily through two groups of texts. The first was texts that informed and reminded readers of the newspaper about historical enemies of the Ukrainian nation—Poles, Jews, Russians/Soviets. The second comprised texts that educated readers on Ukrainian history, historical memory, historical figures (Shevchenko, Franko,

Shashkevych) and discussed national issues (such as *latynnyky* or mixed marriages).

The first group of texts overlapped with one of the primary goals of the German authorities in the General Government: to put its multiethnic population through a "school of hate," that is, propaganda of negative ethnic stereotypes and ethnic hatred aimed at dividing the population along ethnic lines and forming attitudes based on group identity. Anti-Semitism constituted the core of German propaganda in the General Government for the entirety of its existence. At the beginning of the German occupation, official propaganda also engaged with the Poles, primarily to convince them that their prewar state was unviable. The Soviets were a blind spot until June 22, 1941 after which they were returned to their usual Nazi category of Judeobolshevism—the mortal enemy of the Aryan race. On the surface, the original texts of *Krakivski Visti*, texts that represented its own ideological layer, followed Nazi propaganda: they also attacked Jews, Poles and Soviets. However, it would be superficial to assume, just because of this, that *Krakivski Visti* was a "Nazi" newspaper. Nuance matters: these original texts engaged in campaigns against Jews, Poles and Russians/Soviets for reasons that had little or nothing to do with National Socialism.

Krakivski Visti's first campaign was directed at Poles. To a large extent it was a release of resentment for the previous two decades of Polish rule over Western Ukrainians, which treated them as second-class citizens. Ironically, the leading role in the campaign was played by members of the Western Ukrainian party—UNDO—which before the war had attempted to reach a modus vivendi with the Polish state (the normalization of 1935). Two prominent UNDO members, Ivan Kedryn and Stepan Baran, wrote a series of anti-Polish articles each. Kedryn's series was also republished as a book. Besides the sophisticated series of Kedryn and Baran, *Krakivski Visti* also published plenty of primitive texts that were vehemently anti-Polish and often lowered themselves to name-calling. Polishness was presented as antithetical to the values of justice and order. Some Ukrainian authors essentially desired a reversal of the prewar situation and advocated anti-Polish measures just for the sake of Ukrainians' benefit.

Anti-Polish materials were significantly reduced in frequency after June 1941 when the primary focus was shifted to anti-Soviet propaganda due to the German invasion of the Soviet Union. Again, *Krakivski Visti*'s authors had their own reasons to attack the Soviets: two famines (1921-1922 and 1932-1933), collectivization, Stalinist purges and Russification of the 1930s, deportations of 1939-1941 and the June 1941 Soviet massacre of prisoners in Western Ukraine. Unlike Nazi propaganda the original Ukrainian texts identified the Soviet Union with Russians in the first place, not Jews, though the latter also appeared in them. The main themes of the anti-Soviet materials were the civilizational divide between Ukrainians and Russians/Soviets and the inhumane crimes that the latter committed against the former. On two occasions, *Krakivski Visti* ran specific campaigns covering such crimes—the Soviet prison murders of 1941 and the Vinnytsia massacres of 1937—in July-August 1941 and June-September 1943, respectively. In both campaigns victims and perpetrators were ethnicized: the former as Ukrainians and the latter as Russians and Jews. In reality, at least one-third of the victims were non-Ukrainians, and some Ukrainians must certainly have been among the perpetrators.

Besides the two campaigns of 1941 and 1943, *Krakivski Visti* had published hundreds of anti-Soviet articles by the end of the war. Among them was a remarkable series on the history of Bolshevik terror against the Ukrainian nation by the outstanding Ukrainian poet and essayist Evhen Malaniuk. The main themes of his series—Ukrainians shielded Europe from Bolshevism; terror is the essence of Bolshevism; the famines of 1921-1922 and 1932-1933 were manmade; Bolshevik actions against various Ukrainian social groups were part of a single anti-Ukrainian policy—became cornerstones of the Ukrainian martyrology developed in the Ukrainian diaspora in the West during the Cold War.

While anti-Polish texts appeared in *Krakivski Visti* mostly before the German invasion of the Soviet Union and anti-Russian/Soviet texts only after the invasion, the anti-Jewish materials were printed throughout the whole time. Again, besides the official anti-Semitic propaganda, mostly republished from the foreign (usually Axis) press, the newspaper featured original solicited and unsolicited articles written by Ukrainian authors. The primary case of the solicited materials was the campaign of summer 1943, when *Krakivski Visti* was ordered by the occupation authorities to publish a series of anti-Semitic materials. Five Ukrainian authors contributed to the campaign—Oleksander Mokh, Kost Kuzyk, Olena Kysilevska, Luka Lutsiv and Oleksander Mytsiuk. But even without the campaign, the newspaper featured enough original anti-Semitic content submitted by Ukrainian authors, for example, Vasyl Grendzha-Donskyi, of their own volition. Interestingly enough, anti-Semitic materials published in *Krakivski Visti* made no reference to the Jewish pogroms in Ukraine in 1919.

Besides ascertaining the fact of the original Ukrainian anti-Semitism in *Krakivski Visti*, it is also important to determine its typology. It would be inaccurate to equate it with Nazi anti-Semitism. To use an African analogy, the two were different in a similar fashion as contemporary anti-White rhetoric of postcolonial Black nativism in Africa differs from the anti-Black racism of South African apartheid. Most of the original anti-Semitic texts in the newspaper were filled with anticolonial rhetoric driven by a nativist attitude and directed against those who were identified as alien exploiters—Jews. It is remarkable how many of these pieces would be indistinguishable from the Black nativist postcolonial rhetoric if "Jews" were to be replaced with "Whites." It is also important to note that original articles against Poles, Jews, and Russians/Soviets continued prewar trends of Ukrainian nationalism. *Krakivski Visti* might have amplified them, but it certainly did not start them.

The second group of the original ideological layer—numerous articles on Ukrainian history, historical memory and national issues—often evoked and appealed to emotions, but it was not produced to satisfy sentimental needs. Behind it stood a rational and calculated understanding of nation-building, which was the primary (though not openly declared) goal of the UCC's leadership. Kubijovyč wanted to make Ukrainians into a nation ready for statehood even though it became clear to him quickly enough that the occupation authorities had no plans for a Ukrainian state. Ukrainian history played a major role in this pursuit. In a narrow sense, it served the immediate political goals of the UCC, providing historical legitimacy to its claim over the Chełm and Podlasie regions as "Ukrainian territories" in the General Government (*Krakivski Visti* reminded its readers about this in almost every issue in 1940-1941). Curiously, the Lemko region was mentioned less. There is no explanation for this disparity in the editorial archive so I can only speculate on this matter: perhaps the UCC and Kubijovyč felt that their claim over the Lemko region was more secure. In the broader sense, Ukrainian history was used to instill in the readers that they belonged to a nation with a long, rich, and glorious past. It was true that this nation had lost its state, but since then it made several attempts to regain it. What was not said but implied in the newspaper is that when the next opportunity comes, Ukrainians should be better prepared to seize a state.

Of all Ukrainian states of the past, the medieval Halych-Volyn state was emphasized the most in *Krakivski Visti*, which is somewhat intriguing. The Cossack state, Hetmanate (*Hetmanshchyna*), was a better candidate for glorifying the Ukrainian past, especially in terms of military history. Perhaps the authors of *Krakivski Visti* preferred the medieval Halych-Volyn state to the Hetmanate because most of them were Western Ukrainians. Historically speaking, Cossackdom was not a significant phenomenon in the history of Western Ukraine. But on the other hand, and this is even more puzzling, the newspaper mentioned the Western Ukrainian People's Republic of 1918-1919 far less than the Ukrainian Cossacks, though the history of the Republic would have fitted nicely into the German anti-Versailles narrative, which *Krakivski Visti* followed.

Both amateur and professional historians contributed historical material to the newspaper. Among the latter were Mykola Andrusiak, Myron Korduba and Dmytro Doroshenko. The first submitted an overview of Ukrainian history from early Slavic settlement to the Lublin Union (1569), the second—a history of the Halych-Volyn state under its last ruler Bolesław-Yurii II (1323-1340), the third—a memoir about Viacheslav Lypynskyi, Ukrainian historian and political thinker. Though their submissions were different in subject, style and genre, all three underscored the importance of the state in Ukrainian history: they implied that a national collective can fully realize itself only within its own state and to achieve it Ukrainians would need strong leadership and reliable allies. *Krakivski Visti* also paid significant attention to Ukrainian historical memory with articles about the cult of sacrifice for the national cause, Ukrainian graves (both real and symbolic) and commemoration of Ukrainian historical figures such as Taras Shevchenko, Ivan Franko and Markiian Shashkevych—though the latter's inclusion into the Ukrainian pantheon was questionable and had to be defended.

The importance of history and historical memory for the Ukrainian nation remained a constant factor in *Krakivski Visti*. But regarding the nation itself, its boundaries and criteria of inclusion and exclusion (ethnic background, consciousness, language and religion), the newspaper offered mainly two different views. June 1941 was a visible watershed in these discussions. Before the inclusion of Galicia into the General Government, *Krakivski Visti* argued that the Vistula River constituted a historical border between the Ukrainian and Polish nations and favored the inclusion of *latynnyky* (Roman Catholic peasants who used Ukrainian in everyday life) into the Ukrainian national body. There was a clear attempt to widen the national net and prioritize Ukrainianhood not through religion, language or ethnic background but through attitude—in other words, anyone who felt Ukrainian and wanted to help Ukrainian national efforts should be considered a part of the Ukrainian nation.

Most likely, this trend reflected (at least to a degree) attempts of the UCC leadership to expand its horizontal and vertical power within the General Government before the German-Soviet war (see chapter 1). The German invasion of the Soviet Union changed these discussions profoundly. The subject of the Vistula as the westernmost border of the Ukrainian nation had disappeared entirely and by 1943 there were even reminders that not sacrificing the Chełm region in 1918 for the sake of Ukrainian control over Galicia had resulted in losing both territories to Poland. The same happened to the call for an inclusive approach to the Ukrainian nation. Instead, the 1943 discussion over mixed marriages as an existential threat showed a return to the biological, or ethnic, understanding of the Ukrainian nation. The discussion also explored sensitive themes of cultural disparity between Ukrainians and Poles, Ukrainian inferiority and national character.

The importance of *Krakivski Visti* extends beyond ideological matters. Historians who study ethnic killings between Poles and Ukrainians in the General Government (especially in 1943-1944) mostly search for their reasons in the prewar history of the Polish-Ukrainian relationship. These killings would be better understood in the context of the German occupation regime and its brutalization of the occupied populations. Violence and hate can be taught by action and by propaganda. The anti-Polish materials of the Ukrainian legal press should be added into the explanatory framework of the killings. The texts perfectly embodied the logic of ethnic hatred and only lacked a direct call for violence. The same applies to anti-Jewish and anti-Russian/Soviet materials in the legal press: they might provide additional insight into Ukrainian attitudes to the Holocaust and to the postwar anti-Soviet insurgency in Western Ukraine.

Bibliography

Primary Sources

Krakivski Visti. 1940-1944 (Cracow)

Archives

Chomiak, Michael. Fonds PR3260. Provincial Archives of Alberta (Edmonton).

Rudnytsky, Ivan L., fonds. Accession nos. 1984-155, 1991-138, 2020-005. University of Alberta Archives (Edmonton).

Nazaruk, Osyp. Fond 359. Central State Historical Archives of Ukraine in Lviv (TsDIAL of Ukraine).

Audio interview with Mykhailo Khomiak (1975 or 1977). Private archive, Chrystia Chomiak (Edmonton).

Video interview with Benedict Blawacky (2010). Private archive, Maria Hopchin (Edmonton).

Published sources

Berdykhovska, Bogumila, ed. *Yezhy Gedroits ta ukrainska emigratsiia: lystuvannia 1950-1982 rokiv*. Kyiv: Krytyka, 2008.

Bilas, Lev. *Ohliadaiuchys nazad. Perezhyte 1922-2000 i peredumane*. Lviv: Instytut ukrainoznavstva im. I. Krypiakevycha NAN Ukrainy, 2005.

Chernetskyi, Antin. *Spomyny z moho zhyttia*. Kyiv: Osnovni tsinnosti, 2001.

Grendzha-Donskyi, Vasyl. *Shchastia i hore Karpatskoi Ukrainy: Shchodennyk. Moi spohady*. Uzhhorod: Zakarapattia, 2002.

Hentosh, Liliana. "Pro stavlennia mytropolyta Sheptytskoho do nimetskoho okupatsiinoho rezhymu v kontektsi dokumenta z kantseliarii Alfreda Rozenberga," *Ukraina Moderna* no. 20 (2013): 296-317.

Kamenetsky, Ihor, ed. *The Tragedy of Vinnytsia: Materials on Stalin's Policy of Extermination in Ukraine during the Great Purge 1936–1938*. Toronto-New York: Ukrainian Historical Association in cooperation with Bahriany Foundation Inc. and Ukrainian Research and Documentation Center, 1989.

Kedryn, Ivan. *Zhyttia-podii-liudy*. New York, NY: Chervona Kalyna, 1976.

Kolisnyk, Roman. "Moie znaimostvo z profesorom Volodymyrom Kubiiovychem." In *Profesor Volodymyr Kubiiovych*, edited by Oleh Shablii, 356-360. Lviv: Vydavnychyi tsentr LNU imeni Ivana Franka, 2006).

Korovytskyi, Ivan, ed. *Lysty Dmytra Doroshenka do Viacheslava Lypynskoho.* Philadelphia: W. K. Lypynsky East European Research Institute, 1973.

Kubijovyč, Volodymyr. *Meni 70.* Munich: Logos, 1970.

Kubijovyč, Volodymyr. *Meni 85.* Munich: Molode zhyttia, 1985.

Liakhotskyi V.P. et al., eds. *Pamiatky. Tom 2: Epistoliarna spadshchyna Ivana Ohiienka (mytropolyta Ilariona) 1907-1968.* Kyiv: Ukrainskyi derzhavnyi naukovo-doslidnyi instytut arkhivnoi spravy ta dokumentoznavstva, 2001.

Lukasevych, Levko. *Rozdumy na skhylku zhyttia.* New York: St. Sophia Ukrainian Orthodox Publishers, 1982.

Lysiak-Rudnytskyi, Ivan. *Shchodennyky,* edited by Yaroslav Hrytsak and Frank Sysyn. Kyiv: Dukh i Litera, 2019.

Piotrowski, Stanisław. *Hans Frank's Diary.* Warszawa: Państwowe Wydawnictwo Naukowe, 1961.

Romaniv, Oleh, ed. *Narodovbyvstvo v Ukraini: ofitsiini materialy pro masovi vbyvstva u Vinnytsi.* Lviv: Lvivska oblasna istoryko-kulturolohichna orhanizatsiia "Memorial," 1995.

Rudnytska, Milena. *Statti, Lysty, Dokumenty.* Lviv: Misioner,1998.

Shevelov, Yurii. *Ya – mene – meni... (i dovkruhy).* vol. 1. Kharkiv: Vydavets Oleksandr Savchuk, 2017.

Strutynska, Mariia. *Daleke zblyzka.* Winnipeg: Vydavnycha Spilka "Tryzub," 1975.

Tarnavskyi, Ostap. *Literaturnyi Lviv, 1939-1944: Spomyny.* Lviv: Prosvita, 1995.

Veryha, Wasyl, comp. *The Correspondence of the Ukrainian Central Committee in Cracow and Lviv with the German Authorities, 1939-1944.* 2 vols. Edmonton, AB: Canadian Institute of Ukrainian Studies Press, 2000.

Volchuk, Roman. *Spomyny z peredvoiennoho Lvova ta voiennoho Vidnia.* Kyiv: Krytyka, 2002.

Volchuk, Roman. *Spomyny z povoennoi Avstrii ta Nimechchyny.* Kyiv: Krytyka, 2004.

Zabolotna, Inna. "Roky nimetskoi okupatsii na Zakhidnii Ukraini za spohadamy Ivana Krypiakevycha." *Ukrainskyi arkheohrafichnyi shchorichnyk* 10 no. 7 (Kyiv – New York: Vydavnytstvo M. P. Kots, 2002): 389-410.

Secondary Literature

Articles

Abramson, Henry. "'This is the Way it Was!' Textual and Iconographic Images of Jews in the Nazi-sponsored Ukrainian Press of Distrikt Galizien." In *Why Didn't the Press Shout? American & International Journalism and the Holocaust*, edited by Robert Moses Shapiro, 537-556. New York: Yeshiva University Press, 2003.

Berdychowska, Bogumiła. "Od nacjonalisty do lewicowca (Przypadek Borysa Łewyckiego)." *Zeszyty Historyczne* 145 (524) 2003: 214-230.

Bergen, Doris L. "The Nazi Concept of 'Volksdeutsche' and the Exacerbation of Anti-Semitism in Eastern Europe, 1939-45." *Journal of Contemporary History* 29, no. 4 (1994): 569-82.

Berkhoff, Karel C. "Ukraine under Nazi Rule (1941-1944): Sources and Finding Aids: Part I." *Jahrbücher für Geschichte Osteuropas* 45, no. 1 (1997): 85-103.

Brock, Peter. "Vahylevych and the Ukrainian National Identity." In *Nationbuilding and the Politics of Nationalism: Essays on Austrian Galicia*, edited by Andrei Markovits and Frank Sysyn, 111-148. Cambridge: Harvard Ukrainian Research Institute, 1982.

Chornovol, Ihor. "Markiian Shashkevych: mekhanizmy kultu." *Krytyka* no. 1-2 (2005): 1-2.

Dashkevych, Yaroslav. "Vstupne slovo, abo pro problemy kolaborantstva." In *Persha Ukrainska dyviziia Ukrainskoi natsionalnoi armii: istoriia stvorennia ta natsionalno-polityhne znachennia. Materialy naukovo-praktychnoi konferentsii. Dopovidi ta povidomlennia*, edited by Yaroslav Dashkevych, 7-9. Lviv: Novyi chas, 2002.

Fife, Robert. "Freeland knew her grandfather was editor of Nazi newspaper." *The Globe and Mail*, March 7, 2017, https://www.theglobeandmail.com/news/politics/freeland-knew-her-grandfather-was-editor-of-nazi-newspaper/article34236881/

Friedrich, Klaus-Peter. "Die deutsche polnischsprachige Presse im Generalgouvernement (1939-1945): NS-Propaganda für die polnische Bevölkerung." *Publizistik: Vierteljahreshefte für Kommunikationsforschung* 46 no. 2 (2001): 161-188.

Friedrich, Klaus-Peter. "Publizistische Kollaboration im sog. Generalgouvernement: personengeschichtliche Aspekte der deutschen Okkupationsherrschaft in Polen (1939-1945)." *Zeitschrift für Ostmitteleuropa-Forschung* 48 no. 1 (1999): 51-89.

Habor, Vasyl. "Nove Selo." In *Ukrainski chasopysy Lvova 1848-1939 rr. Istoryko-bibliohrafichne doslidzhennia. Tom 3, Knyha 2: 1929-1939 rr.*, edited by M.M. Romaniuk and M.V. Halushko,135-147. Lviv: Svit, 2003.

Himka, John-Paul. "Ethnicity and the Reporting of Mass Murder: *Krakivs'ki visti*, the NKVD Murders of 1941, and the Vinnytsia Exhumation." In *Shatterzone of Empires: Coexistence and Violence in the German, Habsburg, Russian, and Ottoman Borderlands*, edited by Omer Bartov and Eric D. Weitz, 378-398. Bloomington: Indiana University Press, 2013.

Himka, John-Paul. "The Galician Triangle: Poles, Ukrainians and Jews under Austrian Rule." *Cross Currents: A Yearbook of Central European Culture* no. 12 (1993): 125-146.

Himka, John-Paul. "*Krakivski visti* and the Jews, 1943: A Contribution to the History of Ukrainian-Jewish Relations during the Second World War." *Journal of Ukrainian Studies* 21, no. 1-2 (Summer-Winter 1996): 81-95.

Himka, John-Paul. "*Krakivs'ki visti*: An Overview." *Harvard Ukrainian Studies*, Vol. 22, (1998): 251-261.

Himka, John-Paul. "Western Ukraine between the Wars." *Canadian Slavonic Papers* 34, no. 4 (December 1992): 391-412.

Hnatiuk, Ola. "Conditio sine qua non." *East/West: Journal of Ukrainian Studies* IV, no. 2 (2017): 275-290, http://dx.doi.org/10.21226/T20D1V

Hnatiuk, Ola. "Piotr Dunin-Borkowski." *Zeszyty Historyczne* 155 (2006): 188-225.

Hrytsak, Yaroslav. "Ivan Franko—selianskyi syn?" *Ukraina: kulturna spadshchyna, natsionalna svidomist, derzhavnist* no. 15 (2006-2007): 531-542.

Kenez, Peter. "The Ideology of the White Movement." *Soviet Studies* 32, no. 1 (1980): 58-83.

Kenez, Peter. "Pogroms and White Ideology in the Russian Civil War." In *Pogroms: Anti-Jewish Violence in Modern Russian History*, edited by John D. Klier and Shlomo Lambroza, 293-313. Cambridge, UK: Cambridge University Press, 1992.

Kucheruk, Oleksandr. "'… Vse, shcho zviazane z vyzvolenniam Ukrainy' (Do genezy vidnosyn Orhanizatsii Ukrainskykh Natsionalistiv ta Ukrainskoho Tsentralnoho Komitetu na pochatku Druhoi svitovoi viiny)." *Ukrainskyi vyzvolnyi rukh* no. 18 (2013): 25-38.

Kurylo, Taras and Ivan Khymka [John-Paul Himka]. "Yak OUN stavylasia do ievreiv? Rozdumy nad knyzhkoiu Volodymyra Viatrovycha." *Ukraina Moderna* no. 13 (2008): 252-265.

Lazurko, Lidiia. "Sviatkuvannia ukraiinskykh natsionalnykh iuvileiv u Halychyni (kinets XIX—pochatok XX st.)." *Z istoriii zakhidnoukrainskykh zemel* vyp. 10–11 (2015): 184-206.

Lutskyi, Oleksandr. "Lviv pid radianskoiu okupatsiieiu 1939—1941 rr." *Ukrainskyi vyzvolnyi rukh* no. 7 (2006): 89-119.

Lysiak-Rudnytskyi, Ivan. "Nazaruk i Lypynskyi: istoriia ikhnioi druzhby ta konfliktu." In *Lysty Osypa Nazaruka do Viacheslava Lypynskoho*, edited by Ivan Lysiak-Rudnytskyi, xv-xcvii. Philadelphia: W. K. Lypynsky East European Research Institute, 1976.

Markiewicz, Paweł. "Volodymyr Kubijovych's Ethnographic Ukraine: Theory into Practice on the Western Okrainy." *Jahrbücher für Geschichte Osteuropas* 64, no. 2 (April 2016): 228-259.

Mecklenburg, Frank. "Von der Hitlerjugend zum Holocaust. Die Karriere des Fritz Arlt." In *Deutsche, Juden, Völkermord. Der Holocaust als Geschichte und Gegenwart*, edited by Jürgen Matthäus and Klaus M. Mallmann, 87-102. Darmstadt: Wiss. Buchges., 2006.

Nakhlik, Yevhen. "Frankovi 'Konkistadory': poetyzatsiia zdobuvnytskoho heroizmu." May 28, 2018, https://zbruc.eu/node/80144

Pahiria, Oleksandr. "Polska storinka teroru v Karpatskii Ukraini (1938-1939 rokiv)." In *Ukrainofobia yak iavyshche ta polittekhnolohiia*, edited by Ya. Harasym et al, 34-59. Vyp. 1. Lviv, 2014.

Paperno, Irina. "Exhuming the Bodies of Soviet Terror." *Representations* 75, no. 1 (2001): 89–118.

Pavlyshyn, Oleh. "Dylema identychnosty, abo istoriia pro te, yak 'latynnyky' (ne) staly ukraintsiamy/poliakamy (Halychyna, seredyna XIX—persha polovyna XX st.)." *Ukraina Moderna* no. 21 (2014): 179-218.

Pikh, Oleh and Maryna Cheban. "Myron Korduba i Mykola Andrusiak: do istorii vzaiemyn." *Ukraina-Polshcha: istorychna spadshchyna ta suspilna svidomist* no. 5 (2012): 158-178.

Prymak, Thomas M. "Dmytro Doroshenko: A Ukrainian Émigré Historian of the Interwar Period." *Harvard Ukrainian Studies* 25, no. 1/2 (Spring 2001): 31-56.

"Round-Table Discussion." In *Ukrainian-Jewish Relations in Historical Perspective*, edited by Howard Aster and Peter J. Potichnyj, 479-512. 2nd ed. Edmonton: Canadian Institute of Ukrainian Studies, University of Alberta, 1990.

Rudling, Per Anders. "'They Defended Ukraine': The 14. Waffen-Grenadier-Division der SS (Galizische Nr. 1) Revisited." *The Journal of Slavic Military Studies*, 25 no. 3, (2012): 329-368.

Sereda, Ostap. "'As a Father among Little Children': The Emerging Cult of Taras Shevchenko as a Factor of the Ukrainian Nation-building in Austrian Eastern Galicia in the 1860s." *Kyiv-Mohyla Humanities Journal* no. 1 (2014): 159–188.

Shprinher, Tetiana. "Oleksandr Mokh yak literaturnyi krytyk, zhurnalist i vydavets." *Visnyk Lvivskoho universytetu. Seriia zhurnalistyka.* Vyp. 36 (2012): 168-178.

Shumylo, Natalia. "Mykola Yevshan (1889-1919)." In Yevshan, Mykola. *Krytyka. Literaturoznavstvo. Estetyka*, edited by Natalia Shumylo, 3-11. Kyiv: Osnovy, 1998.

Simons, Paula. "'School of hate': Was Foreign Affairs Minister Chrystia Freeland's grandfather a Nazi collaborator?" *Edmonton Journal*, March 8, 2017, https://edmontonjournal.com/news/politics/paula-simons-school-of-hate-was-foreign-affairs-minister-chrystia-freelands-grandfather-a-nazi-collaborator

Stasiv, Bohdan. "Chomu my ishly do dyvyzii 'Halychyna'?" In *Persha Ukrainska dyviziia Ukrainskoi natsionalnoi armii: istoriia stvorennia ta natsionalno-politychne znachennia. Materialy naukovo-praktychnoi konferentsii. Dopovidi ta povidomlennia*, edited by Yaroslav Dashkevych, 56-62. Lviv: Novyi chas, 2002.

Books

Amar, Tarik Cyril. *The Paradox of Ukrainian Lviv: A Borderland City between Stalinists, Nazis, and Nationalists.* Ithaca; London: Cornell University Press, 2015.

Armstrong, John A. *Ukrainian Nationalism, 1939-1945.* New York, NY: Columbia University Press, 1955.

Bergen, Doris. *War and Genocide: A Concise History of the Holocaust.* 3rd ed. Lanham, MD: Rowman & Littlefield, 2016.

Berkhoff, Karel C. *Harvest of Despair: Life and Death in Ukraine under Nazi Rule.* Cambridge, MA: Belknap Press of Harvard University Press, 2004.

Bohachevsky-Chomiak, Martha. *Feminists despite Themselves: Women in Ukrainian Community Life, 1884-1939.* Edmonton: Canadian Institute of Ukrainian Studies Press, University of Alberta, 1988.

Cheban, Maryna. *Mykola Andrusiak: istoriia istoryka.* Lviv: Instytut ukrainoznavstva im. I. Krypiakevycha, 2015.

Confino, Alon. *A World without Jews: The Nazi Imagination from Persecution to Genocide.* New Haven, CT: Yale University Press, 2014.

Dobroszycki, Lucjan, ed. *The Chronicle of the Łódź ghetto, 1941-1944.* New Haven, CT: Yale University Press, 1984.

Dobroszycki, Lucjan. *Die legale polnische Presse im Generalgouvernement, 1939-1945.* München: Selbstverlag des Instituts für Zeitgeschichte, 1977.

Dobroszycki, Lucjan. *Reptile Journalism: The Official Polish-Language Press under the Nazis, 1939-1945*. New Haven, CT: Yale University Press, 1994.

Zabarevskyi M. [Doroshenko, Dmytro]. *Viacheslav Lypynskyi i ioho dumky pro ukrainsku natsiiu i derzhavu*. Vienna: Vyd. zakhodamy O. Zherebka, 1925.

Dziuba, I. M. *Taras Shevchenko. Zhyttia i tvorchist*. Kyiv: Kyievo-Mohylianska Akademia, 2008.

Fedaka, P. M., ed. *Materialy naukovoi konferentsii, prysviachenoi pamiati Ivana Pankevycha (23-24 zhovtnia 1992 roku)*. Uzhhorod: Uzhhorodska typohrafiia, 1992.

Fedevych K. K. *Halytski ukraintsi u Polshchi. 1920-1939 rr. (Intehratsiia halytskykh ukraintsiv do Polskoi derzhavy u 1920-1930-ti rr.)*. Kyiv: Osnova, 2009.

Fest, Joachim C. *The Face of the Third Reich*. Translated by Michael Bullock. London: Weidenfeld & Nicolson, 1970.

Frank, Niklas. *Bruder Norman!: "Mein Vater war ein Naziverbrecher, aber ich liebe ihn."* Bonn: Dietz, 2013.

Frank, Niklas. *Der Vater: eine Abrechnung*. München: C. Bertelsmann, 1987.

Fritz, Stephen G. *Ostkrieg: Hitler's War of Extermination in the East*. Lexington, KY: University Press of Kentucky, 2011.

Gross, Jan Tomasz. *Polish Society under German Occupation: The Generalgouvernement, 1939-1944*. Princeton, NJ: Princeton University Press, 1979.

Himka, John-Paul. *Religion and Nationality in Western Ukraine: The Greek Catholic Church and the Ruthenian National Movement in Galicia, 1867-1900*. Montreal; Kingston, Ontario; London; Ithaca: McGill-Queen's University Press, 1999.

Holovata, Larysa. *"Ukrainske vydavnytstvo" u Krakovi-Lvovi, 1939-1945: Bibliohrafichnyi dovidnyk*. Kyiv: Krytyka, 2010.

Holovata, Larysa. *Ukrainskyi legalnyi vydavnychyi rukh Tsentralno-Skhidnoi Yevropy, 1939-1945* (Kyiv-Lviv, 2013).

Homo politicus [Kedryn, Ivan]. *Prychyny upadku Polshchi*. Krakiv: Ukrainske Vydavnytstvo, 1940.

Housden, Martyn. *Hans Frank: Lebensraum and the Holocaust*. New York: Palgrave Macmillan, 2003.

Hundorova, Tamara. *Franko ne kameniar. Franko i kameniar*. Kyiv: Krytyka, 2006.

Hrendzha-Donska, Zirka. *"My ie lyshen korotki epizody": zhyttia i tvorchist Vasylia Hrendzhi-Donskoho*. Uzhhorod: Sribna zemlia, 1993.

Hryciuk, Grzegorz. *"Gazeta Lwowska"* 1941-1944. Wrocław: Wydaw. Uniwersytetu Wrocławskiego, 1996.

Hrynevch, Vladyslav. *Nepryborkane riznoholossia: Druha svitova viina i suspilno-politychni nastroi v Ukraini, 1939 – cherven 1941 rr.* Kyiv-Dnipropetrovsk: Vydavnytstvo "Lira," 2012.

Hrytsak, Yaroslav. *Prorok u svoii vitchyzni: Franko ta ioho spilnota, 1856-1886.* Kyiv: Krytyka, 2006.

Iliushyn, I. I. *OUN-UPA i ukrainske pytannia v roky Druhoi svitovoi viiny (v svitli polskykh dokumentiv).* Kyiv: Instytut Istorii Ukrainy NAN Ukrainy, 2000.

Iliushyn, I. I. *Protystoiannia UPA i AK (Armii Kraivoi) v roky Druhoi svitovoi viiny na tli diialnosti polskoho pidpillia v Zakhidnii Ukraini.* Kyiv: Instytut Istorii Ukrainy NAN Ukrainy, 2001.

Jockheck, Lars. *Propaganda im Generalgouvernement: die NS-Besatzungspresse für Deutsche und Polen 1939-1945.* Osnabrück: Fibre, 2006.

Kiebuzinski, Ksenya and Alexander Motyl, eds. *The Great West Ukrainian Prison Massacre of 1941: A Sourcebook.* Amsterdam: Amsterdam University Press, 2017.

Kosarenko-Kosarevych, Vasyl. *Moskovskyi sfinks: mit i syla v obrazi Skhodu Evropy.* New York, 1957.

Korduba, Myron. *Istoria Kholmshchyny i Pidliashshia.* Krakiv: Ukrainske Vydavnytsvo, 1941.

Kubijovyč, Volodymyr. *Ukraintsi v Heneralnii Hubernii, 1939-1941: istoriia Ukrainskoho tsentralnoho komitetu.* Chicago, IL: Vyd-vo Mykoly Denysiuka, 1975.

Kuchabsky, Vasyl. *Western Ukraine in Conflict with Poland and Bolshevism, 1918-1923.* Toronto: Canadian Institute of Ukrainian Studies Press, 2009.

Kurylyshyn, Kostiantyn. *Ukrainske zhyttia v umovakh nimetskoi okupatsii (1939-1944 rr.): za materialamy ukrainomovnoi lehalnoi presy.* Lviv: Lvivska natsionalna naukova biblioteka im. V. Stefanyka, 2010.

Kutsenko, Leonid. *Kniaz dukhu: statti pro zhyttia i tvorchist Yevhena Malaniuka.* Kirovohrad: [s.n.], 2003.

Lewandowski, Józef. *"Goniec Krakowski" (27.X.1939 - 18.I.1945): próba monografii.* Warszawa: [s.n.], 1978.

Magocsi, Paul Robert. *The Shaping of a National Identity: Subcarpathian Rus', 1848-1948.* Cambridge, MA: Harvard University Press, 1978.

Magocsi, Paul Robert. *With Their Backs to the Mountains: A History of Carpathian Rus' and Carpatho-Rusyns.* Budapest/New York: Central European University Press, 2015.

Majer, Diemut. *"Non-Germans" under the Third Reich: The Nazi Judicial and Administrative System in Germany and Occupied Eastern Europe, with Special Regard to Occupied Poland, 1939-1945.* Lubbock, TX: Texas Tech University Press in association with the United States Holocaust Memorial Museum, 2013.

Markiewicz, Pawel. *Unlikely Allies: Nazi German and Ukrainian Nationalist Collaboration in the General Government during World War II.* West Lafayette, IN: Purdue University Press, 2021.

Matysiakevych, Zynovii. *Ukrainskyi istoryk Yakiv Holovatskyi.* Lviv: Litopys, 2002.

Mick, Christoph. *Lemberg, Lwów, L'viv, 1914-1947: Violence and Ethnicity in a Contested City.* West Lafayette, IN: Purdue University Press, 2016.

Motyka, Grzegorz. *Od rzezi wołyńskiej do Akcji "Wisła": konflikt polsko-ukraiński 1943-1947.* Kraków: Wydawnictwo Literackie, 2011.

Motyl, Alexander J. *The Turn to the Right: The Ideological Origins and Development of Ukrainian Nationalism, 1919-1929.* Boulder, CO: East European Quarterly; New York, NY: distributed by Columbia University Press, 1980.

Mushynka, Mykola, ed. *Ivan Pankevych ta pytannia literaturnoi movy. Statti ta materialy* = *Mušinka, Mikuláš,* ed. *Ivan Paňkevyč a otázky spisovného jazyka. Štúdie a materiály.* Priashiv, 2002.

Mytsiuk, Oleksander. *Ahraryzatsiia zhydivstva na tli zahalnoi ekonomiky.* Prague, 1933.

Pasternak, Yaroslav. *Staryi Halych: arkheolohichno-istorychni doslidy u 1850-1943 rr.* Krakiv-Lviv: Ukrainske vydavnytstvo, 1944.

Pelenski, Jaroslaw, ed. *Harvard Ukrainian Studies* vol. 9 no. 3/4 (December 1985): The Political and Social Ideas of Vjačeslav Lypyns'kyj.

Perederiï, I. H. *Viacheslav Lypynskyi: etnichnyj poliak, politychnyj ukrainets.* Poltava: PoltNTU, 2012.

Pikh, Oleh. *Myron Korduba (1876-1947).* Lviv: Instytut ukrainoznavstva im. I. Krypiakevycha, 2012.

Rawska, Jolanta. *"Sprawa polska" w prasie "gadzinowej" (lipiec 1944-styczeń 1945).* Warszawa: [s.n.], 1980.

Rein, Leonid. *The Kings and the Pawns: Collaboration in Byelorussia during World War II.* New York: Berghahn Books, 2011.

Rudnytska, Milena, ed., *Zakhidnia Ukraina pid bolshevykamy.* New York: Ameryka, 1958.

Rudnytsky, Ivan L. *Essays in Modern Ukrainian History,* edited by Peter L. Rudnytsky. Edmonton: Canadian Institute of Ukrainian Studies, 1987.

Salyha, Taras. *Vohon, shcho ne zhasa...* Kyiv: Lybid, 2017.

Sawa, Mariusz. *Ukraiński emigrant: działalność i myśl Iwana Kedryna-Rudnyckiego (1896-1995).* Lublin: Instytut Pamięci Narodowej - Komisja Ścigania Zbrodni przeciwko Narodowi Polskiemu, Oddział w Lublinie, 2016.

Schenk, Dieter. *Hans Frank: Hitlers Kronjurist und Generalgouverneur.* Frankfurt am Main: S. Fischer, 2006.

Shankovskyi, Lev. *Pokhidni hrupy OUN: prychynky do istorii pokhidnykh hrup OUN na tsentralnykh zemliakh Ukrainy v 1941-1943 rr.* Munich: Ukrainskyi samostiinyk, 1958.

Shapoval, Yu. H. *I v Ukraini sviatylos te slovo.* Lviv: PAIS, 2003.

Shkandrij, Myroslav. *Ukrainian Nationalism: Politics, Ideology, and Literature, 1929-1956.* New Haven, CT: Yale University Press, 2015.

Sidak V. et al. *Polkovnyk Petro Bolbochan: trahediia ukrainskoho derzhavnyka.* 2nd ed. Kyiv: Tempora, 2009.

Skakun, Roman. *"Patsyfikatsiia": polski represii 1930 roku v Halychyni.* Lviv: Vydavnytstvo Ukrainskoho katolytskoho universytetu, 2012.

Stasiuk, Oleksandra. *Vydavnycho-propahadyvna diialnist OUN (1941-1953 rr.).* Lviv: Tsentr doslidzhen vyzvolnoho rukhu, Instytut ukrainoznavstva im. I. Krypiakevycha, 2006.

Steblii F. I. *Spodvyzhnyk Markiiana Shashkevycha: Yakiv Holovatskyi – diiach ukrainskoho natsionalnoho vidrodzhennia.* Lviv: In-t ukrainoznavstva im. I. Krypiakevycha, 2004.

Świstak, Maria. *Nowy Kurier Warszawski: próba monografii.* Warszawa: [s.n.], 1978.

Uchman, Tomasz Andrzej. *Gazeta Lwowska 1941-1944: próba monografii.* Warszawa: Uniwersytet Warszawski, 1977.

Vasyliev, Valerii and Roman Podkur. *Radianski karateli. Spivrobitnyky NKVS – vykonavtsi "Velykoho teroru" na Podilli.* Kyiv: Vydavets V. Zakharenko, 2017.

Volkov S. V. *Ofitsery rossiiskoi gvardii: Opyt martirologa.* Moskva: Russkii put, 2002.

Wehrhahn, Torsten. *Die Westukrainische Volksrepublik: zu den polnisch-ukrainischen Beziehungen und dem Problem der ukrainischen Staatlichkeit in den Jahren 1918 bis 1923.* Berlin: Weissensee, 2004.

Wójcik, Władysława. *Prasa gadzinowa Generalnego Gubernatorstwa: (1939-1945).* Kraków: Wydawnictwo Naukowe WSP, 1988.

Woldan, Alois and Olaf Terpitz, eds. *Ivan Franko und die jüdische Frage in Galizien Interkulturelle Begegnungen und Dynamiken im Schaffen des ukrainischen Schriftstellers*. Wien: Vienna University Press; Göttingen: V&R unipress, 2016.

Woźniakowski, Krzysztof. *Polskojęzyczna prasa gadzinowa czasów okupacji hitlerowskiej 1939-1945: studia i szkice zebrane*. Opole: Wydawnictwo Naukowe Scriptorium, 2014.

Woźniakowski, Krzysztof. *Polskojęzyczna prasa gadzinowa w tzw. Starej Rzeszy (1939-1945)*. Kraków: Wydawnictwo Naukowe AP, 2001.

Woźniakowski, Krzysztof. *W kręgu jawnego piśmiennictwa literackiego Generalnego Gubernatorstwa (1939-1945)*. Kraków: Wydawnictwo Naukowe WSP, 1997.

Yehreshii, Oleh. *Yepyskop Hryhorii Khomyshyn: portret reliihno-tserkovnoho i hromadsko-politychnoho diiacha*. Ivano-Frankivsk: Nova Zoria, 2006.

Zaitsev, O. Yu. *Ukrainskyi integralnyi natsionalizm (1920-1930-ti) roky: narysy intelektualnoi istorii*. Kyïv: Krytyka, 2013.

Dissertations

Kovaliv, Solomiia-Mariia. "Literaturoznavchi kontseptsii Luky Lutsiva." Dysertatsiia na zdobuttia naukovoho stupenia kandydata filolohichnykh nauk. Lviv: Lvivskyi Natsionalnyi Universytet imeni Ivana Franka, 2018.

Sereda, Ostap. "Shaping of a National Identity: Early Ukrainophiles in Austrian Eastern Galicia, 1860–1873." PhD diss., Central European University, 2003.

Index of Names

Amar, Tarik Cyril 39n116
Andrei, Metropolitan 69-70, 84n296, 128
Andrusiak, Mykola 68, 71-72, 145-151, 162, 204
Arlt, Fritz 42-43
Armstrong, John A. 10
Bahrianyi, Ivan 64
Bandera, Stepan xii-xiii, 2, 26
Baran, Stepan 74n261, 84-87, 118-119, 201
Barna, S. 91
Bartel, Kazimierz 81
Battaglia, Otto Forst de 120
Berkhoff, Karel C. 11
Bilas, Lev 24n55, 29, 75-76
Bisanz, Alfred 43n131
Blawacky, Benedict 10
Bolbochan, Petro 161, 166
Bolesław-Yurii II 68, 151-153, 204
Cameron, James 71
Casimir III the Great 153
Chaikivskyi, V. 61
Charles Robert 153
Cheban, Maryna 145
Chernetskyi, Antin 168-169, 183-184
Chomiak, Alexandra. *See* Khomiak, Alexandra
Chomiak, Chrystia ix, 10
Chomiak, Michael. *See* Khomiak, Mykhailo
Chubynskyi, Pavlo 131
Ciano, Galeazzo 49
Cyril 148
Dashkevych, Yaroslav 16-17, 19

Daszyński, Ignacy 83
Dobroszycki, Lucjan 7, 13-15, 73
Dobrowolski, Kazimierz 31n79
Dolnytskyi, Mstyslav 61
Doroshenko, Dmytro 49, 154-162, 204
Dostoevsky, Fiodor 131
Drahomanov, Mykhailo 131, 157, 163
Dudtko, Fedir 61
Dunin-Borkowski, Piotr 82
Durbak, Ivan 55, 61
Dziuba, Ivan 168n589
Eberle, Joseph 120
Egán, Ede 132
Fedenko, Panas 49
Fest, Joachim 25
Ford, Henry 120
Frank, Hans xii, 24-28, 30, 33-34, 38, 41-43, 66n226, 86-87, 105, 199
Franko, Ivan 98, 121-124, 157, 166, 168, 170-173, 175, 200, 205
Freeland, Chrystia ix-x, 138
Freeland, Halyna ix
Gassner, Emil 52, 58, 70
Gobineau, Arthur de 40
Goebbels, Joseph 26, 48
Goethe, Johann Wolfgang von 174
Gogol, Nikolai 131
Göring, Hermann 48
Grendzha-Donskyi, Vasyl 69, 136-137, 203
Gross, Jan Tomasz 19n47
Günther, Hans F. K. 40

Gustaf V 62
Halaichuk, Bohdan 61
Halan, Yaroslav 53, 95
Halit, Bohdan 134
Hardy, Emily x
Herder, Johann Gottfried von 174
Himka, John-Paul ix, 5, 10n10, 12-13, 17, 57, 102-103, 108-109, 117, 119n434-435, 128, 129n467, 141
Himmler, Heinrich 25n61, 146n512
Hitler, Adolf xi, 19, 24-25, 29, 33n91, 38, 40, 48, 66n226, 87, 96, 146n512, 200
Hnatyshak, Mykola 175
Holian, Roman 61
Holovata, Larysa 13, 17, 57n190
Holovatskyi, Yakiv 172, 175
Holovinska, Slava 135
Hołówko, Tadeusz 83
Hopchin, Bruce 10
Hopchin, Maria 10
Hordynskyi, Sviatoslav 51, 61
Horniatkevych, Damian 49, 61
Hoshovskyi, Bohdan 61, 164, 172
Hrushevskyi, Mykhailo 150, 158
Humenna, Dokiia 64
Hunka, Yaroslav x
Ilarion, Archbishop 69-70
Kachmar, Vasyl 61
Károly Róbert. See Charles Robert
Kedryn, Ivan 35n98, 36n104, 45n141, 55n185, 57-58, 61, 66-67, 71, 78-84, 87, 94, 151, 201
Khmelnytskyi, Bohdan 157-158, 163, 168
Khomiak, Alexandra 57

Khomiak, Mykhailo ix, 5, 8-10, 12, 21-22, 52-63, 67-74, 77-78, 94, 110, 132-133, 138-141, 150-151, 160, 162-163, 190n661, 200
Khvyliovyi, Mykola 169
Koch, Erich 105
Konovalets, Myron 183-189
Konovalets, Yevhen 166, 184
Korduba, Myron 49, 68, 145, 150-154, 162, 204
Kosach, Yurii 49
Kosak, Marian. See Kozak, Mariian
Kosarenko-Kosarevych, Vasyl 133
Koshelnyk, Yurii 193-195
Kostiuk, Hryhorii 49, 64
Kotliarevskyi, Ivan 126
Kotorovych, Hennadii 70, 105
Kotsur, Ivan 59-60
Kovalenko, (Liudmyla?) 64
Kovaliv, Stefan 124
Kovshyk, Fedir 61
Kozak, Mariian 61-63, 107-110, 118-119, 120n436, 200
Kriukov, Borys 61
Krypiakevych, Ivan 32-34, 49, 158
Kubiiovych, Volodymyr. See Kubijovyč, Volodymyr
Kubijovyč, Volodymyr xi-xii, 11-12, 16-17, 22, 30-47, 51-52, 54-56, 58-60, 62, 70-71, 79, 86-87, 94, 98, 102-103, 143, 177, 183n639, 199, 203-204
Kuchabskyi, Vasyl 165
Kupchynskyi, Roman 63
Kurdydyk, Anatol 71, 105, 110-111, 118, 120, 121n441

Index of Names

Kurylyshyn, Kostiantyn 14-17, 19
Kuzelia, Zenon 49
Kuzyk, Kost 61, 119, 121-125, 128, 203
Kvashenko, Mykyta 53n175
Kysilevska, Olena 67-68, 119, 127-128, 203
Leary, Timothy 197
Lepkyi, Bohdan 49, 63, 175
Lepkyi, Lev 61, 63, 171
Levynskyi, Volodymyr 162-163
Levytskyi, Borys 54-56
Levytskyi, Vitalii 61
Lewytzkyj, Borys. *See* Levytskyi, Borys
Lieberman, Herman 83
Liubchenko, Arkadii 51
Lukasevych, Levko 33-34, 119
Lukiianovych, Denys 49
Lutsiv, Luka 119, 125-127, 174-175, 203
Lypa, Yurii 49, 118-119
Lypynskyi, Viacheslav 62, 78n274, 154-162, 204
Lysiak, Ivan. *See* Rudnytsky, Ivan L.
Lysiak, Pavlo 108-109
Lysiak, Yu. *See* Rudnytsky, Ivan L.
Majer, Diemut 24, 58
Malaniuk, Evhen 49, 111-114, 119, 165-166, 202
Marples, David R. xiv, 5
Martel, René 69
Martynets, Volodymyr 171n602
Masikevych, Omelian 61
Melnyk, Andrii xii, 37-38
Mesnil-Marigny, Jules Du 120

Methodius 148
Mieszko I 147
Mikhnovskyi, Mykola 184n641
Mirchuk, Ivan 189-192, 196
Mitrynga, Ivan 54
Mokh, Oleksander 61, 119-121, 163n565, 203
Mościcki, Ignacy 81
Moses 170, 172
Mudryi, Vasyl 49, 60
Mussolini, Benito 22, 33n91
Mylianych, Atanas 96
Mytsiuk, Oleksander 119, 129-133, 203
Nakonechna, Hanna 72n251
Navrotskyi, Volodymyr 131
Nazaruk, Osyp 57, 69, 77-79, 162
Nedilko, Oleksander 68-69
Nemyrych, V. 88, 134
Nimchuk, Ivan 55n185, 61, 63, 145, 181-183, 191-193, 196
Nyzhankivskyi, Bohdan 61, 63
Ohiienko, Ivan. *See* Ilarion, Archbishop
Ohloblyn, Oleksander 49
Onatskyi, Yevhen 49, 68
Osadchuk, Bohdan 146n513
Osmachka, Todos 64n222
Ostroverkha, Mykhailo 90
Ottokar, O. 91
Paliiv, Dmytro 43n131
Pankevych, Ivan 173-175
Papini, Giovanni 120
Parfanovych, Sofiia 49
Pasternak, Yaroslav 46
Pavlyk, Mykhailo 131
Pelenskyi, Yevhen Yulii 45, 55
Pétain, Philippe 18
Petliura, Symon 161, 166

Petriv, Vsevolod 163
Podolynskyi, Serhii 131
Pushkin, Aleksandr 131
Putin, Vladimir x
Radiievych, Yu. 134
Rakovskyi, Ivan 39
Rataj, Maciej 83
Reid, Zoe x
Remarque, Erich Maria 127
Revai, Yuliian 52n170
Rosenberg, Alfred 116
Rudling, Per Anders ix
Rudnytska, Milena 29, 69, 73, 79n280, 82-83
Rudnytsky, Ivan L. ix-x, 28-29, 57, 73, 108-109, 197-198
Rudnytskyi, Ivan. See Kedryn, Ivan
Rydz-Śmigły, Edward 81
Ryvak, Vasyl 61
Šafárik, Pavel Jozef 174
Sahaidachnyi, Petro 61
Saltykov-Shchedrin, Mikhail 131
Savaryn, Denys 61, 195-196
Schlegel, August 174
Schlegel, Friedrich 174
Schneider, Robert 120
Shandruk, Pavlo 51
Shashkevych, Markiian 166, 172-175, 201, 205
Shebeko, Nikolai 159
Sheptytskyi, Andrei. See Andrei, Metropolitan
Shevchenko, Taras 46, 131, 166-173, 175, 177, 200, 205
Shevelov, Yurii (George) 34, 49, 64, 72-73
Shkandrij, Myroslav ix
Shkrumeliak, Ihor 61

Shlemkevych, Mykola 63
Shumoskyi, Kost 90
Skoropadskyi, Pavlo 154-155, 159-160, 162
Sławek, Walery 81, 83
Sombart, Werner 120
Spengler, Oswald 62
Stalin, Joseph xi, xii, 96
Stroński, Stanisław 83
Strutynska, Mariia 29, 64
Sushko, Roman 30, 35-36
Szabłowski, Witold 183n638
Tarkovych, Yurii 135
Tarnavskyi, Myron 166
Tarnavskyi, Ostap 59, 61, 63, 64n222, 65n224, 66, 70, 105n382, 140-141
Tarnovych, Yulian 164
Tomashivskyi, Stepan 147, 149, 162
Trąmpczyński, Wojciech 83
Trotsky, Leon (Lev) v
Turskyi, Andrii. See Mylianych, Atanas
Tvorydlo, Mykola 61
Umland, Andreas 5
Vahylevych, Ivan 172-173
Veresh-Sirmianskyi, Vasyl 67
Vlasov, Andrei 18
Volchuk, Roman 76, 196-197
Volodymyr the Great 86, 146-148
Vovk, Fedir 131
Vozniak, Mykhailo 49
Vynnychenko, Rozaliia 184
Vynnychenko, Volodymyr 184
White, Arnold 120
Witos, Wincenty 81, 83
Yaroslav the Wise 148
Yefremov, Serhii 175

Yendyk, Rostyslav 39-40
Yevshan, Mykola 174-175
Zaremba, Ya. 61
Zdziechowski, Marian 120
Zelensky, Volodymyr x
Zerov, Mykola 169
Zilynskyi, Ivan 60

UKRAINIAN VOICES

Collected by Andreas Umland

1   Mychailo Wynnyckyj
    Ukraine's Maidan, Russia's
    War
    A Chronicle and Analysis of the
    Revolution of Dignity
    With a foreword by Serhii
    Plokhy
    ISBN 978-3-8382-1327-9

2   Olexander Hryb
    Understanding
    Contemporary Ukrainian
    and Russian Nationalism
    The Post-Soviet Cossack Revival
    and Ukraine's National Security
    With a foreword by Vitali Vitaliev
    ISBN 978-3-8382-1377-4

3   Marko Bojcun
    Towards a Political Economy
    of Ukraine
    Selected Essays 1990–2015
    With a foreword by John-Paul
    Himka
    ISBN 978-3-8382-1368-2

4   Volodymyr Yermolenko
    (ed.)
    Ukraine in Histories and
    Stories
    Essays by Ukrainian
    Intellectuals
    With a preface by Peter
    Pomerantsev
    ISBN 978-3-8382-1456-6

5   Mykola Riabchuk
    At the Fence of Metternich's
    Garden
    Essays on Europe, Ukraine, and
    Europeanization
    ISBN 978-3-8382-1484-9

6   Marta Dyczok
    Ukraine Calling
    A Kaleidoscope from
    Hromadske Radio 2016–2019
    With a foreword by Andriy
    Kulykov
    ISBN 978-3-8382-1472-6

7   Olexander Scherba
    Ukraine vs. Darkness
    Undiplomatic Thoughts
    With a foreword by Adrian
    Karatnycky
    ISBN 978-3-8382-1501-3

8   Olesya Yaremchuk
    Our Others
    Stories of Ukrainian Diversity
    With a foreword by Ostap
    Slyvynsky
    Translated from the Ukrainian by
    Zenia Tompkins and Hanna Leliv
    ISBN 978-3-8382-1475-7

9   Nataliya Gumenyuk
    Die verlorene Insel
    Geschichten von der besetzten
    Krim
    Mit einem Vorwort von Alice
    Bota
    Aus dem Ukrainischen übersetzt
    von Johann Zajaczkowski
    ISBN 978-3-8382-1499-3

10 Olena Stiazhkina
    Zero Point Ukraine
    Four Essays on World War II
    Translated from the Ukrainian
    by Svitlana Kulinska
    ISBN 978-3-8382-1550-1

11 *Oleksii Sinchenko, Dmytro Stus, Leonid Finberg (Compilers)*
    Ukrainian Dissidents
    An Anthology of Texts
    ISBN 978-3-8382-1551-8

12 *John-Paul Himka*
    Ukrainian Nationalists and the Holocaust
    OUN and UPA's Participation in the Destruction of Ukrainian Jewry, 1941–1944
    ISBN 978-3-8382-1548-8

13 *Andrey Demartino*
    False Mirrors
    The Weaponization of Social Media in Russia's Operation to Annex Crimea
    With a foreword by Oleksiy Danilov
    ISBN 978-3-8382-1533-4

14 *Svitlana Biedarieva (ed.)*
    Contemporary Ukrainian and Baltic Art
    Political and Social Perspectives, 1991–2021
    ISBN 978-3-8382-1526-6

15 *Olesya Khromeychuk*
    A Loss
    The Story of a Dead Soldier Told by His Sister
    With a foreword by Andrey Kurkov
    ISBN 978-3-8382-1570-9

16 *Marieluise Beck (Hg.)*
    Ukraine verstehen
    Auf den Spuren von Terror und Gewalt
    Mit einem Vorwort von Dmytro Kuleba
    ISBN 978-3-8382-1653-9

17 *Stanislav Aseyev*
    Heller Weg
    Geschichte eines Konzentrationslagers im Donbass 2017–2019
    Aus dem Russischen übersetzt von Martina Steis und Charis Haska
    ISBN 978-3-8382-1620-1

18 *Mykola Davydiuk*
    Wie funktioniert Putins Propaganda?
    Anmerkungen zum Informationskrieg des Kremls
    Aus dem Ukrainischen übersetzt von Christian Weise
    ISBN 978-3-8382-1628-7

19 *Olesya Yaremchuk*
    Unsere Anderen
    Geschichten ukrainischer Vielfalt
    Aus dem Ukrainischen übersetzt von Christian Weise
    ISBN 978-3-8382-1635-5

20 *Oleksandr Mykhed*
    „Dein Blut wird die Kohle tränken"
    Über die Ostukraine
    Aus dem Ukrainischen übersetzt von Simon Muschick und Dario Planert
    ISBN 978-3-8382-1648-5

21 *Vakhtang Kipiani (Hg.)*
    Der Zweite Weltkrieg in der Ukraine
    Geschichte und Lebensgeschichten
    Aus dem Ukrainischen übersetzt von Margarita Grinko
    ISBN 978-3-8382-1622-5

22 *Vakhtang Kipiani (ed.)*
    World War II, Uncontrived and Unredacted
    Testimonies from Ukraine
    Translated from the Ukrainian by Zenia Tompkins and Daisy Gibbons
    ISBN 978-3-8382-1621-8

23 *Dmytro Stus*
   Vasyl Stus
   Life in Creativity
   Translated from the Ukrainian by
   Ludmila Bachurina
   ISBN 978-3-8382-1631-7

24 *Vitalii Ogiienko (ed.)*
   The Holodomor and the
   Origins of the Soviet Man
   Reading the Testimony of
   Anastasia Lysyvets
   With forewords by Natalka
   Bilotserkivets and Serhy
   Yekelchyk
   Translated from the Ukrainian by
   Alla Parkhomenko and
   Alexander J. Motyl
   ISBN 978-3-8382-1616-4

25 *Vladislav Davidzon*
   Jewish-Ukrainian Relations
   and the Birth of a Political
   Nation
   Selected Writings 2013-2021
   With a foreword by Bernard-
   Henri Lévy
   ISBN 978-3-8382-1509-9

26 *Serhy Yekelchyk*
   Writing the Nation
   The Ukrainian Historical
   Profession in Independent
   Ukraine and the Diaspora
   ISBN 978-3-8382-1695-9

27 *Ildi Eperjesi, Oleksandr
   Kachura*
   Shreds of War
   Fates from the Donbas Frontline
   2014-2019
   With a foreword by Olexiy
   Haran
   ISBN 978-3-8382-1680-5

28 *Oleksandr Melnyk*
   World War II as an Identity
   Project
   Historicism, Legitimacy
   Contests, and the (Re-)Con-
   struction of Political Commu-
   nities in Ukraine, 1939–1946
   With a foreword by David R.
   Marples
   ISBN 978-3-8382-1704-8

29 *Olesya Khromeychuk*
   Ein Verlust
   Die Geschichte eines gefallenen
   ukrainischen Soldaten, erzählt
   von seiner Schwester
   Mit einem Vorwort von Andrej
   Kurkow
   Aus dem Englischen übersetzt
   von Lily Sophie
   ISBN 978-3-8382-1770-3

30 *Tamara Martsenyuk,
   Tetiana Kostiuchenko (eds.)*
   Russia's War in Ukraine
   During 2022
   Personal Experiences of
   Ukrainian Scholars
   ISBN 978-3-8382-1757-4

31 *Ildikó Eperjesi, Oleksandr
   Kachura*
   Shreds of War. Vol. 2
   Fates from Crimea 2015–2022
   With an interview of Oleh
   Sentsov
   ISBN 978-3-8382-1780-2

32 *Yuriy Lukanov*
   The Press
   How Russia Destroyed Media
   Freedom in Crimea
   With a foreword by Taras Kuzio
   ISBN 978-3-8382-1784-0

33 *Megan Buskey*
   Ukraine Is Not Dead Yet
   A Family Story of Exile and
   Return
   ISBN 978-3-8382-1691-1

34 *Vira Ageyeva*
Behind the Scenes of the Empire
Essays on Cultural Relationships between Ukraine and Russia
With a foreword by Oksana Zabuzhko
ISBN 978-3-8382-1748-2

35 *Marieluise Beck (ed.)*
Understanding Ukraine
Tracing the Roots of Terror and Violence
With a foreword by Dmytro Kuleba
ISBN 978-3-8382-1773-4

36 *Olesya Khromeychuk*
A Loss
The Story of a Dead Soldier Told by His Sister, 2nd edn.
With a foreword by Philippe Sands
With a preface by Andrii Kurkov
ISBN 978-3-8382-1870-0

37 *Taras Kuzio, Stefan Jajecznyk-Kelman*
Fascism and Genocide
Russia's War Against Ukrainians
ISBN 978-3-8382-1791-8

38 *Alina Nychyk*
Ukraine Vis-à-Vis Russia and the EU
Misperceptions of Foreign Challenges in Times of War, 2014–2015
With a foreword by Paul D'Anieri
ISBN 978-3-8382-1767-3

39 *Sasha Dovzhyk (ed.)*
Ukraine Lab
Global Security, Environment, and Disinformation Through the Prism of Ukraine
With a foreword by Rory Finnin
ISBN 978-3-8382-1805-2

40 *Serhiy Kvit*
Media, History, and Education
Three Ways to Ukrainian Independence
With a preface by Diane Francis
ISBN 978-3-8382-1807-6

41 *Anna Romandash*
Women of Ukraine
Reportages from the War and Beyond
ISBN 978-3-8382-1819-9

42 *Dominika Rank*
Matzewe in meinem Garten
Abenteuer eines jüdischen Heritage-Touristen in der Ukraine
ISBN 978-3-8382-1810-6

43 *Myroslaw Marynowytsch*
Das Universum hinter dem Stacheldraht
Memoiren eines sowjet-ukrainischen Dissidenten
Mit einem Vorwort von Timothy Snyder und einem Nachwort von Max Hartmann
ISBN 978-3-8382-1806-9

44 *Konstantin Sigow*
Für Deine und meine Freiheit
Europäische Revolutions- und Kriegserfahrungen im heutigen Kyjiw
Mit einem Vorwort von Karl Schlögel
Herausgegeben von Regula M. Zwahlen
ISBN 978-3-8382-1755-0

45 *Kateryna Pylypchuk*
The War that Changed Us
Ukrainian Novellas, Poems, and Essays from 2022
With a foreword by Victor Yushchenko
Paperback
ISBN 978-3-8382-1859-5
Hardcover
ISBN 978-3-8382-1860-1

46 Kyrylo Tkachenko
Rechte Tür Links
Radikale Linke in Deutschland,
die Revolution und der Krieg in
der Ukraine, 2013-2018
ISBN 978-3-8382-1711-6

47 Alexander Strashny
The Ukrainian Mentality
An Ethno-Psychological,
Historical and Comparative
Exploration
With a foreword by Antonina
Lovochkina
Translated from the Ukrainian
by Michael M. Naydan and
Olha Tytarenko
ISBN 978-3-8382-1886-1

48 Alona Shestopalova
From Screens to Battlefields
Tracing the Construction of
Enemies on Russian Television
With a foreword by Nina
Jankowicz
ISBN 978-3-8382-1884-7

49 Iaroslav Petik
Politics and Society in the
Ukrainian People's Republic
(1917–1921) and
Contemporary Ukraine
(2013–2022)
A Comparative Analysis
With a foreword by Mykola
Doroshko
ISBN 978-3-8382-1817-5

50 Serhii Plokhy
Der Mann mit der
Giftpistole
Eine Spionagegeschichte aus dem
Kalten Krieg
ISBN 978-3-8382-1789-5

51 Vakhtang Kipiani
Ukrainische Dissidenten
unter der Sowjetmacht
Im Kampf um Wahrheit und
Freiheit
Aus dem Ukrainischen übersetzt
von Christian Weise
ISBN 978-3-8382-1890-8

52 Dmytro Shestakov
When Businesses Test
Hypotheses
A Four-Step Approach to Risk
Management for Innovative
Startups
With a foreword by Anthony J.
Tether
ISBN 978-3-8382-1883-0

53 Larissa Babij
A Kind of Refugee
The Story of an American Who
Refused to Leave Ukraine
With a foreword by Vladislav
Davidzon
ISBN 978-3-8382-1898-4

54 Julia Davis
In Their Own Words
How Russian Propagandists
Reveal Putin's Intentions
With a foreword by Timothy
Snyder
ISBN 978-3-8382-1909-7

55 Sonya Atlantova, Oleksandr
Klymenko
Icons on Ammo Boxes
Painting Life on the Remnants of
Russia's War in Donbas, 2014-21
Translated from the Ukrainian by
Anastasya Knyazhytska
ISBN 978-3-8382-1892-2

56 Leonid Ushkalov
Catching an Elusive Bird
The Life of Hryhorii Skovoroda
Translated from the Ukrainian
by Natalia Komarova
ISBN 978-3-8382-1894-6

57 Vakhtang Kipiani
Ein Land weiblichen
Geschlechts
Ukrainische Frauenschicksale
im 20. und 21. Jahrhundert
Aus dem Ukrainischen übersetzt
von Christian Weise
ISBN 978-3-8382-1891-5

58 Petro Rychlo
„Zerrissne Saiten einer
überlauten Harfe ..."
Deutschjüdische Dichter der
Bukowina
ISBN 978-3-8382-1893-9

59 Volodymyr Paniotto
Sociology in Jokes
An Entertaining Introduction
ISBN 978-3-8382-1857-1

60 Josef Wallmannsberger
(ed.)
Executing Renaissances
The Poetological Nation of
Ukraine
ISBN 978-3-8382-1741-3

61 Pavlo Kazarin
The Wild West of Eastern
Europe
A Ukrainian Guide on Breaking
Free from Empire
Translated from the Ukrainian
by Dominique Hoffman
ISBN 978-3-8382-1842-7

62 Ernest Gyidel
Ukrainian Public
Nationalism in the General
Government
The Case of *Krakivski Visti*,
1940–1944
With a foreword by David R.
Marples
ISBN 978-3-8382-1865-6

63 Olexander Hryb
Understanding
Contemporary Russian
Militarism
From Revolutionary to New
Generation Warfare
With a foreword by Mark Laity
ISBN 978-3-8382-1927-1

64 Orysia Hrudka, Bohdan Ben
Dark Days, Determined
People
Stories from Ukraine under Siege
With a foreword by Myroslav
Marynovych
ISBN 978-3-8382-1958-5

65 Oleksandr Pankieiev (Ed.)
Narratives of the Russo-
Ukrainian War
A Look Within and Without
With a foreword by Natalia
Khanenko-Friesen
ISBN 978-3-8382-1964-6

66 Roman Sohn, Ariana Gic
(eds.)
Unrecognized War
The Fight for Truth about
Russia's War on Ukraine
With a foreword by Viktor
Yushchenko
ISBN 978-3-8382-1947-9

67 Paul Robert Magocsi
Ukraina Redux
Schon wieder die Ukraine ...
ISBN 978-3-8382-1942-4

68 Paul Robert Magocsi
L'Ucraina Ritrovata
Sullo Stato e l'Identità Nazionale
ISBN 978-3-8382-1982-0

69 Max Hartmann
Ein Schrei der Verzweiflung
Aquarelle von Danylo Movchan
zu Russlands Krieg in der
Ukraine
Mit einem Vorwort von Mateusz
Sora
Paperback
ISBN 978-3-8382-2011-6
Hardcover
ISBN 978-3-8382-2012-3

70 Vakhtang Kebuladze (Hg.)
Die Zukunft, die wir uns
wünschen
Essays aus der Ukraine
ISBN 978-3-8382-1531-0

71 *Marieluise Beck, Jan Claas Behrends, Gelinada Grinchenko und Oksana Mikheieva (Hgg.)*
Deutsch-ukrainische Geschichten
Bruchstücke aus einer gemeinsamen Vergangenheit
ISBN 978-3-8382-2053-6

72 *Pavlo Kazarin*
Der Wilde Westen Ost-Europas
Der ukrainische Weg aus dem Imperium
Aus dem Ukrainischen übersetzt von Christian Weise
ISBN 978-3-8382-1843-4

73 *Radomyr Mokryk*
Die ukrainischen »Sechziger«
Chronologie einer Revolte
ISBN 978-3-8382-1873-1

74 *Leonid Finberg*
My Ukraine
Rethinking the Past, Building the Present
ISBN 978-3-8382-1974-5

75 *Joseph Zissels*
Consider My Inmost Thoughts
Essays, Lectures, and Interviews on Ukrainian Matters at the Turn of the Century
ISBN 978-3-8382-1975-2

76 *Margarita Yehorchenko, Iryna Berlyand, Ihor Vinokurov (eds.)*
Jewish Addresses in Ukraine
A Guide-Book
With a foreword by Leonid Finberg
ISB 978-3-8382-1976-9

77 *Viktoriia Grivina*
Kharkiv—A War City
A Collection of Essays from 2022–23
ISBN 978-3-8382-1988-2

78 *Hjørdis Clemmensen, Viktoriia Grivina, Vasylysa Shchogoleva*
Kharkiv Is a Dream
Public Art and Activism 2013–2023
With a foreword by Bohdan Volynskyi
ISBN 978-3-8382-2005-5

79 *Olga Khomenko*
The Faraway Sky of Kyiv
Ukrainians in the War
With a foreword by Hiroaki Kuromiya
ISBN 978-3-8382-2006-2

80 *Daria Mattingly, Jonathon Vsetecka (eds.)*
The Holodomor in Global Perspective
How the Famine in Ukraine Shaped the World
With a foreword by Anne Applebaum
ISBN 978-3-8382-1953-0

81 *Olga Khomenko*
Ukrainians beyond Borders
Nine Life Journeys Through the History of Eastern Europe
With a foreword by Zbigniew Wojnowski
ISBN 978-3-8382-2007-9

82 *Mykhailo Minakov*
From Servant to Leader
Chronicles of Ukraine under the Zelensky Presidency, 2019–2024
With a foreword by John Lloyd
ISBN 978-3-8382-2002-4

83 *Volodymyr Hromov (ed.)*
A Ruined Home
Sketches of War, 2022–2023
ISBN 978-3-8382-2008-6

84 Olha Tatokhina (ed.)
Why Do They Kill Our People?
Russia's War Against Ukraine as
Told by Ukrainians
With a foreword by Volodymyr
Yermolenko
ISBN 978-3-8382-2056-7

*85 Mieste Hotopp-Riecke,
Sarah Reinke (Hrsg.)*
Die Krimtataren
Geschichte – Kultur – Politik
ISBN 978-3-8382-1986-8

Book series "Ukrainian Voices"

Coordinator
Andreas Umland, National University of Kyiv-Mohyla Academy

Editorial Board
Lesia Bidochko, National University of Kyiv-Mohyla Academy
Svitlana Biedarieva, George Washington University, DC, USA
Ivan Gomza, Kyiv School of Economics, Ukraine
Natalie Jaresko, Aspen Institute, Kyiv/Washington
Olena Lennon, University of New Haven, West Haven, USA
Kateryna Yushchenko, First Lady of Ukraine 2005-2010, Kyiv
Oleksandr Zabirko, University of Regensburg, Germany

Advisory Board
Iuliia Bentia, National Academy of Arts of Ukraine, Kyiv
Natalya Belitser, Pylyp Orlyk Institute for Democracy, Kyiv
Oleksandra Bienert, Humboldt University of Berlin, Germany
Sergiy Bilenky, Canadian Institute of Ukrainian Studies, Toronto
Tymofii Brik, Kyiv School of Economics, Ukraine
Olga Brusylovska, Mechnikov National University, Odesa
Mariana Budjeryn, Harvard University, Cambridge, USA
Volodymyr Bugrov, Shevchenko National University, Kyiv
Olga Burlyuk, University of Amsterdam, The Netherlands
Yevhen Bystrytsky, NAS Institute of Philosophy, Kyiv
Andrii Danylenko, Pace University, New York, USA
Vladislav Davidzon, Atlantic Council, Washington/Paris
Mykola Davydiuk, Think Tank "Polityka," Kyiv
Andrii Demartino, National Security and Defense Council, Kyiv
Vadym Denisenko, Ukrainian Institute for the Future, Kyiv
Oleksandr Donii, Center for Political Values Studies, Kyiv
Volodymyr Dubovyk, Mechnikov National University, Odesa
Volodymyr Dubrovskiy, CASE Ukraine, Kyiv
Diana Dutsyk, National University of Kyiv-Mohyla Academy
Marta Dyczok, Western University, Ontario, Canada
Yevhen Fedchenko, National University of Kyiv-Mohyla Academy
Sofiya Filonenko, State Pedagogical University of Berdyansk
Oleksandr Fisun, Karazin National University, Kharkiv
Oksana Forostyna, Webjournal "Ukraina Moderna," Kyiv
Roman Goncharenko, Broadcaster "Deutsche Welle," Bonn
George Grabowicz, Harvard University, Cambridge, USA
Gelinada Grinchenko, Karazin National University, Kharkiv
Kateryna Härtel, Federal Union of European Nationalities, Brussels
Nataliia Hendel, University of Geneva, Switzerland
Anton Herashchenko, Kyiv School of Public Administration
John-Paul Himka, University of Alberta, Edmonton
Ola Hnatiuk, National University of Kyiv-Mohyla Academy
Oleksandr Holubov, Broadcaster "Deutsche Welle," Bonn
Yaroslav Hrytsak, Ukrainian Catholic University, Lviv
Oleksandra Humenna, National University of Kyiv-Mohyla Academy
Tamara Hundorova, NAS Institute of Literature, Kyiv
Oksana Huss, University of Bologna, Italy
Oleksandra Iwaniuk, University of Warsaw, Poland
Mykola Kapitonenko, Shevchenko National University, Kyiv
Georgiy Kasianov, Marie Curie-Skłodowska University, Lublin
Vakhtang Kebuladze, Shevchenko National University, Kyiv
Natalia Khanenko-Friesen, University of Alberta, Edmonton
Victoria Khiterer, Millersville University of Pennsylvania, USA
Oksana Kis, NAS Institute of Ethnology, Lviv
Pavlo Klimkin, Center for National Resilience and Development, Kyiv
Oleksandra Kolomiiets, Center for Economic Strategy, Kyiv

Sergiy Korsunsky, Kobe Gakuin University, Japan
Nadiia Koval, Kyiv School of Economics, Ukraine
Volodymyr Kravchenko, University of Alberta, Edmonton
Oleksiy Kresin, NAS Koretskiy Institute of State and Law, Kyiv
Anatoliy Kruglashov, Fedkovych National University, Chernivtsi
Andrey Kurkov, PEN Ukraine, Kyiv
Ostap Kushnir, Lazarski University, Warsaw
Taras Kuzio, National University of Kyiv-Mohyla Academy
Serhii Kvit, National University of Kyiv-Mohyla Academy
Yuliya Ladygina, The Pennsylvania State University, USA
Yevhen Mahda, Institute of World Policy, Kyiv
Victoria Malko, California State University, Fresno, USA
Yulia Marushevska, Security and Defense Center (SAND), Kyiv
Myroslav Marynovych, Ukrainian Catholic University, Lviv
Oleksandra Matviichuk, Center for Civil Liberties, Kyiv
Mykhailo Minakov, Kennan Institute, Washington, USA
Anton Moiseienko, The Australian National University, Canberra
Alexander Motyl, Rutgers University-Newark, USA
Vlad Mykhnenko, University of Oxford, United Kingdom
Vitalii Ogiienko, Ukrainian Institute of National Remembrance, Kyiv
Olga Onuch, University of Manchester, United Kingdom
Olesya Ostrovska, Museum "Mystetskyi Arsenal," Kyiv
Anna Osypchuk, National University of Kyiv-Mohyla Academy
Oleksandr Pankieiev, University of Alberta, Edmonton
Oleksiy Panych, Publishing House "Dukh i Litera," Kyiv
Valerii Pekar, Kyiv-Mohyla Business School, Ukraine
Yohanan Petrovsky-Shtern, Northwestern University, Chicago
Serhii Plokhy, Harvard University, Cambridge, USA
Andrii Portnov, Viadrina University, Frankfurt-Oder, Germany
Maryna Rabinovych, Kyiv School of Economics, Ukraine
Valentyna Romanova, Institute of Developing Economies, Tokyo
Natalya Ryabinska, Collegium Civitas, Warsaw, Poland
Darya Tsymbalyk, University of Oxford, United Kingdom
Vsevolod Samokhvalov, University of Liege, Belgium
Orest Semotiuk, Franko National University, Lviv
Viktoriya Sereda, NAS Institute of Ethnology, Lviv
Anton Shekhovtsov, University of Vienna, Austria
Andriy Shevchenko, Media Center Ukraine, Kyiv
Oxana Shevel, Tufts University, Medford, USA
Pavlo Shopin, National Pedagogical Dragomanov University, Kyiv
Karina Shyrokykh, Stockholm University, Sweden
Nadja Simon, freelance interpreter, Cologne, Germany
Olena Snigova, NAS Institute for Economics and Forecasting, Kyiv
Ilona Solohub, Analytical Platform "VoxUkraine," Kyiv
Iryna Solonenko, LibMod - Center for Liberal Modernity, Berlin
Galyna Solovei, National University of Kyiv-Mohyla Academy
Sergiy Stelmakh, NAS Institute of World History, Kyiv
Olena Stiazhkina, NAS Institute of the History of Ukraine, Kyiv
Dmitri Stratievski, Osteuropa Zentrum (OEZB), Berlin
Dmytro Stus, National Taras Shevchenko Museum, Kyiv
Frank Sysyn, University of Toronto, Canada
Olha Tokariuk, Center for European Policy Analysis, Washington
Olena Tregub, Independent Anti-Corruption Commission, Kyiv
Hlib Vyshlinsky, Centre for Economic Strategy, Kyiv
Mychailo Wynnyckyj, National University of Kyiv-Mohyla Academy
Yelyzaveta Yasko, NGO "Yellow Blue Strategy," Kyiv
Serhy Yekelchyk, University of Victoria, Canada
Victor Yushchenko, President of Ukraine 2005-2010, Kyiv
Oleksandr Zaitsev, Ukrainian Catholic University, Lviv
Kateryna Zarembo, National University of Kyiv-Mohyla Academy
Yaroslav Zhalilo, National Institute for Strategic Studies, Kyiv
Sergei Zhuk, Ball State University at Muncie, USA
Alina Zubkovych, Nordic Ukraine Forum, Stockholm
Liudmyla Zubrytska, National University of Kyiv-Mohyla Academy

Friends of the Series

Ana Maria Abulescu, University of Bucharest, Romania
Łukasz Adamski, Centrum Mieroszewskiego, Warsaw
Marieluise Beck, LibMod—Center for Liberal Modernity, Berlin
Marc Berensen, King's College London, United Kingdom
Johannes Bohnen, BOHNEN Public Affairs, Berlin
Karsten Brüggemann, University of Tallinn, Estonia
Ulf Brunnbauer, Leibniz Institute (IOS), Regensburg
Martin Dietze, German-Ukrainian Culture Society, Hamburg
Gergana Dimova, Florida State University, Tallahassee/London
Caroline von Gall, Goethe University, Frankfurt-Main
Zaur Gasimov, Rhenish Friedrich Wilhelm University, Bonn
Armand Gosu, University of Bucharest, Romania
Thomas Grant, University of Cambridge, United Kingdom
Gustav Gressel, European Council on Foreign Relations, Berlin
Rebecca Harms, European Centre for Press & Media Freedom, Leipzig
André Härtel, Stiftung Wissenschaft und Politik, Berlin/Brussels
Marcel Van Herpen, The Cicero Foundation, Maastricht
Richard Herzinger, freelance analyst, Berlin
Mieste Hotopp-Riecke, ICATAT, Magdeburg
Nico Lange, Munich Security Conference, Berlin
Martin Malek, freelance analyst, Vienna
Ingo Mannteufel, Broadcaster "Deutsche Welle," Bonn
Carlo Masala, Bundeswehr University, Munich
Wolfgang Mueller, University of Vienna, Austria
Dietmar Neutatz, Albert Ludwigs University, Freiburg
Torsten Oppelland, Friedrich Schiller University, Jena
Niccolò Pianciola, University of Padua, Italy
Gerald Praschl, German-Ukrainian Forum (DUF), Berlin
Felix Riefer, Think Tank Ideenagentur-Ost, Düsseldorf
Stefan Rohdewald, University of Leipzig, Germany
Sebastian Schäffer, Institute for the Danube Region (IDM), Vienna
Felix Schimansky-Geier, Friedrich Schiller University, Jena
Ulrich Schneckener, University of Osnabrück, Germany
Winfried Schneider-Deters, freelance analyst, Heidelberg/Kyiv
Gerhard Simon, University of Cologne, Germany
Kai Struve, Martin Luther University, Halle/Wittenberg
David Stulik, European Values Center for Security Policy, Prague
Andrzej Szeptycki, University of Warsaw, Poland
Philipp Ther, University of Vienna, Austria
Stefan Troebst, University of Leipzig, Germany

[Please send requests for changes in, corrections of, and additions to, this list to andreas.umland@stanforalumni.org.]

ibidem.eu